TED HOOD
Through Hand and Eye
An Autobiography

TED HOOD

Through Hand and Eye
An Autobiography

By Ted Hood
And Michael Levitt

Mystic Seaport
75 Greenmanville Ave., PO Box 6000
Mystic, CT 06355-0990

www.mysticseaport.org

Designed by Richard Hood, Flow Media Design, Newport, RI

Consulting provided by B. Devereux Barker IV

ISBN (cloth): 0-939511-14-2

Cataloging-in-Publication Data

Hood, Ted.
   Ted Hood : through hand and eye : an autobiography / by Ted Hood and Michael Levitt.-1st ed.
-Mystic, CT : Mystic Seaport, c2006.
     p. : ill., ports. ; cm.
     Includes index.
     Contents: Beginnings -- The sailmaker -- Victories and losses -- Robin -- Nefertiti -- The
designer -- America's Cup trials 1974 -- A successful defense -- Success, growth & changes -
America's Cup 1977 -- The boatbuilder -- Goodbye Marblehead -- Powerboats.

     1. Hood, Ted. 2. Sailmakers -- United States. 3. America's Cup. 4. Yacht racing -- United States.
5. Yacht designers -- United States. 6. Yacht building -- United States. I. Title.

VM140.H6 A3 2006

Books by Michael Levitt
The North Sails Story;
The America's Cup—the History of Sailing's Greatest Competition in the Twentieth Century (co-author Dennis Conner);
The Official Record of West McLaren Mercedes 1998;
The Official Record of West McLaren Mercedes 1997;
Around the World in Seventy-Nine Days (co-author Cam Lewis);
Learn to Sail (co-author Dennis Conner);
America's Cup 1851-1992: The Official Record (winner of a 1992 Benjamin Franklin Award);
Sail Like A Champion (co-author Dennis Conner);
The Art and Science of Sails (co-author Tom Whidden);
Upset: Australia Wins the America's Cup (co-author Barbara Lloyd);
A Tissue of Lies: Nixon versus Hiss (co-author Dr. Morton Levitt).

Acknowledgments

This book tells stories from my life that I wanted to tell. Most of these stories are about the ideas I have pursued–some of which were built, and others of which may be built one day. Thinking up better ways of doing things and building them is my passion.

But this book also tells of the many people who have added so much to my life. To all of you, I am truly grateful for helping me to pursue my dreams and for enriching my life by simply being a part of it.

Above all, I thank my wife of over 50 years, Susan, to whom I dedicate this book. She has been at my side for all these years, providing the foundation that allowed me to pursue my dreams and yet raise a wonderful family of four children at the same time. Thank you, Sue for your love and support for all these years. I could not have done it without you.

Thanks to Michael Levitt for his hard work in putting my story into words - not an easy task!

Thanks to my son Rick for his work in creating the book design.

Very special thanks to Don McGraw, a very dear friend, whose help made this book possible.

Ted Hood

Contents

Ted Hood
Taken by Michael Levitt during the Ocean Triangle Race
of the Southern Ocean Racing Conference
1974

Foreword

Ted Hood

To think Ted Hood might have built houses for a living. What a loss that would have been to boating. Frederick E. "Ted" Hood was drafted out of high school in the waning days of World War II. Coming home to Marblehead, Massachusetts, he finished high school in the same class as his younger brother, Bruce, and then attended Wentworth Institute of Technology, courtesy of the GI Bill, to study building construction, design and engineering, and business.

He designed a house for his father's friend. He dug the foundation and started framing it, when a neighbor, a lawyer, objected. The house would ruin his water view. The attorney offered the owner everything he had in it, plus $5,000. "That was a lot back then. So the guy took it, and that was the end of my homebuilding career. I enjoyed it, however; I often think I would have done pretty well at it, but I returned to sailmaking."

David Vietor, who graduated from Yale and took a Ph.D. from Stanford in German before working for Hood as a sailmaker, sees his former boss as a seminal figure in the sport. "He's as important to yachting as was Nathanael Herreshoff. Whatever he touches–and he touches practically everything –ends up significantly better than what was there before."

Herreshoff, who designed and built five yachts that defended six America's Cups from 1893 to 1920, has a fine museum that sings his praises. If as worthy, Ted Hood has no museum, probably never will. A man of measured words, in keeping with his Yankee heritage, he is the embodiment of the expression: "Still waters run deep."

The America's Cup Hall of Fame, founded by Herreshoff's grandson Halsey Herreshoff, describes Hood as "the quietest man to defend the America's Cup."

If Ted Hood won't tell you much, I will. He established the first international sailmaking business, which still bears his name if no longer his imprimatur. Hood Sailmakers predominated in the business from about 1958 to 1983. By weaving his own polyester (Dacron) sailcloth, Hood made better sails than everyone else. Not incidentally, his sails were on every America's Cup defender from 1962 to 1977. *Yachting* magazine billed him as "Sailmaker to the Twelves." He was the sole protagonist in a 12,000-word profile in the *New Yorker* (August 26, 1967) simply titled "Sailmaker."

So superior was Hood cloth, and such a national treasure was Hood, that the New York Yacht Club (NYYC), the keeper of the America's Cup for 132 years, established a country-of-origin "litmus test" for sailmakers, yacht designers, and boatbuilders that was in effect through the 2003 America's Cup. In truth, it might just as easily have been called the "Ted Hood rule."

There were 19 Hood lofts. The first satellite loft was in Australia. "That wouldn't be big today, but it was back then," said Hood.

Tom Whidden is president of North Sails, now the largest sailmaking organization in the world. He is also the preeminent tactician in the America's Cup, having sailed with Dennis Conner since 1980. As such he has won the America's Cup three times. When Whidden was 17, he taught sailing at the Wianno Yacht Club in Osterville, Massachusetts, on Cape Cod.

Said Whidden, "I got to know Jack Fallon, a real-estate developer, fairly well. I mentioned to him my dream of sailing in the America's Cup. He knew Ted Hood, the famous sailmaker. At the time Hood was preparing a 12-Meter, *Nefertiti*, a boat of his design, for the America's Cup. Fallon got me aboard. I worked a coffee-grinder winch. But whenever I could, I would sneak a peek back into the cockpit at Hood. I was amazed how quiet he was. Hood barely uttered five words the entire day. He spent all of his time looking at sails; he made a lot of notes; he even wrote notes on the sails. While I wasn't sure what he was doing then, I understand it now. He had an extraordinary eye for what a sail should look like.

"Being young and a complete stranger to this level of the game, I was really taken by it all. Even then, I realized that Ted Hood was the greatest of the great. That day had as much to do with shaping my future as anything or anyone ever has."

There's a saying in the business: "If you didn't go to Harvard, you went to Hood." Among that group of alumni of "Hood U." is Robbie Doyle, who went to Harvard and to Hood. Doyle now runs Doyle Sailmakers. There is, as mentioned, David Vietor, who went to Yale and Hood. Other well-known alumni include Phil Stegall, Tim Stearn, Scott Loomis, Deiter Empacher, Lee Van Gemert, Ed Botterell, Jeff Neuberth, Ted Fontaine, Jim Taylor, Larry Rosenfeld, Tim Woodhouse, Jim Mullen, Bruce Livingston Jr., Bob Reimens, Brit Chance, Phil Bennett, Mark Ellis, Walter Greene, Art Fraser, and Chris Bouzaid.

If sailmaking was all, it would be enough. But Hood does everything—including powerboats—well.

From Ted Hood the sailmaker, we move to Ted Hood the sailor. Indeed, the two are inexorably entwined, as he built a career on the principle of "victories at sea." A reluctant Ted Hood skippered *Courageous* to victory in the 1974 America's Cup. Earlier that year, he also won the Southern Ocean Racing Conference (SORC) aboard his *Robin Too II*; this writer was aboard for one of the races, the Ocean Triangle, which he won. Add the America's Cup to the SORC and, not surprisingly, Hood was the Rolex Yachtsman of the Year in 1974.

In 1956 he won the Mallory Cup, the US Sailing Men's Championship. In the process, he defeated such well-known sailors as Bus Mosbacher, Buddy Melges, and Bill Ficker—all of whom would go on to skipper successful America's Cup defenders—and Bill Buchan, a two-time Star-boat Olympic gold medalist. Hood was overall winner of the 1968 Bermuda Race on *Robin*, a boat he designed. He won the 1961 Marblehead-Halifax Race in a 36-foot keel-boat built in Japan and in 1971 in a 50-foot sloop built in Holland.

Then there is Hood the yacht designer and/or builder. When he was twelve, he designed and built an eight-foot sailboat, and when he was fifteen, he designed and built the twelve-foot dinghy *Doohdet*—Ted Hood spelled backwards.

Much later, he designed and built *American Promise*, a Little Harbor 60 for Dodge Morgan, a Maine businessman. In 1985, Morgan sailed her alone and nonstop around the world in 150 days, shaving some two months off the nonstop solo record of Chay Blythe. This was also nine days faster than Philippe Jeantot's winning time in the 1982-83 BOC, which included four stops.

There have been 1,100 copies of Hood-designed production yachts for the likes of Bristol, Tartan, Wauquiez, Hinckley, and Hatteras, and more than 250 of his Little Harbor yachts, from 35 to 75 feet, are sailing today. Among them is *Palawan VII*, a 75-footer built originally for the late Tom Watson, the former head of IBM. Wrote Watson about his new yacht, "The designer and the type of boat were selected by my blessed wife Olive who has patiently followed me for 51 years. It was her turn to pick a boat suited to her need and that is what we have in the new *Palawan*."

Hood built a full-size cardboard and plywood mockup of the interior to be certain everything fit. This way, Watson could try the yacht on for size.

Palawan, now owned by Joseph Hoopes, won her class in the 2002 Newport-Bermuda Race. Said Hood, "The only boat that ever started the Bermuda with the Bimini up."

Having a Yankee's eye for value, he has built yachts in Japan, Holland, Marblehead, Taiwan, China, Portsmouth, Rhode Island, and most recently, Poland and Turkey. He helped modernize and pioneer the boatbuilding industry in many of these countries.

Ted Hood Design Group got its start in 1958. It has designed yachts from 30 to 150 feet. Hood has designed such

America's Cup 12-Meter yachts as *Nefertiti* and *Independence*. The former finished second to *Weatherly* in the four-boat trials in 1962 and second to *Constellation* in the four-boat trials in 1964. The latter finished second to *Courageous* in the four-boat trials in 1977. His *Dynamite*, a two-tonner, won the 1972 Canada's Cup for Llwyd Ecclestone.

He developed the important Stoway Mast and the Stoboom. Why this emphasis on the taming of the mainsail? Because Ted Hood hates mainsails, believing they are hard to handle when shorthanded and inefficient when compared to a jib. Headsails haven't escaped his creative musings either. He also designed the grooved headstay (Sea-Stay and Gemini), a racing standard, and jib roller-furling and reefing (SeaFurl), a cruising standard. Nearly all of these devices were built under licenses belonging to Hood.

For 37 years, Ted Hood was the personification of sailing in Marblehead, following in the tradition of his friend and one-time business associate C. Raymond Hunt, designer of the 110, 210, Concordia yawl, 12-Meter *Easterner*, the ubiquitous Boston Whaler, and, perhaps most important, the deep-vee hull for powerboats.

Then in 1986, Hood gathered up his wife Sue, daughter Nancy, and three sons: Ted, Bob, and Rick, and moved lock, stock, and barrel to Melville—a section of Portsmouth, Rhode Island. He developed 11 acres on Narragansett Bay on property warehoused by the Navy. This was formerly the Navy's Atlantic Fleet Fuel Station. Next door was the former PT base where the likes of John F. Kennedy trained. His was one of 30 bids for the property. Simply put, he and then-partner Everett Pearson would develop the property and design, build, and service yachts.

There was nothing simple about it, however; it was a bet-your-financial-life proposition. Hood had to invest $7 million within five years and employ 250 people. Then he would own the property. Here, Hood the almost-homebuilder built a huge nautical mall, a nautical Mall of America.

But property development didn't stem the creative flow. Hood was among the first to sense "a change in the wind." He became almost as well known for powerboats as sailboats, as would Hinckley, Alden, and Freedom-Legacy. In 1986, he purchased Black Watch powerboats. Wife Sue wanted a powerboat to explore the Sakonnet River, which led Hood to purchase the company. The Black Watch 26 and 30 became his most popular fishing boats. Some 160 were built.

Hood's powerboats were strongly influenced by Ray Hunt's deep-vee shape—the Black Watch 26 and 30 hulls were Ray Hunt designs—still the most eloquent answer to rough-water running. Hood looked back for inspiration, but in typical fashion, back to the future, as well. For example, he created Ted Hood Whisperjets. The waterjet propulsion system allows shallow draft and no protruding propellers, plus it keeps noise and engine vibration well aft, providing a more comfortable and quieter ride. Hood enjoys throwing the shift from forward to reverse, without skipping a beat and with nary a warning. Coming from someone thought to be so traditional, it attracted inordinate attention.

Today, one leaves his office overlooking Narragansett Bay, and there is *America³* and *Il Moro*—defender and challenger in the 1992 America's Cup—and sundry megayachts. The yard looks like it has been here forever. Hood sailed on *Vim* in the 1958 America's Cup, and Hood and his father and his father's friends created the revolutionary bendy boom for this yacht. Hood is sure *Vim*'s bendy boom is here, but doesn't know exactly where. There, too, are companies like North Sails—a bit incongruous, perhaps—and Alden. US Sailing is there, as is Garry Hoyt, founder of Freedom Yachts. However, a new name predominates: Hinckley, which in 1999 purchased all of the manufacturing capability of Hood and molds for Little Harbor sailboats, Black Watch, and the Whisperjet line of powerboats, and most of the property. In 2002 the yacht design business was purchased from Hinckley by Ted Fontaine, Ted's long-time yacht design manager, and carries on under the name Fontaine Design Group.

As I write this in the summer of 2005, Ted Hood is 78 years old, but the creative juices still flow, indeed course like a rapids. Hood has begun building "powercats." The first of these is a catamaran, measuring 52 feet long and 25 feet wide. Once again, he is developing the industry.

Listen to this supposedly quiet man: "A catamaran, I think, has a big advantage for a powerboat. The old commuters were narrow boats. They'd go fast, with very little power. Of course, they'd roll, didn't have much space in them. The test tank says the boat with twin 300s will go 18 or 22 knots. Talked to a guy who does hydrofoils, and he said you'd go 30 with them. I can try hydrofoils later. This is a displacement boat, 45,000 pounds. Seaworthy boat, with enough fuel to go across the ocean."

He is building a motorsailer too. "Trying to make a motorsailer for someone who sails and wants to go to power or someone who powers and wants to go to sail."

And he dreams and schemes about building a huge marina on the southern edge of the property.

Who says big dreams are only for young men? For Hood, the only nod to the past is this book.

– Michael Levitt

At the helm of *Marjay*
1932

Chapter 1

Beginnings

"Once, we had to fit a new garboard plank to Shrew *[an R-boat]. It was a really tricky place, with all kinds of curves and twists and bevels—the sort of place where an average shipwright would ruin two or three planks before he got the right fit. Ted looked at it, planed the wood, looked at it again and did some more planing. Then he put it to the hull, and it went in perfectly. It was nice to give him things to do. His eyes and his hands were so well connected."*

— *the* New Yorker, *August 26, 1967*

Two early events perhaps explain the course of my life. I was born in May 1927 at Beverly, Massachusetts, because Danvers, where my family lived, didn't have a hospital. My father was an ardent sailor, but my mother, Helen Hood, decided I needed a month of seasoning before taking me out on a sailboat. When I did first venture to sea, I was in a basket placed on the cabin sole of my father's old 40-foot Friendship sloop *Marjay*.

"Ted's been trying to make up for that lost month ever since," my late father, Ralph Stedman Hood, liked to say.

The next season, when I was a year old, I fell out of a bunk on the same boat and landed on my head. "He never recovered from that blow," my father often said.

Danvers is about eight miles inland from Marblehead on Boston's North Shore, although it does have a small river that leads to the ocean. At the time it was a manufacturing and farming town. There we lived in a fairly sizable house that was home to three generations. My grandfather and grandmother who originally owned the house still lived there, as did the mother of my grandfather's fiancée, who died before they were married. My mother and father took over the house when my grandparents could no longer afford it. My brother, Bruce, would join us two years later, and my father's unmarried younger sister lived with us, too. We also had an extra bedroom for a guest or two and an attic with two bedrooms, which were used occasionally.

My grandfather, Ralph Otis Hood, was an electrical engineer with a degree from Tufts. He was an inventor with many patents to his name. He developed, for example, a high-pressure steam automobile. Interestingly, high-pressure steam has not been perfected to this day. Another invention was a self-starter and generator for automobiles. I understand that he sold the rights to Charles Kettering of General Electric, and with the money he received for this he went into the automobile business. The late Briggs Cunningham, the racecar driver, manufacturer of the Cunningham C4R automobile, and America's Cup skipper (*Columbia*, 1958), once said, "The way to make a small fortune in the automobile business is to start with a large one." My grandfather started with a small one.

He designed and began building the "Gas-Au-Lec," which stood for gas, auxiliary, and electric. It had its debut at the Boston Automobile and Motor Boat Exhibition in 1905. According to a contemporary article in the *Salem News* written by Jim McAllister, the Gas-Au-Lec–built at the Corwin Manufacturing Company in South Peabody–had a gas engine and an electric generating motor. The electric generating motor would start the car–thus being the first car with a self-starter–but it would also assist the car when climbing hills or maneuvering in traffic and could act as a primary source of power for short distances. To me, it sounds like the new hybrid vehicles being developed now, a hundred years after Ralph Hood's Gas-Au-Lec.

Wrote McAllister, "Unfortunately, the Gas-Au-Lec's inventor was also responsible for the car's demise. When Hood refused to replace the vehicle's problematic magnetic valves with more compatible mechanical ones, his backers withdrew their financial support and production came to an immediate halt." Several custom automobiles built by my grandfather are still around. One of these is in my brother's garage waiting for restoration, and another is in my cousin's garage awaiting the same attention.

After failing in the automobile business, my grandfather did consulting work for George Poor of Sylvania Electric, and at the same time he developed a speedometer for boats. It featured a small tube about the size of the end of a pencil,

Ted in the driveway of 7 Ash Street, Danvers
1929

which only stuck out a half inch from the bottom of a boat. It was a simple Pitot tube system, and yet it worked well. The Kenyon speedometer, the major competition in those days, had a much more cumbersome apparatus; it stuck out about 10 inches from the bottom of the boat and was prone to being broken off. My grandfather made them in the workshop in the basement of our house and would sell them to sailors.

He was often my babysitter, from the time I was eight to about ten, and I'd accompany him on sales and service trips to Marblehead. We'd stop to see Charles Foster, who ran the present Boston Yacht Club, which was a gentleman's club in those days. He developed the Foster Rig: a mule mizzen, the luff of which went on the backstay with a short boom. We'd also visit yacht designer Murray G. Peterson, several of whose designs were inspired by coasting schooners. On one of these sales trips my grandfather asked if I'd like a ginger ale. I said, "Oh sure," so we went into Matties Sail Loft Bar and Grill in Marblehead. My grandfather enjoyed a couple stronger libations that I wasn't supposed to know about (if my mother only knew).

My father was similarly inventive and had several patents on radio components. He had studied at Tufts, like his father before him, and was an electrical, chemical, and mechanical engineer and good at all three. He published a book on shortwave radios. As a kid, he had a sailing canoe. We used to call him "the Professor," mostly because he was a little absent-minded, although he did teach in a Midwestern college for a year. He worked for the Merrimack Chemical Company, a division of Monsanto Chemical, in Everett, Massachusetts, and supported the entire family.

My mother, Helen Emmart Hood, came from New Bedford, Massachusetts. Emmart is my middle name. Her great-great-grandfather was the captain of a whaleship and was lost at sea. His surname was Gardner, my son Ted's middle name. Later, the family went into the textile business.

Our house had a sizable workshop in the basement, and there was a second workshop in the two-story barn in the backyard. The one in the basement was used by my grandfather for metalworking and by my father for his woodworking

Ted's grandfather's "Gas-Au-Lec" automobile
1905

hobby. Automobiles in various states of decomposition littered the barn. After school, I'd spend time with my grandfather in the basement, where he taught me a lot. I think that is something young people miss today, because generations of families don't live together anymore.

I showed more aptitude in the workshop than I did in school. I was never going to win a spelling bee. Mr. Dodge, my English teacher, said I was his worst pupil. My prospects for graduation increased, perhaps, when I gave him a shot out of a bottle we had snuck into a school dance. If poor at spelling and English, I was, however, good in math and science.

I would hurry home from school and work on a boat–in the early years model boats–when other kids would be playing baseball. My father told a writer from the *New Yorker* (published August 26, 1967), "Once, we had to fit a new garboard plank to *Shrew* [an R-boat]. It was a really tricky place, with all kinds of curves and twists and bevels–the sort of place where an average shipwright would ruin two or three planks before he got the right fit. Ted looked at it, planed the wood, looked at it again and did some more planing. Then he put it to the hull, and it went in perfectly. It was nice to give him things to do. His eyes and his hands were so well connected."

My younger brother, Bruce, was more well-rounded. For one thing, he was gifted academically. The Professor said, "Bruce, like most boys, had periods when he wanted to be doing other things, but Ted, from his first voyages in a basket in the bottom of the cockpit, never wanted to do anything but go sailing." Later, Bruce attended the Massachusetts Institute of Technology.

Ted and Bruce
1931

Ted, 2nd Grade
1935

The R-boat *Shrew*
1934

In 1933 the old Friendship sloop gave way to a Universal Rule R-boat that was called *Shrew*. [1] This 40-foot boat was practically new when my father bought her for $900. This was during the Depression; people were selling things at low cost because they needed money. My father, however, was lucky to have a good job.

I started racing with my father on *Shrew* when I was seven years old. These were Saturday races off Marblehead, where we might have a total of 150 boats participating each week. He would be the skipper, and my grandfather trimmed the spinnaker. Also in the crew were Stan Pidgeon, the son of Harry Pidgeon of Pidgeon Hollow Spars, East Boston, who originally made spars for Boston clippers and other merchant ships, and Nat Nichols, a good small-boat sailor. There would be quite a bit of arguing. My father didn't like to argue, but my grandfather did.

Although sometimes we got lucky, we never did that well because of very poor sails. We couldn't afford new sails, and we were racing against yachtsmen who had several new sails every year. New cotton sails had to be broken in, and many of our competitors would have their captains doing that during the week. To do this, you would first set them in good dry air–but not too breezy–and sail around on a reach, gradually stretching them. (You never wanted to use a new sail in damp, wet conditions, which would cause it to shrink and stretch unevenly.) It could take up to 10 hours of gentle sailing before you could race with them. New cotton sails didn't look very good when you first put them up. If they looked good then, they probably wouldn't after they were used a while.

I had an aptitude for recognizing yachts at a distance. My father told the *New Yorker*, "We used to go out off Marblehead on Sunday afternoons, and the whole horizon would be trimmed with boats. Ted would point to one so far away that you could barely see it and say, 'That's the *Andiamo*.' Sure enough, when we drew closer, it would be the *Andiamo*. He'd recognized the rig." The *Andiamo*, by the way, was a

---

[1] The Universal Rule, under which *Shrew* was rated, was created by Nathanael G. Herreshoff in 1898; its adoption in 1904 by the New York Yacht Club and then other eastern yacht clubs can be traced to yachts like *Reliance*, the largest yacht to compete in the America's Cup, in 1903. Interestingly, *Reliance* was designed by Herreshoff. The Universal Rule produced a rating in linear feet.

The Rating Formula:

$$.18\,L \times \sqrt{SA} + 3\sqrt{D}$$

Where L = Length, SA = Sail Area, and D = Displacement

Class boats were designated by a letter, I through S. "I" ended up being the largest. They were never built, however. J-Class yachts were. There were also M-boats, K-boats, Os, Ps, Qs, Rs, Ss and Ts–the smallest one. The S-boat was the only one that didn't seem to fit the Universal Rule. The boats were about 27 feet overall and about 20 feet on the water and they are exceptionally fast. R-boats had a maximum allowable rating of 20.

Shrew (#11) racing with the R-boat fleet off of Marblehead
1934

beautiful Marconi-rigged New York 50 designed and built by
Nathaniel Herreshoff. If you loved boats as I did, there was
no mistaking her.

In the America's Cup of 1937, the J-Class yacht _Ranger_,
skippered by Harold S. "Mike" Vanderbilt, easily beat
Endeavour II, skippered by Thomas Octave Murdock "T.O.M."
Sopwith. That event was followed by the New York Yacht
Club's Annual Regatta and Annual Cruise. For the J-Class
yachts, the season ended in Marblehead. This included _Ranger_,
both _Endeavours_, _Rainbow_, and _Yankee_. There were five races, all
won by _Ranger_, considered the best J-Class yacht ever. In 1937,
her one and only season, she won 35 of 37 races.

The assemblage, which included the huge steam yachts
that accompanied the racers, created quite a stir in our town.
Not the least of reasons was that _Ranger_'s primary designer
was W. Starling Burgess of Marblehead. [2] He also designed
such J-Class yachts as _Enterprise_, the successful defender in

[2] A 28-year-old Olin Stephens worked with Burgess on the design of _Ranger_. To protect his reputation, which was tarnished somewhat by _Rainbow_'s performance in
1934—the New York Yacht Club was lucky to retain the Cup—Burgess insisted that
who did what be kept secret. For years the controversy raged: Was Stephens or
Burgess responsible for the lines of _Ranger_, considered the fastest racing boat ever
built? After Burgess's death, a leading English journal wrote that Stephens designed
the boat. Mike Vanderbilt thought likewise. Respecting Burgess's wish, Stephens
remained silent on the matter for 20 years. In 1956 Vanderbilt wrote in the _New
Yorker_ magazine that Olin Stephens was responsible for _Ranger_. Stephens felt com-
pelled to answer the question at last. He wrote to the magazine: "Models for tank
testing were drawn up by Burgess and myself, individually, and by draftsmen under
close supervision, and the model selected to become _Ranger_, as the result of the
tank tests, was a Burgess model." Stephens went on to design such successful
America's Cup yachts as _Columbia_ (1958), _Constellation_ (1964), _Intrepid_ (1967),
Courageous (1974), and _Freedom_ (1980)—four of which used my sails.

Ralph Stedman Hood

"My father had several patents in radios. He was an electrical, chemical, and mechanical engineer and good at all three. He published a book on shortwave radios. We used to call him "the Professor," mostly because he was a little absent-minded, although he did teach in a midwestern college for a year."

As a student at Tufts University
1920

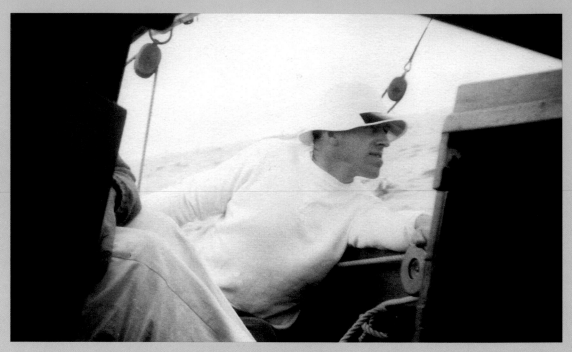

At the helm of the R-boat *Shrew*
1934

He was still working on a sail fabric development from his hospital bed a few days before he died. Such was the indomitable spirit and tenacity of Stedman Hood (at the loft we called him "The Professor" or simply "Prof.") whose body failed him on March 8, 1982. He was Ted Hood's father, but all of us at Hood knew him and loved him as our own.

Professor Hood was the patriarchal engineering genius of the family. His background in the textile and chemical industries provided an invaluable asset to his two sons, Bruce and Ted. He helped Ted in the development of sailcloth in both weaving and finishing. Without his expertise and his sheer determination to do the impossible, Hood Sailmakers would not be in the unique position it enjoys as a leader in sail technology. Without his humor and his vigor, life around the Marblehead loft would not have been nearly so enjoyable.

In addition to assisting Ted in the sailmaking business, Prof. also helped Bruce develop and operate a company which manufactures foam products.

The Professor would have enjoyed his memorial service. A small Dixieland combo played the music that he loved, and at one time loved to play. Not mournful or sad, just the tunes he knew. There were no tears among his family, who remembered a father and grandfather who was a cheerful man not given to the emotional weakness not all of us could suppress. He was eulogized by the Reverend Charles F. Hood, associate minister of Marblehead's Old North Church. Prof. would have been pleased at this gathering of family, coworkers, and friends. The real sadness is that we have been deprived of his friendship, wisdom, and the accumulated knowledge of his 82 years.

Professor Hood was associated with the Monsanto Chemical Corporation in Everett, Massachusetts, and the Hood family lived in Danvers and sailed on the Danvers River. Prof. had a workshop in the cellar, and there all three generations of Hoods (he, his father, Ted, and Bruce) constructed gadgets and fittings for whatever boats they had at the time.

Ted and Stedman on the Corinthian Yacht Club pier
1950

Egyptian cotton, which had become difficult to obtain after the war. While other sailmakers, upset by the new unforgiving material, were finding it hard to cope with, Ted and Prof. did some experimenting of their own with synthetic fibers. They concluded that the Orlon® and Dacron® cloth then available was not good enough to allow them to make a sail that would hold its shape under hard use. They purchased four looms and set them up in the back of the State Street loft with the help of a part-time fixer from the old Pequot Mills in Salem.

I will always remember Prof. saying to me, "If they (DuPont) can't do it, then I can." At the time he was building a machine to specially treat the Dacron yarn which would be used in cloth for a super-lightweight 12-Meter mainsail.

Professor Hood was instrumental in the development of all of Hood's priority fabrics, from rayon to the latest polyesters, nylons, composite cloths, and most recent innovations, Hood Eclipse, Laminar fabrics, and the Duroseam chafe-resistant treatment.

Professor Hood was a very special person to all of us; his presence here will be missed.

– Chris Bouzaid

Professor Hood started sailing as a very young boy off Salem, first in sailing canoes, then in a 27-foot gaff keelboat named *Wizard*. In the late 1920s, he became a charter member of the Salem Willows Yacht Club and moved up to a 40-foot Friendship sloop called *Marjay*.

After the 1938 hurricane, the Professor had an opportunity to purchase the 40-foot, Rhodes-designed cutter, *Narwhal*. Built in 1931, she had just come back from the Bermuda Race, for which she had been equipped with a modern rig and gear. Although, through damage sustained in the hurricane, she had been declared a total loss, the Professor and Ted repaired *Narwhal* and successfully cruised and raced her.

The family, who had been living in Danvers, Massachusetts, summered in Marblehead aboard *Narwhal* in 1942 and 1943, and in 1943 they moved to Marblehead Neck permanently.

In 1948, to keep the family hand in racing, the Professor bought an International One-Design, which he called *Princess*, and with which the Hoods won four season championships. Prof. also sailed with Ted on his 44-foot Alden yawl, which Ted bought and rebuilt after the 1954 hurricane.

Professor Hood owned two more boats after this; an S&S designed 50-footer, *Caravan*, (sistership to Irving Johnson's *Yankee*) on which he cruised south to the islands for several seasons, and a 42-foot Bristol trawler that he took down the Intracoastal Waterway to Florida for several years.

In the late 1950s, Professor Hood took early retirement from Monsanto to help his sons in their respective businesses. Sailmaking had been thrown into an upheaval by the introduction of synthetic cloth for sails as opposed to

Ted with "Prof." at one of the Hood looms
1960s

Narwhal with her new rig
1938

1930, and *Rainbow*, the successful defender in 1934. Burgess's father, Edward, likewise designed three successful America's Cup defenders, *Puritan*, *Mayflower*, and *Volunteer*, before dying young. Interested in automobiles and aviation as well as boat design, Starling Burgess trained with the Wright brothers and obtained their license to develop a seaplane.

During World War I, Burgess and the aviator Greely Curtis became well-known in the airplane business. In their factory at Little Harbor in Marblehead, they employed 800 people and turned out about eight seaplanes a month. In 1918, at the end of the war, the plant mysteriously burned to the ground and was never rebuilt. I would set up shop on this very site in 1954; I even used part of his foundation that had survived. I'd remain there until relocating the business to Portsmouth, Rhode Island, in 1988.

The visit of the J-Class yachts made quite an impression on me, too, then 10 years old. We went out on our R-boat *Shrew* to view the racing. My friend Brad Noyes was on the committee boat, which his father owned and loaned for the regatta. To see 20 sailors in white suits lined up on the deck pulling up the mainsail was memorable. We kids managed to sneak aboard a few of those J-Class yachts, which seemed a lot larger and more luxurious than they do today. They were unambiguously yachts, and kind of shocking even to my 10-year-old eyes as the Great Depression still lingered.

Vanderbilt and Sopwith and all the other J-Class owners had a day of racing aboard "Brutal Beasts," the 12-foot cat-rigged skiffs that kids of all ages raced at Marblehead. Friends and families loaned the boats for these races among the Cup luminaries. Vanderbilt actually swamped his boat, which wasn't too hard to do, as I found out racing and crewing on these boats in years to come.

This was, seemingly, the "last hurrah" for J-Class yachts. By 1941 seven of the ten ever built were gone, most of them scrapped for the war effort. Only *Endeavour*, *Shamrock*, and *Velsheda* remain; we saw them at the America's Cup Jubilee in Cowes, England, in 2001. They are still an impressive sight, as were the other older America's Cup boats that were racing—some with gaff rigs and topsails. [3]

On September 21, 1938, a hurricane ravaged New England. Called the "Great Hurricane of 1938" it had gusts of 186 mph, the highest ever recorded in New England, and the strongest sustained winds: 121 mph. It also produced the greatest storm tide of 19 feet on the south coast of New England. Six hundred people died, and property damage was $306 million in 1938–$20.8 billion in today's money. This included hundreds of yachts.

[3] In 2003, a re-creation of *Ranger* was launched. Also, *Cambria*, which predated the J-Class yachts, was recently converted to this type.

[4] Rhodes was also the designer of *Kirawan*, winner of the Bermuda Race in 1936. Later, there was his popular Rhodes 19 and *Weatherly*, winner of the 1962 America's Cup.

One storm-damaged yacht was *Narwhal*, a 40-foot Phil Rhodes-designed cutter built at Minneford Yacht Yard in City Island, New York. She was a great racer and an outstanding yacht on Long Island Sound in 1931–the boat that made Phil Rhodes famous. [4] Art Shuman, a young designer who worked with Frank Paine and C. Raymond Hunt at the George Lawley & Sons yard in Neponset, Massachusetts, had redesigned the rig of *Narwhal* for the 1938 Bermuda Race for Bob Leeson of Padanaram (South Dartmouth), Massachusetts. The boat had stainless-steel tube spreaders and through-the-boom roller-reefing, the first I ever saw. She also had double headstays side by side to make jib changing quicker. She had a beautiful wood mast and, of course, a whole new set of cotton racing sails made by Prescott Wilson, one of the best sailmakers of the day.

The hurricane nearly demolished the boat. One side was completely gone, including the deck and part of the cabin. It looked pretty hopeless. However, my father bought *Narwhal* from the insurance company, and she was hauled out at Palmer Scott's yard in nearby New Bedford, alongside the railway between the yacht-building shed and the river. We rebuilt her right there at Palmer Scott's. My father, grandfather, and I spent nearly every winter weekend there working outdoors. When it was warm enough, we would sleep on the boat and eat baked beans warmed on a kerosene heater. Otherwise, we'd bunk in a small room or with relatives in the New Bedford area. One of my mother's relatives ran Wamsutta Mills in New Bedford, where they wove sailcloth for Bob Bainbridge, of Howe & Bainbridge.

I was just 11, but Palmer Scott himself taught me how to caulk a boat. It was a pleasure to work all of those weekends on *Narwhal* and sneak off to watch the men building production-line sailboats: Shuman 36 Singlehanders, 37-foot Alden Coastwise Cruisers, Alden Overnighters, Sparkman & Stephens Weekenders, and a whole line of 42-foot Coast Guard picket boats. I can recall them so clearly to this day. It was amazing what I learned watching these boats being built: steaming frames, planking, pouring lead, and so many other procedures. I was shy, but I did ask a lot of questions. I soaked it all in. I guess it is like a young person learning a language: I learned boatbuilding just by watching, asking questions, and then working on boats myself.

My own first boat was a rowboat that I converted into a sailboat when I was 12. I did this in the yard at the house in Danvers. I added a centerboard trunk and centerboard, built a rudder, put on rudder pintles, made floorboards, and installed a deck on the forward three feet through which the mast went, to help support the top of the centerboard trunk. I made the spruce mast and boom, and I bought most of the hardware in the five-and-dime: all the screws, nuts and bolts, wire, and turnbuckles. The boat had a Marconi main and a genoa jib. I taught myself to make both of the sails by read-

Narwhal with Ted's father at the helm, his mother, her sister, and Ted's grandfather (in the companionway)
1940

Ted sailing his first boat, a converted rowboat
1939

ing a book I got out of the library called *Gray's Sailmaking*.

The boat was about five feet wide and eight feet long, with high freeboard. It showed great stability–the only small boat in Marblehead you could take out in a nor'east gale when the races were called off. At such times, we would jump in our boat to sail around. That was the beginning of my designing and building beamy boats with big jibs.

Drawing boats was a passion of mine: profiles, interiors, and sail plans. I once drew a 60-footer based on *Blitzen*, a 56-foot Sparkman & Stephens sloop built in 1938. I actually had dreams of building the 60-footer in our backyard and started making a list of materials to build it. My father eventually convinced me to build a smaller boat–a 12 footer–when I was 15. He suggested that it would be useful to build a model out of cardboard first. This two-foot model helped me to figure out how to construct the boat. Be it planking or framing, the cardboard behaved the same as did the wood in a larger vessel. The model also gave me a good idea of what needed to be changed in terms of design.

I began by going to a lumberyard and buying a 16-foot-long piece of Philippine mahogany that was about 18 inches wide and $1^1/_2$ inches thick. I put it in my little kiddy cart and hauled it two miles to a sawmill on the Danvers

Doohdet
1942

riverfront. I had them split it down the middle; the result was two pieces over a half inch thick. Next, I had them plane them down to $3/_8$ inch thick. I took these beautiful, thin, 17-inch-wide planks home in my cart and used one for each side of the boat. I had to split them into three pieces each to fit them to the shape of the hull so that all top three planks on both sides matched each other as if they were from one piece of wood.

It took most of the winter to build the boat. I would come home from school each day, steam a few ribs, and put them in place on the form that I built. Fortunately, we had steam heat in the house, and I hooked up a tube to the heater and put it in the end of an old wooden gutter pipe to use as a steam box. The frames were only $5/_8$ by $1/_2$ inch sections; the oak stem was laminated with Weldwood glue, and all the seams of the boat were edge-fastened and glued as well.

I called the boat *Doohdet*: Ted Hood spelled backwards. The dictionary said it means a well-dressed female, and the boat was definitely that. She had a tall, double-spreader rig, hollow spruce mast, and bronze-wire rigging, which I spliced

and soldered, serving all the splices. I made the sails out of a special Zelan-treated DuPont finish on cotton cloth, which made them waterproof and, thus, not so susceptible to rain and wet weather that would affect their shape when sailing. This was the beginning of my research on sailcloth. *Doohdet* had a dagger-centerboard that was adjustable fore and aft as well as up and down. This was also the start of my infatuation with centerboards.

After several years on the hard, *Narwhal* resumed her racing career, proving quite successful for us. Summers, we lived aboard her in Marblehead Harbor–gas rationing during World War II made driving back and forth to Danvers impossible. My brother had his own Brutal Beast to race, but I would crew with other people any chance I could. I would also do odd jobs like repairing house porches or fences, working in boatyards, or doing sail repair. I would describe us as "making do" rather than "well to do."

One summer my friend Bradley Noyes and I started a lobster business with over 60 traps that we built. The real lobstermen thought we were just kids taking business away from them, so one of them cut our traps loose. From 60 traps we were down to 20. We were pretty angry at the time, and Bradley was sitting out there guarding our traps with a gun. I don't think he intended to use it, but we were angry. We had worked hard building the traps and then had them cut loose. Nevertheless, the gain from our summer of lobstering was $200. We also sold the boat for $100 more than it cost us–not the last boat I'd sell at a profit.

When I was 10, I learned the Viennese waltz at Miss Harriet James's School of Dance at Hamilton Hall in nearby Salem. This was at first a command performance orchestrated by my mother, but I came to enjoy it. I must have shown some skills at it because Miss James, at the time 80 years old, let me become an instructor in the Viennese waltz. My talents with the Viennese waltz helped me to win the most important person in my life.

After the summer of 1942, we didn't move back to Danvers but stayed on *Narwhal* through the end of October; again gas rationing due to the war made the commute back to Danvers unworkable. Besides gas rationing, it was also a period of blackouts. No bright lights were allowed at night so as not to tip off enemy planes or submarines. I did my homework aboard *Narwhal* by candlelight; any other light would be too bright. I'd take papers to school often covered with candle wax, as were my books. We commuted to school in a hearse; it became the school bus for eight of us living on Marblehead Neck at the time.

Then we moved into a brown-shingled house with four bedrooms on Marblehead Neck, high on a cliff with a 180-degree ocean view. To the south the windows took in Boston Harbor, Hingham, and Scituate, and to the northeast you could see Gloucester Harbor. It was beautiful waterfront property that cost all of $12,500 during the war—waterfront property wasn't too valuable then. My brother, various friends, and I did work on the house. We replaced the entire roof with slate. The house is now probably worth $2 million —times change.

Security was tight in those days. You couldn't get onto Marblehead Neck without a pass, and, as mentioned, the top two-thirds of the headlights of the cars were painted black. At night, all the curtains in the house had to be drawn. The Army had several barracks on Marblehead Neck, and there were Coast Guard structures. There were tall antisubmarine watchtowers on the heights along the shoreline in Gloucester, Manchester, Marblehead, Nahant, and south to the Cape Cod Canal. Convoys for Europe would make up outside Boston during the war, and I believe about 15 ships were sunk in Massachusetts Bay during this period. The shoreline was covered with such a thick oil slick from sunken ships that you couldn't walk on the beach. Oil-soaked lifejackets and other wreckage, as well as dead and dying birds, would wash up on the beach.

I enlisted in the Navy in 1945 while a junior in high school, about a month before I was to be drafted. They sent me to boot camp for 10 weeks in Sampson, New York. I returned home on leave before being assigned to more training or duty. There, I became very ill, and an ambulance took me to the Navy hospital in the Fargo Building in Boston. Finally, I was diagnosed with viral pneumonia. There is no medication for such a virus. I was in the hospital for more than two weeks. The guy in the bed next to me had the same thing and died of it. I remember eating nothing for seven days. Back then my family had a hard time finding out how I was doing in the hospital.

After I recovered, I went to Newport for further military training. I got off the bus, walked into the Navy base, was told I was AWOL, and wound up in the brig. It was a frightening experience for an 18-year-old. In time, they found out I had been in the Navy hospital, and they released me.

In Newport, I spent my time studying navigation and went to firefighting school. Also, we went out on a 10-day training cruise on the *Ticonderoga*-class aircraft carrier *Randolph*, which was in Newport for repairs. It was my luck to be picked for KP duty; I had to cut 1,000 grapefruit in half and peel potatoes for 2,000 men.

Seaman Hood
1945

FREDERICK EWART HOOD

To you who answered the call of your country and served in its Armed Forces to bring about the total defeat of the enemy, I extend the heartfelt thanks of a grateful Nation. As one of the Nation's finest, you undertook the most severe task one can be called upon to perform. Because you demonstrated the fortitude, resourcefulness and calm judgment necessary to carry out that task, we now look to you for leadership and example in further exalting our country in peace.

Harry Truman

THE WHITE HOUSE

Truman's call for leadership
1945

Ted in uniform
1945

**The International One Design *Princess*
sailing off of Marblehead**
1949

Off Bermuda, we were hit by a hurricane. The *Randolph* –all 27,100 tons of her–was heeling what seemed like five degrees. We were taking solid spray over the flight deck. Destroyer escorts looked like submarines. My first experience with big ships in bad weather made me realize the strength of the sea.

I was eventually assigned to the naval gun factory in Washington, D.C., specifically to a 125-foot tug, a very modern diesel-electric vessel. Coming from Massachusetts made me unpopular. I was considered a "Yankee bastard" by the other two ranking members of the crew, who were tough rednecks from the South. I got the short end of all the duties. There was only one other coxswain on the boat. I painted the whole tug myself from the waterline up.

The 243-foot presidential yacht *Williamsburg* was berthed next to us, and President Harry S. Truman often went out on her to relax. Nearby was the 50-foot powerboat used by Admiral Chester W. Nimitz. I used to cast off their lines and take care of them. I remember President Truman tipping his hat to me when I handled the *Williamsburg*'s lines.

We'd take the guns made in Washington and deliver them to the Aberdeen Proving Ground, up Chesapeake Bay. The pay was $56 a month, and I would actually save money from that.

After 18 months in the Navy, I returned home and finished my last year in high school, winding up in the same class as my younger brother. Upon graduating, I considered going to the Massachusetts Maritime Academy but decided to attend business-school classes instead. I did one year and then transferred to Wentworth Institute in Boston, where I studied building construction, engineering, design, and the business of building houses. I learned how to cut frames, lay brick, plaster walls, and estimate building cost. I even learned business law. Many students were older, experienced builders sent by their companies for more education. We all learned from them.

While attending Wentworth, I would drive my father and three others to work at Merrimack Chemical in Everett. One was a sales engineer, one a sales manager, one in management, and my father was in charge of research, development, engineering, and design. From them, I learned a lot about the various aspects of business. I would leave the car at the plant and walk to catch the elevated train to Boston. At the end of the day, I'd have the car waiting for them and drive them home. This continued for three years.

All this schooling was paid for by the GI Bill, which made it easier on my family, which was putting my brother Bruce through MIT. During summers I augmented the family finances by repairing sails, recutting slow sails, and making new ones. Boats would come into the harbor with torn sails, and the launch men would send them over to see me at home, where I did the work in my bedroom.

After completing my schooling at Wentworth Institute I

started in the construction business. My first project was a three-bedroom cape near the waterfront in Marblehead. John Bainbridge, brother of Bob Bainbridge of Howe & Bainbridge sailcloth, hired me to design and build the house. John was one of the men I had driven to Merrimack Chemical before going on to school.

I had the foundation in and some of the framing up when the next-door neighbor, a well-to-do lawyer, began complaining that this house would spoil his view. He offered Bainbridge everything he had invested in the property and materials plus $5,000, a lot of money back then.

Suddenly out of a job, I had to choose; should it be houses or boats? I then decided to give sailmaking a try and opened my first loft. History, I think, would prove it a good choice. Nevertheless, I often think I would have done fairly well at homebuilding.

We belonged to the Corinthian Yacht Club, where we raced *Narwhal*, a cruising yacht, and then *Princess*, an International One Design (IOD), purchased after I got out of the United States Navy in 1946.

One night I went to the yacht club for a dance. A girl from Salem whom I had dated brought a friend along. My brother started dancing with her, but I was smitten so I cut in. I tried to impress this girl, Sue Blake, with my skill at the Viennese waltz.

Waltzing wasn't all of it, however. I remember Sue fell down while dancing fast. I was sort of a wild dancer back then. I took her home late. It wasn't long before her next-door neighbor learned that Sue was dating one of the Hood boys and asked Sue's mother which one. "Ted," she said. The neighbor said, "Well, that is better than his brother, Bruce, but they are both pretty bad."

I enjoyed life: racing sailboats, partying, drinking, and dancing. Work hard, play hard. Sue was six years younger than I was, but we dated steadily. There was moonlight sailing on an International One Design. Four weeks after meeting Sue I asked her to marry me. She gave me no answer.

My lifelong friend Brad Noyes recalled stopping by my house to see me during this period. My mother told him that I had gone to South Hadley, Massachusetts. Brad couldn't understand it as we always did things together; he knew everything about me, and I knew everything about him. South Hadley is the home of Mount Holyoke College, where Sue attended school. "It was then," Brad said years later, "that I recognized this relationship was serious. Very serious."

Another significant hurricane to strike New England was Carol, which made landfall on August 31, 1954. By the time Carol departed the Northeast, 65 people were dead, 4,000 homes were destroyed, and 3,500 automobiles and a like number of boats were lost. A couple of days later I drove down to Padanaram on Buzzards Bay, looking for wrecks to fix up. It was almost like family history repeating itself as I spotted

Salvaging *Nova*
1954

***Princess* racing off Marblehead**
1956

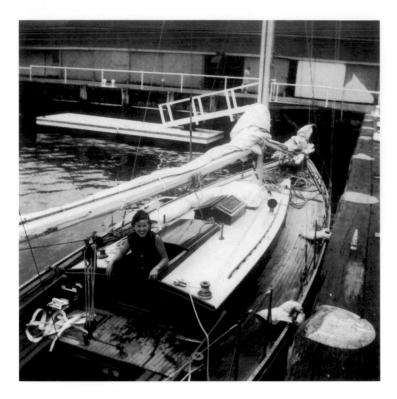

Sue during the honeymoon aboard *Princess*
1955

**Family cruise: Ted surrounded by his children
Rick, Bob, Ted, and Nancy**
1969

Nova, a 44-foot Alden yawl. She had sailed right over the top of the highway bridge into a small cove and ended up perched on a seawall and a jetty. She was lying on her side, which was pretty badly damaged, as were the rails and other things. The rig was still in her, however. The insurance company said she was a total loss, one of the reasons being that they couldn't figure out how to get a boat with six feet of draft out of a cove with three feet of water at high tide.

In any event, I bought the boat and started working on her. Then the owner of the house, whose seawall the boat had landed on, sued us for damages. We had to pay $450–as much as we had paid for the boat. Nevertheless, it could have cost that much, or even more, to litigate this in the courts. As it was, a deputy sheriff was sitting next to the boat so we couldn't work on it anyhow.

Once that matter was taken care of, we began salvaging the boat. My father and I, with the help of another person, dug a very narrow channel just for the keel, to get her through the drawbridge and to a boatyard on the other side. This we accomplished in the muck at low tide, the boat high and dry. Then we jacked the boat up somewhat so we could patch her with timber and canvas, in hopes that she would float. We built a makeshift cradle under the boat. For floats, we bought two large Navy inflatable pontoons from Grossman's Surplus Company–$48 for the pair. We placed them on one side of the boat, so the boat would float at an angle of 30 degrees and, thus, present less draft. Then we waited for the full moon high tide to arrive, at 4:00 a.m. When the water rose, we inflated the pontoons with canisters of carbon dioxide. My poor father, who was holding the hose from the canisters against the pontoon, got his hand so chilled that he just about froze his thumb and finger off. It took a week to heal.

When the pontoons were filled, the boat floated. It was quite amazing to see it float at such an angle of heel. With a skiff we slowly pulled the heeled-over yacht toward the drawbridge. We had pumps aboard in case the patching was inadequate, but we found that the boat was leaking faster–considerably faster–than the pumps could pump. Furthermore, the drawbridge wasn't manned until 9:00 a.m. Fortunately, we remembered to bring a garbage can full of sawdust. Using a tin can on a stick, we forced the sawdust under the hull as close to the leaks as we could. The sawdust was sucked into the leaks, eventually blocking them and giving the pumps the upper hand. This is a trick we'd learned from an old boatyard foreman.

At 9:00 a.m. we passed through the bridge, and an hour later we were hauled out at the Concordia Yard, about 500 feet away. A week later, *Nova* arrived in Marblehead on her own bottom under her own fixed-up engine. That winter we restored her and renamed her *Princess*, the name we had used on our old International One Design.

I met Sue Blake when she was in her second year of a five-year nursing program at Mount Holyoke College. At this time, I had been working as a sailmaker for two years. Two years later we were cruising aboard a chartered schooner with my father, mother, brother, and his girlfriend. One night in Quissett Harbor, on Buzzards Bay, Sue woke me up and finally replied, "Yes! I'll marry you."

We got married the next summer, on July 3, 1955. We couldn't hold the ceremony on the 4th of July as that is a race day in Marblehead, and most of those in the wedding party, and a lot of those coming to the party, were sailors. After the reception, my brother took us to a hotel in Boston, where we spent the night. It was a 100-degree heat wave, and the air conditioner in the room kept blowing fuses, so the hotel gave us a box of fuses to keep it running.

The next day, we took a train across the Cape Cod Canal to Falmouth Harbor, where my father and Sue's father had delivered our 44-foot yawl *Princess*. We cruised to Nantucket for a honeymoon, and afterwards we lived on the boat in Marblehead Harbor. I would row Sue ashore very early on Monday mornings so she could make the two-and-a-half-hour drive in my old Ford convertible to Hartford Hospital to begin work at 8:00 a.m. She would spend the workweek in Hartford. This lasted until the fall when she graduated. Our four children followed: Rick in July 1957, Ted in April 1959, Robert in April 1962, and Nancy in February 1965.

As I write this 50 years later, Sue remains my wife and life companion, and often an important member of the crew of our ocean-racing yachts. She had most of the responsibility of raising our four fine children. All of them have worked at my company full-time or during summers. Sue would often tell me she should have married a doctor because of all the phone calls I would get, particularly when in the sailmaking business. We did a lot of sailing when the children were younger. We always took off the last week of the summer to go cruising together. There is nothing like cruising to keep the family together. Today there are so many other choices for youngsters that it is hard to get them away on the boat. Those were great years.

As for me, I continue to sail and to race—even at 78 years old—and continue to design, build, and dream about boats, be they sail or power. I guess I'm still trying to make up for that month of sailing missed so early.

Ted at the sewing machine
1970s

Chapter 2

The Sailmaker

"(Hood) borrowed his grandmother's fifty-year-old Singer sewing machine, installed it in his bedroom, and hustled up some orders. It wasn't long before Ted was improving sails as well as repairing them. If a sail was brought to him for a little restitching, he liked to take it completely apart and put it back together discreetly recut and reshaped. He enjoyed the feel of the cotton canvas in his hands and the smell of the seizing twine that helped hold grommets, hanks, and snap hooks in place, and there was a physical satisfaction in working with steel needle and leather palm, carrying the thread through several heavy layers of cloth."

— the New Yorker *magazine*

My formal training in sailmaking was limited. When I was 12, I borrowed a thin little book called *Gray's Sailmaking* from the library and read it carefully. Years later, I applied for a job at Clooney Sailmakers in nearby Gloucester. Clooney mostly made sails for fishing boats but did make the occasional sail for yachts. I was told I had to join the union and apprentice for seven years. As a young man in a hurry, that wasn't for me.

If my formal training was limited, my hands-on experience in sailmaking was more extensive. With the impulsiveness of youth, I decided to let the marketplace decide if I were a sailmaker or not. My parents did not discourage me from following this entrepreneurial road, which is an uncertain path for anyone just starting out. It was, in fact, just the opposite for my younger brother, Bruce, and me. It was as if we were raised to take such risks.

My father was facing his own challenges in this regard. After years as an executive with Merrimack Chemical Company, a division of Monsanto Chemical, he refused a transfer to St. Louis and decided to place a bet on his own talents. The timing was such that he could help his two sons who were doing much the same thing.

So ready or not, a sailmaker I became in 1950. The launch

**An early Hood spinnaker on an
International 210 Class boat**
1952

drivers would steer customers my way. There was no other sailmaker in town, and they knew me—as I was always hanging around the waterfront—and what I did. They knew all the kids and looked out for them.

I would sew sails in my bedroom on my grandmother's 50-year-old Singer sewing machine—which I still have and cannot believe I built sails with—and lay them out in the living room, after rolling up the carpet. I'd repair some fairly sizable sails, for boats up to 40 feet or so. My mother didn't mind as long as I cleaned up afterwards.

I was busy enough that soon I moved to a decrepit boat-yard next to the Boston Yacht Club in Marblehead. I rented a sizable space that had formerly been a spar loft. So dirty and rough was the floor that I had to put paper down to keep the sails clean and undamaged. My first employee was Gertrude Nicholson, an elderly Marblehead widow who worked as a seamstress. The pay for such work back then was $1 an hour. Much of our work was building mains and jibs for Interclub dinghies, and for International 110s and 210s—all were C. Raymond Hunt designs.

I was fortunate that Marblehead was home to the noted designer C. Raymond Hunt.[1] A gifted helmsman who had learned to sail on shallow Duxbury Bay, he had gained an uncommon mastery of wind and tide in Duxbury Ducks. As a teenager, he twice won the Sears Cup, awarded to the best junior sailor in the Northeast.[2] He went on to compete in R-boats, Q-boats, and the J-Class yacht *Yankee*, a contender in the 1934 America's Cup. Hunt had worked for Frank Paine, *Yankee*'s Boston-based designer, and then joined Waldo Howland as a partner in the Concordia Company. Hunt designed the 24-foot, double-ended, fin-keel International 110

---

[1] The source material on C. Raymond Hunt comes primarily from Joseph Gribbins's "Ray Hunt – New England Archimedes," *Nautical Quarterly* 25.

[2] The Sears Cup is, today, the U.S. Junior Triplehanded Championship.

for Massachusetts Bay racers in 1939. It was one of the first sailboats built of marine plywood. This novel design came off his board about the same time as the classically traditional lines of his career-defining Concordia yawl design. Concordia yawls are prized to this day. After the war, Hunt continued to produce classic and innovative designs, including the International 210, a 30-foot, hard-chine, fin-keel boat; the 5.5-Meter sloops *Quixotic*—which we would sail in the 1956 Olympic trials—and *Chaje II*—which would win the 5.5-Meter World Championship in 1960; and the 12-Meter *Easterner*, which Chandler Hovey entered in the 1958 America's Cup trials. Although Ray Hunt was a sailor and sailboat designer to his core, his best-known and most influential contribution to boating is the deep-vee hull, which has influenced the shape and performance of powerboats since 1960.

In 1950, Bradley Noyes and I accompanied Ray Hunt to Bermuda to crew on *Princess*, my family's International One Design (IOD) in the Amorita Cup. In his gruff way he called Brad "Bilgey" and me "Junior." He maintained a quiet, intense focus during races. Hunt used my sails during this regatta, as did another IOD, I believe. We won the Amorita Cup. Then we won the North American Match Racing Championship for the Prince of Wales Bowl, which was also sailed in Bermuda. This was my first exposure to match racing, which characterizes the America's Cup as well.

Hunt had a design office on the Marblehead waterfront, about a two-minute walk from my loft. He must have liked my sails because shortly after we returned he put a sign in his window saying, "C. Raymond Hunt & Fred E. Hood Associates." He wanted to sell my sails. I was flattered. He helped me considerably because he knew the top sailors. Then, as now, this was a people business that relied on informal relationships.

Hunt may have been Marblehead's preeminent yacht designer at the time, but he wasn't the only one. L. Francis Herreshoff, Nathanael's son, also had a design office there. He worked and lived in the fairly eerie Castle Brattahlid at Crocker Park. He had designed the J-Class yacht *Whirlwind* for the 1930 America's Cup trials and also the beautiful *Tioga*—later famous as *Ticonderoga*—for my friend Brad Noyes's father.

I once asked Herreshoff for a sail plan for a Bounty or some other series yacht he designed. I had a commission to build sails for one. A sail plan—not to be confused with a lines drawing—just shows the yacht in profile and the rig measurements: J, P, E, etc. Such a request is standard from a sailmaker to a yacht designer. Without it, sails won't fit. L. Francis refused me, saying I might steal the design.

From the beginning, I wasn't interested in being a "me-too" sailmaker. In 1951, with but a year under my belt in this business, I developed the crosscut spinnaker. Mains and jibs of those days were crosscut, made up of horizontal panels. Spinnakers, on the other hand, had vertical panels. I reasoned

1951
The Crosscut Spinnaker

"I found out that the crosscut spinnaker was a lot better; it had a number of problems with the shaping of the head but it would fly wider, and projected area is key for a downwind sail."

The vertical-cut spinnaker

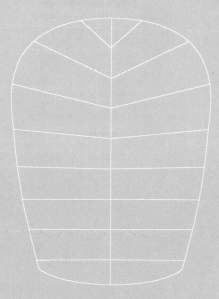

The crosscut spinnaker

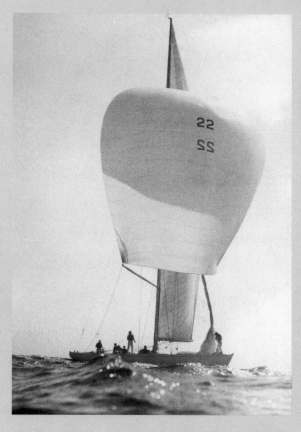

The 12-Meter *Intrepid* with her crosscut spinnaker showing its full shoulders

The first spinnakers were cut with a vertical panel orientation (above left). While this made sense from a sail-construction point of view, the stresses induced by this design cause the shoulders of the spinnaker to collapse toward the middle of the sail, reducing the sail's projected area.

The crosscut spinnaker panel layout (above middle) focused the stress to the middle of the sail, allowing the relatively stress-free shoulders to expand, increasing projected area.

The use of crosscut spinnakers on the 12-Meter *Vim* during the 1958 America's Cup campaign established the crosscut spinnaker as a breakthrough design that quickly became the worldwide standard.

The crosscut spinnaker remained the standard for many years, until the advent of the radial-head spinnaker in the 1970s.

A perfect example of the high shoulders and large projected area created by the crosscut design is shown at left on the Australian yacht *Teal*

that this crosscut orientation might work well for spinnakers too. In making a chute for a 210, I tried orienting the seams at every possible angle from vertical to horizontal. I then flew the sail on a test pole outside. I kept the clews at the same height and put a stick across and measured the width to see which shape had the greatest projected area. I determined that the crosscut spinnaker was a lot better. It was a challenge for me to shape the head, but it would fly wider, and projected area is of key importance in a downwind sail. I even patented this design.

The crosscut spinnaker was copied by any number of sailmakers. I never really enforced the patent. We would sometimes write letters to people and ask them to stop, but the market was not big enough in those days to make it worth fighting over.

Another thing we did in the early days was to design a mainsail with reinforcing tape, akin to the Tape-Drive sails one hears about today. The tape, used in the mainsail of a 210, ran from the head to the clew, just in front of the battens, where there was a hard spot. The hope was the special Dacron tape would take the load off the battens. It seemed to work, but the tape was primitive and difficult to apply.

The spar loft where I first set up shop was nearly impossible to heat, so I soon moved into a space used by Charlie Parsons, a canvas-maker who in the winter would follow his customers and the sun to Florida. The loft was heated with a coal stove; the trick was to keep it burning through the night. In the summers, Charlie Parsons and I would share the space. In 1952, I hired Alice Benoit as a second stitcher.

These were the waning days of cotton sailcloth. Cotton had an extraordinary run in sailmaking, beginning in about 1820. It was used on American warships and American yachts; flax continued to be used on British warships and British yachts. Cotton, like flax, is a plant fiber. Cotton fibers come from the seed case of the cotton plant. Flax fibers are extracted from the stem of the flax plant.

Recall that famous 1851 race between *America*, a New York Yacht Club schooner, and 15 yachts representing the Royal Yacht Squadron in Cowes, England. *America* won the trophy that became known as the America's Cup in her honor. She sported cotton sails, while the British yachts flew flax. Cotton stretched less.

Low-stretch sails that provided an edge when sailing to windward were among *America*'s secrets; she could sail five or six degrees closer to the wind, a huge advantage. Wrote British journalist Dixon Kemp, "In 1851 the yacht *America* came here, and the superiority of the cut, make, and set of

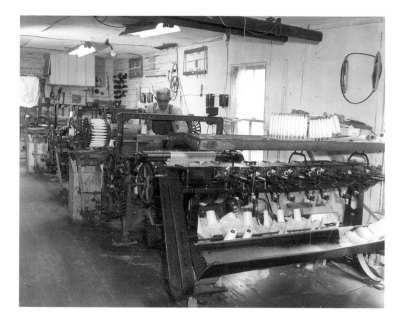

The first looms to weave Hood sailcloth
1952

***Vim* with her crosscut spinnaker leads *Columbia*—note the wider shoulders on *Vim*'s spinnaker, as well as her larger mainsail roach**
1958

her cotton canvas revolutionized sailmaking in England."

I preferred long-staple Egyptian cotton; the longer fibers allowed a tighter weave, minimizing stretch. I bought such cotton sailcloth from Howe & Bainbridge in Boston or Harrington King, which was just down the street from Howe & Bainbridge. Harrington King was much more of a ships' chandlery than a cloth supplier. It had outfitted the clipper ships during the great age of sail. I remember the five-story building well; the elevator would stop on a floor that would have nothing but rope or anchors. Imagine an entire floor of anchors! There would be hemp, anchor chain, sail hooks, slides, thimbles, and blocks from the old shipping days. The smell was evocative. It was a history lesson as much as a visit to a supplier.

I'd go through every roll of cloth at either establishment and pull them in the long direction, called the warp, in the short direction (the fill), and on the diagonal—the bias direction. Sailmakers sometimes refer to this process of touching sailcloth to ascertain its qualities as "hand." I'd take my time; sometimes it would take me hours. I truly enjoyed it. Thinking about cloth and thinking about sails in this way was the beginning of my formal education in sailmaking. Often I'd take what was considered second-quality cloth because the seconds were better than the firsts for my purposes.

Ted checks out a sail on the loft roof test mast
1960s

Ted on the loft floor re-cutting a sail
1950s

I'd look for different things for different sails. Mechanical loadings in a headsail and a mainsail are different, so it is important for a sailmaker to match cloth strength to load. The weaving process is so complex that one can almost say no two bolts of cloth are the same. Of course, finally, I had to take what I could get.

By 1952, Orlon had largely replaced cotton in sailmaking. Orlon is the trademark name for acrylic fiber, developed by DuPont. Although I enjoyed working with cotton, I embraced the new material. Orlon has many benefits. It is resistant to sunlight, it doesn't shrink, it resists moisture, and it shows high tensile strength. As important for a relatively new sailmaker like me, it was a revolutionary change in materials that put us all on nearly equal footing.

Rather than trying to find appropriate Orlon cloth from suppliers like Howe & Bainbridge or Harrington King, I began to weave it myself, beginning in 1952. In the back of the space I shared with Charlie Parsons, I put in four pillow-case looms purchased from Pequot Mills, in Salem. They were the right width for sailcloth, and I paid just $50 apiece. They were junk; we had to rebuild them. I'd keep the looms weaving Orlon and later Dacron, or polyester, all during the week, and then I'd have a loom fixer come in on Saturdays and tune them up. This was important because they were worked extraordinarily hard. The looms required a fair amount of babysitting, too. I could fix small things; bigger problems required the attention of Tony Caron, a loom technician.

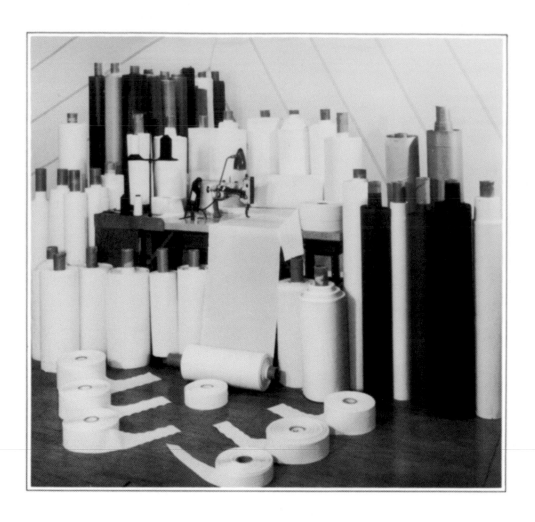

The sailcloth no sailmaker can buy.

If you ask a number of sailmakers what kind of cloth they use, they'll name quite a number of brands. But one that they won't mention is Hood sailcloth. That's because we don't sell it to them.

There are good reasons why we don't sell it commercially. First, we just don't have enough Hood sailcloth to spread around. Our two mills struggle mightily to meet the demands of our lofts around the world. And it's taken a fantastic investment in research, machinery development, and training to bring those mills to their present state of productivity. We can't increase our output without similar long-term effort.

Second, we think other sailmakers would be reluctant to pay the costs of our cloth — the out-of-pocket costs of buying it, the costs of working with it, and the costs of learning a whole new technology of sailmaking.

And we mean that — a whole new technology of sailmaking.

Our picture shows a sample of each of the different sailcloths we now make and use in Hood sails. There are more than 40 types, not to mention a rainbow of colors. All are engineered for specific purposes in sailmaking. They give our sailmakers the greatest cloth resources of any sailmakers in the world.

We could buy the same cloths any other sailmaker buys. But we make our own.

Hood makes a difference. And we want you to know it.

HOOD SAILMAKERS, INC.
Little Harbor Way
Marblehead, Mass. 01945

Costa Mesa, Calif. • Annapolis, Md. • Jericho, Long Island, N.Y. • Vancouver, B.C. • Kingston, Ont. • Lymington, Hants, England • Nice, France • Sidney, Australia • Auckland, New Zealand

This advertisement for Hood Sailmakers points out the advantages of Hood's own sailcloth

1972

Superior Hood Sailcloth

"In some ways, their constant chatter gave me energy. In other ways, it gave me fear. I had to make good sails and sell them—otherwise the din from the weaving machines would slow. Or stop. That said, being the only sailmaker to weave his own cloth then, helped me to make good sails and sell them. It spoke to our purposefulness and helped to distinguish Hood Sailmakers from the rest."

Hood Sailcloth*

The Competitors Cloth*

*Enlarged 107 diameters by Scanning Electron Microscope—both samples show equal areas of 4.5 oz. sailcloth. Note that the individual filaments are of equal size in both samples.

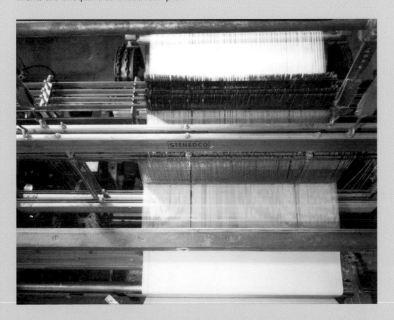

The key to the superiority of Hood sailcloth was how tightly the cloth was woven.

The photos above show the extremely tight weave of Hood cloth compared to other sailcloth available. This tight weave locked the fibers together, creating much higher stretch resistance in the weak bias (diagonal) direction.

The keys to obtaining a tight weave were the looms that Ted reconfigured for weaving his cloth. The photo at left shows one of the many Hood sailcloth looms, modified to weave narrow but extremely tightly woven cloth.

Ted checking out a sail on the loft floor with Dev Barker
1960s

The sail loft building at Little Harbor
1960

Marblehead Manufacturing ("M^2")
1968

The looms were separated from the main loft space by a curtain to diminish the noise, but also because of the need to keep the humidity up when weaving. The yarns get brittle if the air is too dry. The weaving mills that congregated in Fall River and New Bedford, Massachusetts, benefited because those cities are near the water, where the humidity is naturally high. They were known as "steam-cotton companies" as they used steam to supply additional humidity. The looms were also isolated because we didn't wish to share our secrets with the rest of the sailmaking world.

In some ways, the looms' constant chatter gave me energy. In other ways, it filled me with fear. It was like a scorekeeper. I had to make good sails and sell them; otherwise, the din from the weaving machines would slow. Or stop. That said, being the only sailmaker at the time weaving his own cloth helped me to make good sails and sell them. I could better control the characteristics of the finished sails by controlling the manufacture of the cloth. As important, it spoke to our purposefulness and helped to distinguish Hood Sails from the rest of the sailmaking industry.

Eventually we built a proper loft in Marblehead—more later—and added about 18 looms, bringing the total to 22. Then we built a second facility called "M^2" for Marblehead Manufacturing, where eventually there were 50 looms. There was also a tower there, allowing us to extrude polypropylene that we used to make "Floater Cloth" for light-air spinnakers. Then we expanded further to Fall River with an additional 60 looms in rented space, until the owner of the building told us to leave. He feared the weaving process was threatening his building's structural integrity. That's how hard we pushed the weaving process. An expansion to Ireland followed, which is running to this day, although owned by another. In time there were 110 looms weaving.

In weaving, I would vary the size of the yarns depending on the application. For mainsails, which, as I mentioned, were crosscut, I wanted fill-oriented cloth. To accomplish this in the weaving process, we made the fill yarns thicker than the warp yarns. The larger fill yarns tend to be straighter and more resistant to stretch. The thinner warp yarns bend around the thicker fill yarns. A crimped yarn will stretch like a crimped telephone cord. It was helpful, too, to limit bias stretch in such sails.

For headsails, I wanted equal stretch in all directions. That meant the fill and warp needed to be fairly balanced, with yarns of about the same size. Different cloth for mainsails and jibs was, perhaps, a first in sailmaking. We could do it as we wove our own cloth.

The cloth I wove was 20 inches wide—the size of a pillowcase. Commercially available sailcloth typically came in 36-inch-wide bolts. The smaller panels, which would shrink even more in the finishing, allowed me to move the shuttle less distance and to weave the material tighter than commercial fin-

Constantly taking notes on how to improve the shape of Hood sails
1970s

ishers could. This was important because sailcloth is the most tightly woven textile in the world. A tight weave contributes to low stretch and to windward ability in the sail; this is as key to modern sailmaking as it was to *America*'s sails in 1851. More, but narrower, panels also gave me more opportunities to shape the sail, and the result was a smoother shape.

Indeed, smaller panels became a signature of mine, as did the brown thread I used to assemble them. People called me "Brown Thread Ted from Marblehead." I did it less to distinguish myself—although that was important to me—than because dark thread allows you to see your mistakes and correct them, and made it easier to see when the stitching was chafing and in need of repair. White thread, on the other hand, could disguise sloppy workmanship. I wanted to see my mistakes and rectify them.

Sailmaking was hard work in those days, but I was young, strong, and very ambitious. When building larger sails—those 60 or 70 feet on the luff—I would haul them to Abbot Hall, a Marblehead building used for meetings or social events, or to the Corinthian Yacht Club. At the latter building, I first danced with Sue Blake, who would later become my wife. Typically, I had to clean either floor first, usually at night. After first layout, I'd haul them back to the loft, where a seamstress would stitch them up. Then I would haul the sail back to either space for a second layout. I can't imagine working that hard today.

Despite all of the physical work, these were great times for me. I made sails and raced sailboats–could life be any better than that?

The Southern Ocean Racing Conference (SORC) was growing popular in the early 1950s. This winter racing series was held in Florida and the Bahamas. I pretended I went only for the "proof of the pudding"–to see my sails perform in competition–but I also went because I loved the racing. In the SORC's Miami-Nassau Race in 1954, I sailed aboard Carleton Mitchell's famous 50-foot yawl *Caribbee* (a Phil Rhodes design, launched by the Nevins yard at City Island in 1937 as *Alondra*), which had a crosscut spinnaker of mine. A sailor, writer, and photographer, Mitchell would eventually be the yachting correspondent for *Sports Illustrated*. With his 1948 book *Islands to Windward*, "Mitch" had practically invented the pastime of cruising in the Caribbean. The *New York Times* described him as the "writer-philosopher of the beat-to-windward generation." Having even just a spinnaker aboard a yacht such as *Caribbee* was important to this young sailmaker.

He was a great organizer, as I would learn in this SORC. Mitchell had an alarm on *Caribbee* that sounded below decks when all hands were needed. Once when off watch this ship-worthy horn started going Honk! Honk! Honk! With that, the crew and I rolled out of our bunks to repair a broken jib halyard, or something. I remember that before we even went on deck, the entire crew lit cigarettes. Not a smoker, it seemed strange to me that they couldn't even wait for fresh air. We won the race.

In 1954, Mitch had Sparkman & Stephens design him a 38-foot shallow-draft centerboard yawl that he named *Finisterre*. She also had my spinnakers–the rest of his sails were made by Ratsey & Lapthorn. *Finisterre* won three consecutive Bermuda Races–1956, 1958, and 1960–which is still a record.

In the 1956 SORC, I raced aboard Thor Ramsey's *Solution*, an Aage Nielsen-designed 46-foot centerboarder that had my sails. It was nice to escape the Marblehead winter for summery Florida. To join the boat, I flew from Boston to LaGuardia Airport in New York. Landing in a snowstorm, I missed my connection. Learning another flight was leaving from Newark, New Jersey, I hopped in a cab. I missed that flight, too, and remember being angry about it. Tragically, that plane crashed upon takeoff, and many of the passengers lost their lives. In some ways it put things into perspective for me. The life I chose, the life I lived, and the people I shared it with seemed even more precious to me after that.

In 1954 I purchased what remained of the Burgess-Curtis aircraft company site in Little Harbor, a rock-strewn cove behind Fort Sewall, just north of the harbor entrance in Marblehead. This, you may recall, was where Starling Burgess, the famous yacht designer of America's Cup fame, built seaplanes during World War I. I paid $25,000 for the property,

On board Carleton Mitchell's *Caribbee* at the end of a race, "Mitch" (with arms folded, center) poses with his crew, including Ted (bottom center) and Brad Noyes (to Mitch's right).
1954

$15,000 of which I'd saved from my first three years in business. Yes, I am frugal. I borrowed the rest. My interest, at first, was only in the land to build a sail loft. The property, however, included a boatbuilding and repair yard. As time went on, I found uses for those things, too.

We built sails by day and worked nights and weekends building the loft. To save money, we incorporated two sides of the old factory foundation, all that remained after the fire that burned the building at the end of World War I. We bought secondhand lumber out of buildings in Marblehead Neck that were being torn down. We also salvaged toilets, doors, flooring, and anything else useable. It only cost $3 a foot to build the building. It wasn't totally without luxury: We put hot-water pipes in the floor to heat it. In sailmaking you work on the floor so much that this is important.

I may have thought inexpensive, but I never thought small. I made the loft big enough to build really large sails, like a mainsail for a 12-Meter—about 80 feet on the luff and 30 feet on the foot. In time I'd have the opportunity to build sails for such boats, beginning with *Vim* in the 1958 America's Cup.

I built Orlon sails for such boats as the International 110, the 210, and Frank Paine's *Gypsy*, a 55-footer that is still sailing. Ray Hunt helped me secure the *Gypsy* order. Later, we made durable Orlon sails for the *Bluenose II*, a replica of the famous fishing schooner from Nova Scotia that was launched in 1963 to sail the coast. The total sail area on this 161-foot schooner measured over 11,000 square feet, with 4,150 in her mainsail alone. The Orlon sails we made for the 1970 reproduction of the British frigate HMS *Rose*—13,000 square feet in all—lasted 15 years.

After seeing some of my Orlon sails in 1957, Arthur Knapp Jr., who would skipper *Weatherly* in the 1958 America's Cup, ordered 500 yards of the material from me. He never used it, however, as by 1958 Orlon was being supplanted by Dacron in racing boats.

A byproduct of oil refining, Dacron was invented in England in 1941 by H. R. Whinfield and J. T. Dickson. In 1945, DuPont purchased the rights to what was then called "Terylene." DuPont named it "Fiber V" and later "Dacron"—polyester is the generic name for the material produced by others. It would be nearly 10 years before sailcloth was made from it. Ultimately, it was selected because polyester wouldn't mildew, as would cotton, for example. Orlon wouldn't mildew either. However, Orlon would not heat-treat, and Orlon appropriate for sailmaking was getting harder to find. The primary market for Orlon was fashion clothing, and the chemical industry—Orlon was resistant to many chemicals—not sailmaking.

Polyester, on the other hand, would grow tighter when heat-treated. The result was a lower-stretch sail and, as mentioned, low stretch is the most desirable quality for triangular sails. Another desirable quality, certainly, is light weight. This accounted for the march of materials in sailmaking from flax to cotton, to Orlon, Dacron (or polyester), and on to Mylar, Kevlar, spectra, carbon, etc. Think of it as a natural evolution.

Sailmaking was very different in those days. Ratsey & Lapthorn, Ltd., in City Island, New York, and Cowes, England, was the closest thing to an international sailmaker. How Ratsey became the first international loft, at least as far as I know, is interesting. For the America's Cup of 1901, the famous Herreshoff yard in Bristol, Rhode Island, built a new yacht, *Constitution*. In the defense trials, she would race *Columbia*, the defender in 1899, making an encore appearance. *Columbia* was also designed and built by Herreshoff. Her skipper would again be the notable Charlie Barr. The syndicate was headed by the formidable J. Pierpont Morgan, former commodore of the New York Yacht Club and the world's preeminent banker. Morgan is best known for the line about the cost of yachting: "If you have to ask how much it costs, you can't afford it." Herreshoff was a sailmaker as well as a yacht designer and builder, and the only sailmaker capable of building such huge sails: *Columbia* was 132 feet overall, *Constitution* a foot longer. When in 1901, both yachts ordered new mainsails for the America's Cup, Herreshoff made the tough decision to build one for his new boat, which he much fancied. This infuriated J. Pierpont Morgan, who encouraged Ratsey to set up a loft in City Island. Morgan and Herreshoff almost never spoke again.

An advantage I enjoyed, certainly, was that my father—"the Professor"—while not a sailmaker, was an expert in fiber technology through his work at Monsanto. He, in turn, had help from some of his young engineering friends who worked for him, who had an interest in sailing and seemed to enjoy the challenge of sailmaking.

As mentioned, Orlon was getting harder to find. Thus, I was quick to add Dacron or polyester to our line. I still preferred weaving my own cloth. The Dacron fiber would come from DuPont. Then, it was woven on our looms into a cloth strip that was 20 inches wide. Each strand of the fill—running across the cloth—would be hammered under great pressure against the previous one. We would match the fiber characteristics to the use. When making mainsails, for example, we might use double yarns of 220 denier (a fineness measure) in the fill—for a total of 440 denier—and single 250 denier yarn in the warp. In a mainsail, the fill takes much more load than the warp. Headsails would have more balanced cloth: 220 in both directions or 250 in both, depending on the size of the sail and the wind speed for which it was designed.

The coat of sizing that protects the yarns during weaving would be washed off in an aqueous bath, and the material was then dried. Next, it would be taken for calendering, where pressure from steel rollers would beat up the material, further tightening the weave. The rollers were also heated, which would shrink the cloth another 10 percent. The combination of heat and pressure locked the fibers of the cloth together. During calendering, pullers helped control how much and in what direction the cloth would shrink and helped prevent the cloth from wrinkling. If you pulled it too fast, you'd stretch the warp and crimp the fill. That was bad for mainsails, for example. We would run it through the rollers a second time; this was in essence ironing to remove the wrinkles.

Interest in the Hood weaving process peaked after the 1962 America's Cup. When *Gretel*, the first challenger from Australia, surfed past *Weatherly* on that private wave of hers, she flew a Hood spinnaker. She also had in her inventory a Hood mainsail that we had made for *Vim* in 1957. The Australians chartered *Vim* for a trial horse in 1962. After that series, where *Weatherly*, with Bus Mosbacher at the helm and our sails aloft, defended the Cup 4-1, the New York Yacht Club established a "country-of-origin" litmus test for such items. This meant only American yachts could use American-made sails in the America's Cup or benefit from American test tanks or designers. This rule remains in existence to this day, although in altered form. There were reports in the sailing magazines of how America's Cup challengers would take our sails apart, panel-by-panel, and strand-by-strand to try to learn the secrets.

Much of what we did would become fairly standard. What wasn't, however, was the aqueous bath: The Hood secret! The solution was milky white in appearance. In it was a very fine microscopic-balloon material akin to sand. The particles were so small it felt like powder in your hands. Monsanto, for whom my father had worked, made it to increase the friction

Gretel surfs past Weatherly
1962

Lee Van Gemert and Ted check out a sail during the America's Cup trials
1977

of American cotton fiber so it would have the strength of Egyptian cotton. We thought, why not use this fine sand to make the polyester fibers in sailcloth nonskid? That should make for a lower-stretch sail.

Weaving our own cloth, weaving it tighter, varying the thread width depending on the sail, calendaring, and especially the sand-like aqueous bath were the things that distinguished Hood cloth from the rest.

It would be years before another sail-maker—Ratsey & Lapthorn—started to weave its own cloth. Interestingly, there was a Hood connection. One of the companies my father and brother consulted with was in New Hampshire. They made foam-filled bumpers, head-rests, and visors for automobiles. My father and brother basically invented the process. The company they were working for sold the rights to Sir Owen Aisher, an Englishman who campaigned yacht after yacht named *Yeoman*. (His son Robin campaigns *Yeomans* to this day.) With a mutual interest in sailing, my father and Sir Owen became friendly. He was inventive like my father; among other things, Aisher invented the concrete roof tile soon after World War I. He asked a lot of questions about the Hood weaving process. We knew he had some connection to Ratsey so we didn't tell him very much. If

I knew how connected he was, I probably wouldn't have told him anything. When Sir Owen began to run the company, Ratsey began weaving its own sailcloth. Later, a few other sail-makers such as Watts began weaving their own cloth.

We never told anyone very much about the weaving process; not even sailmakers who worked for me for years. We ran Hood Sailmakers on a "need-to-know" basis. We taught key employees about sailmaking—the shapes of the foils—but not weaving.

Obviously we pushed manu-facturing pretty hard. Another example was the Hood Seamer. Before its devel-opment, seamstresses would have to work the on-off pedal with a foot, with their right hand hold-ing the cloth behind the nee-dle and their left hand holding the cloth in front. They'd sew about a foot and have to reposition their hands. It required con-siderable skill to make the two pieces of cloth come together perfectly after 30 feet of sewing. Harry Davis, who worked for me at the loft and became an expert in sewing machines, Lee Van Gemert, a salesman at Hood Sails who was trained as an engineer, and I developed a seamer and folder that guided the two pieces of cloth together so they came out evenly at the end. The principle was akin to a circular saw; with a circu-lar saw you don't push the material straight ahead but against

Lee Van Gemert
1977

Lee Van Gemert came to work at Hood in 1964, as a sails consultant. A key member of the team, he remained at Hood until he retired in 1985. Van Gemert attended the Massachusetts Maritime Academy where he graduated with a third mate's license. During the Second World War he was an officer on different ships owned by the Standard Oil Company in the North Atlantic dodging German U-boats. After the war he taught at King's Point Merchant Marine Academy and co-authored a book on ship stability and trim that became the industry standard. He went to work for Bethlehem Steel Shipbuilding Division in their design section, before joining Hood.

a fence. We protected our secrets, as I've said. When anyone came from the Singer Sewing Machine Company or from a competitor, the devices would be removed. At the end of the day, they were locked in a safe, away from prying eyes.

The sewing machines we used to assemble sails were unique. They were designed by the aforementioned Harry Davis, who when he was a young man started working for me at the loft in Marblehead, becoming loft manager in time. His uncle was a friend of my father's from Monsanto. Davis's special interest was in the rebuilding of sewing machines used in sailmaking. He would cut them in half and rebuild them to make them wider. He and I also worked with the thread company for five years, building better thread for the sewing of polyester sails. The thread would melt as it moved through the heavy Dacron. We changed how the thread was made, how it was twisted, added lubrication to it, and air-cooled and moisturized the needle as it passed through the cloth.

Another thing we developed was the "Hood Ring" for sheets. We made these first out of stainless steel, but the sailcloth would actually bend the material, so in due time we switched to beryllium copper. A ring with teeth on it was put on either side of the sail and then pressed together with a mechanical device. It allowed nice big holes, where two sheets could be easily passed through and knotted, and it saved hours in handwork. Not once was there a failure.

At some point, I allowed my father and my brother to use a small piece of the property in Little Harbor for what they vaguely described as a "research project." Even within the family we operated on a need-to-know basis. I didn't know much about it, other than they hoped to manufacture titanium, a miracle material that was growing popular after the Korean War. The expectation was that everything would be made from titanium, which has such a high melting point. Apparently, it is extremely difficult to manufacture, however, requiring very high temperatures, but my father thought he could make it.

As I would later learn—as would the entire town of Marblehead—to make titanium you basically have to set off an explosion in what amounts to a small reactor. To cool it and to prevent fire, you use liquid sodium. My father and brother worked on this for a couple of years.

Normally, they worked very late at night, so no one would hear or see what they were up to, and waited until the wind was offshore—in case something caught on fire—but one night they were so excited about some process they couldn't wait for favorable winds. A "controlled explosion" quickly got out of control and ignited their work shed. In no time, caustic chemicals and thick smoke blew into Marblehead, literally obscuring it and covering cars. The police and firemen responded. Upon his arrival, the police chief said, "What the Hell are you doing?" Upon his arrival, the fire chief said, "What the Hell are you doing?" The fire chief, in particular,

For centuries the art of sailmaking involved a great deal of handwork.

Rings were sewn onto the sail corners by hand until the invention of the "Hood Ring."

The Hood Ring was composed of two halves cast of high-strength beryllium copper. The halves were placed on either side of the sail and compressed together under enormous pressure and held together by a formed stainless-steel tube. Small points cast into the halves gripped the sailcloth extremely well.

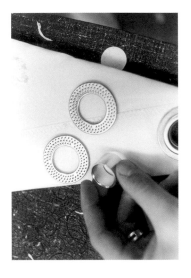

The Hood Ring
1968

had reasons to be concerned, as you can't pump water on a sodium-chloride fire; water just makes it explode. When I got down there, at about 2:00 a.m., I said, "What the Hell are you doing? You're going to put me out of business."

Somehow they got the fire out—even the water was burning. And eventually the town went back to bed. The next morning we found a four-pound chunk of pure titanium in the bottom of the burned reactor. That, however, was the total output of titanium from the Hood family.

I barely had a friend in Marblehead for months.

The 5.5-Meter-Class yacht *Quixotic*
1956

Chapter 3

Victories And Losses

Ratsey & Lapthorn have made the sails for the American defender in the last four Cup races, and they don't intend to miss having their sails in this one. But a young Marblehead sailmaker named Ted Hood is going to turn the trials into a duel as far as sailmaking is concerned. Of the four American contenders, Columbia *has practically all Ratsey sails,* Easterner *has all Hood, while* Vim *and* Weatherly *have split their orders... Depending on who wins with whose sails, either Ratsey or Hood is going to be covered with glory.*

— Sports Illustrated, *July 14, 1958.*

The year 1956 was a pivotal one for me as a sailor and a sailmaker, but not all of it was good. The 5.5-Meter, a sloop of about 30 feet, had been selected for Olympic competition, beginning in 1952. I had hopes of sailing for the U.S. in the 1956 Olympics, which would be held at Melbourne, Australia, in November. Joining me were John J. "Don" McNamara Jr., a friend from Marblehead, and John Collins, then yachting editor of the *Boston Herald*. We had built a 5.5 to a C. Raymond Hunt design during the winter of 1955-56.

Hunt was casual, to say the least, about construction details, and this was no ordinary yacht.[1] It featured a short fin keel with a bulb that extended all the way back to and including the rudder. Then, it had to be built to Lloyd's Scantling Rules. I said to Hunt, "How do you expect me to build that?" He said, "That's your problem!" Fortunately, the designer Fenwick Williams, who lived in Marblehead, did the detail drawings for Ray Hunt; they required Lloyd's approval.

John Collins came up with the name *Quixotic* for the boat. Like a proud parent, he told us the name. This was met with blank stares from McNamara and me. Our lack of comprehension appeared to hurt his feelings. As Collins would then instruct us, it means a romantic if impossible dream.

---

[1] The 5.5-Meter was a much lighter boat than one produced by the International Rule.

Launching *Quixotic*
1955

In July we took *Quixotic* down to Marion, Massachusetts, for the Olympic trials. The first race was won by Bob Mosbacher, with his talented brother "Bus" in the crew. We won the second, third, and fourth races and placed third in the fifth. *Quixotic* was fast but nearly impossible to steer—especially downwind under spinnaker. With two races to go, we only had to beat one boat out of 13 to gain the Olympic berth, and *Rush IV*, sailed by Andy Schoettle, had to win both races. How hard could that be?

In the sixth race, however, we were protested for tacking too close by Pete du Pont, later governor of Delaware, sailing *Lil Flicka*. We finished third, but these were the days of one strike and you're out. Schoettle's *Rush IV* finished first, as the script demanded. Following a protest hearing, we were told we were out. I thought we had completed the tack in time, but the burden of proof was on us. Nevertheless, there was still one race to go and still only one boat out of 12 to beat; again, *Rush IV* had to win.

After the first weather leg, we were up to fourth place. On the second weather leg, following two reaches, we were in second place, behind Dr. Britton Chance—the father of the yacht designer—sailing *Complex II*. Dr. Chance had won a gold medal in 1952 at Helsinki in this class's Olympic debut.

Then, like a bolt from above, *Quixotic's* mainsail fell as the shackle on the halyard opened. Don McNamara climbed the mast using the spinnaker halyard for purchase. Unfortunately, these are three-quarter-rigged boats. Once McNamara ran out of spinnaker halyard, there was nothing more to hold onto but a slippery mast.

Smooth water is not a common feature of windy Buzzards Bay. With the mast carving sickening circles in the sky, he attempted to shinny up the remaining 12 feet with no rigging to help him. However, he was a big guy—we were all big guys—and there was no way he could get to the top. The main halyard was about a foot beyond his grasp. He tried climbing the mast a second time with a boathook, but down he came helpless and hapless, his hands bloody.

We used the spinnaker halyard to hoist the mainsail about two-thirds of the way up, but *Quixotic* was a wounded bird. We watched in horror as *Rush IV* won that race, too, and the twelfth boat slowly but inexorably beat us across the line. *Quixotic's* designer Ray Hunt, alone in his Concordia sloop *Harrier*, witnessed all of this. After *Rush* took the gun and we finished last, he jibed away, heading toward Padanaram. Not a word was spoken. What could anyone say?

After the disastrous Olympic trials in 1956, it was time for some cruising with my friend Bradley Noyes. Brad and I, you'll recall, made a relative fortune in the lobster business

Quixotic during sea trials
1956

Ted, Ray Hunt, and Brad Noyes
1950

Brad Noyes at the helm of *Tioga*
1954

when we were kids. We also crewed for Ray Hunt in my family's International One Design (IOD) in the Amorita Cup and the Prince of Wales Cup in Bermuda in 1950, both of which we won.

Before we departed for Nantucket, we noticed that the Eastern Yacht Club, of which Brad was a member, hadn't nominated a crew for the Mallory Cup. Then the North American Men's Sailing Championship, the Mallory Cup is now the U.S. Sailing Championship. The 1956 trials were slated for Nantucket. Sailing for the Eastern Yacht Club, we won and were named the representative from the Yacht Racing Union of Massachusetts Bay, beating the likes of George O'Day and Charlie Leighton in the process. The finals were in Seattle, and my crew was Noyes—my partner in many such ventures—and Charles Pingree. Also competing were such notables as Bus Mosbacher, Bill Buchan of Seattle, who won this event in 1955, Harry "Buddy" Melges of Wisconsin, and Bill Ficker, from California. All five of us would become involved in the America's Cup.

The Mallory Cup finals that year were sailed in a hybrid design called the "Blanchard Senior Knockabout," a centerboarder with a Star-boat mast but with a spinnaker (which Stars don't fly). With its little cabin, it looked more like a cruising boat than a racer. We finished one race in the dark, with running lights on. Another race we rounded the weather mark, set the chute, and then realized we'd rounded the mark the wrong way. We had to take the spinnaker down and re-round. All that aside, it was nice to win.

During the series I got to know and to enjoy Buddy Melges. A determined competitor, Buddy has a warm and engaging personality. He would go on to win the Mallory Cup in 1960 and 1961 and win a bronze medal in the 1964 Olympics in the FD and gold in the Soling in 1972. In 1992 Melges would act as helmsman on *America*[3], the successful defender in that year's America's Cup, at the tender age of 62. He would also win two world championships in the important Star class—the first when he was 48.

In 1954, I had built sails for *Tioga*, a 50-foot Aage Nielsen-designed yawl owned by Brad Noyes. I was pleased that he had put his trust in me to build sails for *Tioga*. His family was well known in yachting circles, particularly in Marblehead. Brad's father, Harry, built an earlier *Tioga* in 1936, to the design of L. Francis Herreshoff, who lived in Marblehead. Under the Noyeses' stewardship, the 72-foot *Tioga* was on her way to becoming one of the most famous racing yachts ever. Certainly she was one of the most beautiful. From 1936 to 1951 the yacht, later known as *Ticonderoga*, was first to finish 24 times and broke more than 30 elapsed-time records.

The New York Yacht Club's Annual Cruise came to Marblehead in 1956. An important race of the Annual Cruise is the Astor Cup, a fixture since 1899. The Nielsen-designed

Tioga won the Astor Cup race, that year a joint regatta with Eastern Yacht Club. I was aboard her for the Annual Cruise. In fact, *Tioga* won 16 of 19 races in 1956. This was characterized as "One of the greatest records in modern yachting," by Carleton Mitchell in his book *The Summer of the Twelves*.

To grow the sailmaking business, it was necessary to broaden the market beyond the confines of Marblehead. My plan was simple: make better sails and give better service. I hoped that my customers and I would win races using my sails, and the world would take notice. "Victories at sea" is how I thought of it.

Tioga's success was noticed by Alfred Lee Loomis Jr., a member of the New York Yacht Club, who owned the 65-foot yawl *Good News*. Like his namesake father, the noted financier and experimenter in sonic technology who held the patent for Loran, Loomis was a large, forceful, and accomplished man who would become a friend. Since he believed he was a better sailor than Brad Noyes, Loomis concluded that *Tioga's* sails must have made the difference. I was not going to argue with him about who was the better sailor. Lee Loomis ordered a complete suit of sails from me for *Good News*. With them, he started doing better. I sailed with him on occasion.

In 1956, there had not been an America's Cup series for 19 years, since the J-boat era just before World War II–the longest hiatus ever. That year, New York Yacht Club Commodore Henry "Harry" Sears visited England and met with Sir Ralph Gore, commodore of the Royal Yacht Squadron, in Cowes, England, where the whole thing had begun with the New York Yacht Club schooner *America's* unexpected victory over a fleet of yachts from the Royal Yacht Squadron in 1851.

Commodore Gore expressed interest in reviving the event, but not in J-Class yachts, which measured 119 to 136 feet overall and at least 65 feet on the water. These huge racing machines were anachronisms in a postwar world characterized by high taxes, high building and operating costs, and a lack of qualified professionals to sail them. Gore suggested the competition feature 12-Meter yachts.

The 12-Meter class, designed to the International Rule, had been around since 1906.[2] Launched in 1907, *Heatherbell* was the first 12-Meter in Great Britain. She measured 61 feet overall and 40 feet on the water, with a beam of 11 feet and draft of 7 ½ or 8 feet. The 12-Meter class was even used for Olympic competition in 1908, 1912, and 1920. Upon seeing 12-Meters racing in a near-gale in England for the first time, Charlie Barr, a three-time winner of the America's Cup (1899, 1901, and 1903), said, "These are the best-built little vessels I have ever seen. We have no yachts of their size in America [that] would stand that sea without breaking up."

America got its first 12-Meters in 1928, when New York Yacht Club members ordered six Starling Burgess-designed, Abeking & Rasmussen-built one-design yachts. *Onawa*, still

Ted, with crew Charlie Pingree and Brad Noyes, is presented with the Mallory Cup
1956

2   The International Rule was to Europe what the Universal Rule was to America, as discussed in a footnote in Chapter 1. In 1906, 16 European nations met in England to discuss yacht-racing rules. This resulted in the International Rule, where classes would be designated in meters (or metres as spelled in England), such as 12, 10, 8 and 6. The 12-Meter formula is:

$$\frac{L + 2\,d + \sqrt{S} - F}{2.37}$$

The result cannot be greater than 12 Meters or 39.37 feet.

L is the profile length taken above the measured waterline with other corrections for the fullness of the ends. D is the difference between the skin girth and chain girth. It is a measure of how the maximum beam varies from a standard beam. F is the average of three freeboard stations, and S is rated sail area. Other measurements are fixed arbitrarily.

In 1924, a rules conference was held in London for Americans and Europeans to air their differences. It took five years, or until 1929, for the principals to agree to adopt the Universal Rule for boats that rated higher than 46 feet. This ushered in the J-Class era (1930-37) in the America's Cup. Then, the International Rule's 12-Meter class sailed in the America's Cup from 1958 to 1987.

Training aboard *Vim*
1958

competing, is an example of this group. By 1956, some 100
12-Meter yachts had been constructed to standards established by Lloyd's surveyors, and at least half of these sturdy
vessels, including *Heatherbell*, were still sailing in places like
Great Britain, the United States, Norway, Sweden, Germany,
and Italy.

A trend toward smaller, more manageable yachts had been
ongoing in the America's Cup competition since 1903, when
the oversized *Reliance*, a Nathanael Herreshoff design, defended. She was 143 feet on deck but 201 feet from the tip of her
bowsprit to the end of her boom. *Reliance* cost $175,000 to
build—a fortune in 1903. From launch to defense of the
America's Cup, her career lasted just four months. She was
finally broken up in 1913. J-Class yachts were a more practical
answer, beginning in 1930. These were similar but not identical boats, meaning design differences still mattered. Designers
had to make choices: more sail area required less waterline
length, for example. Beginning with the 1930 America's Cup
series—the first raced in J-boats—handicaps were dropped, and
the America's Cup race course was moved from New York to
Newport, Rhode Island. There it remained until 1983.

J-Class yachts had—in fact, still have—an aura about them.
To this day, they are a sight to see and a thrill to sail, particu-

larly in a good breeze. I, for one, have never forgotten the visit of the J-Class yachts to Marblehead in 1937, when I was 10 years old. 12-Meter yachts make a similar statement. This accounts, at least in part, for the fact that so many of them have been restored even–or especially–as the America's Cup has moved on to the wholly new America's Cup Class. (Of course, 12-Meter yachts are often good candidates for restoration as their pedigree includes the "Lloyd's Scantling Rules.")[3] Incidentally, seeing the J, 12-Meter, and America's Cup Classes together at Cowes for the America's Cup Jubilee gave me the impression that the current rule isn't a good one. The America's Cup Class rule is too restrictive and doesn't allow for improvements in yacht design as promoted in the America's Cup Deed of Gift.

Back in 1956, allowing 12-Meter yachts to compete for the America's Cup required two changes to the Deed of Gift that governed the contest. First, the minimum waterline length had to be reduced from 65 feet–that of the J-Class yachts–to the 44-feet minimum of 12-Meters. Second, the requirement that challenging yachts sail to the United States on their own bottoms had to be dropped. Few would wish to sail a 12-Meter across an ocean. These changes to the Deed of Gift were approved by the New York State Supreme Court in 1956.

[3] The informal name for the strict construction standards for International yachts was "Lloyd's Scantling Rules." The formal name was "Rules for the Building and Classification of Yachts of the International Rating Classes."

Sail check aboard *Vim*–John Matthews (left), Ted, and Don Matthews (at the helm)
1958

Thus, in 1958 began the 12-Meter era in the America's Cup, which would last for 10 defenses over 29 years.

In 1957, only *Vim*, a 12-Meter once owned by Harold S. "Mike" Vanderbilt, was a potential defender. Her designer was Olin Stephens, of Sparkman & Stephens (S&S), and she measured 45 feet on the waterline and 69 feet overall. Olin had been a great favorite of Vanderbilt's since the J-boat *Ranger*, which dominated the 1937 America's Cup. Vanderbilt, a three-time winner of the America's Cup during the J-Class era (1930, 1934, and 1937), campaigned *Vim* on England's Solent in 1939. There she won 21 of 27 races and never finished lower than third against a half dozen British 12-Meters. With World War II, she was brought home and left on the blocks at City Island, New York. Coincidentally, Vanderbilt, who wrote the racing rules that we still more or less use—and who also invented the game of Contract Bridge—would serve on the New York Yacht Club's America's Cup Committee that would select the defender in 1958. He was commodore of the New York Yacht Club in 1922-24.

In 1951, John Matthews, a shipping executive from Oyster Bay, New York, was able to purchase *Vim*. Vanderbilt did not normally sell any of his yachts. Rather than seeing them grow threadbare in the hands of less-committed, less-knowledgeable, or less-able owners, he preferred to scrap them. With the best 12-Meter in the world, until proven otherwise, Matthews decided to enter *Vim* in the 1958 America's Cup trials.

In addition, three new yachts would be built to vie for the defense: *Columbia*, also designed by Olin Stephens; *Weatherly*, designed by Philip Rhodes; and *Easterner*, designed by Ray Hunt. One of the four would meet the challenger, *Sceptre*, shaped by David Boyd for the Royal Yacht Squadron, which officially submitted its challenge in 1957, with racing scheduled for 1958.

During *Vim*'s preparations, Lee Loomis mentioned my sails, and presumably me, to John Matthews. They were neighbors in Oyster Bay, and Matthews respected Lee's opinion. Plus, Lee had once owned a 12-Meter. Upon graduating from Harvard Law School, Loomis had wanted to go to Europe, which didn't please his father at all. Having polished his negotiating skills at law school, Lee told his father he'd hang around if he'd buy him a 12-Meter. The result was the Sparkman & Stephens-designed *Northern Light*, launched, like *Vim*, in 1938.

I sailed on *Vim*, beginning in the late summer and fall of 1957, and made sails for her. She was at the time skippered by Matthews's younger son, Don. His half-brother, Dick, was navigator on the boat. Matthews had chartered another 1938 12-Meter, *Nyala*, as a trial horse, and Emil "Bus" Mosbacher Jr. and Arthur Knapp Jr.—both champion International One Design sailors from Long Island Sound—took turns skippering the latter boat.

My father got to know John Matthews fairly well. They were contemporaries. Matthews said to my father, "What can we do to make *Vim* better?" For Hoods—father and son—that's like being handed the keys to the candy store, and the answer proved to be plenty.

Two of my father's friends who like to build things made a flexible boom for *Vim* that would better complement sail shape. By the rules, the boom couldn't be bent mechanically. *Vim*'s new boom was constructed, however, to bend sideways naturally. It was built in two pieces and would slide on Teflon tape. Then there were adjustments on the end, which would stop it from bending further. At 180 pounds, the boom was about 60 pounds heavier than a standard 12-Meter boom. However, it worked well in conjunction with *Vim*'s original mast, built by Bath Iron Works, which had constructed *Ranger* for Vanderbilt. *Vim*'s mast was fabricated, not extruded. The sheet metal was rolled and riveted, and the mast showed a nice taper.

We needed to add inside ballast, so we used tungsten, which is nearly twice as heavy as lead. Unfortunately you couldn't melt the stuff—it has a very high melting point—so we made molds from the deep bilge of *Vim*, and we just stuck in as big a piece of tungsten as we could, wherever we could. Then we filled the rest of the space with molten lead. It was even suggested that we use gold, which is heavier—prohibitive, perhaps, but it only cost about $35 an ounce back then, not $450 like today. No one knew about the tungsten until Australians rebuilt the boat years later. Tungsten and other heavy materials like spent uranium were then outlawed. There wasn't anything illegal about tungsten in 1958, however.

We used a special flaked-copper bottom paint on *Vim*. When mixed with lacquer, it laid down very smooth. However, it dried quickly. You had to do one spot, let it dry and then go back. Then we'd spray a wetting agent—a detergent-like substance—on the bottom just before the races. How much was left by the time we started racing was anyone's guess. My father, from his work in the chemical business, figured this out. This was much in contrast to accepted wisdom. Yards were full of people simonizing the bottoms of racing boats. That's the worst thing you can do. You don't want a waterproof bottom; you want to keep the smooth (laminar) flow of water attached to the hull as long as you can. (It's the same with sails—keep the flow attached.) Did it work on *Vim*? I don't know, but wetting agents and the like, including such high-tech solutions as "Rivlets," developed by 3M and used in the 1987 America's Cup on *Stars & Stripes*, have been declared illegal by the powers-that-be.

Of course, we experimented with sails on *Vim*. While Arthur Knapp Jr. had ordered 500 yards of Orlon from me

Vim sailing close-hauled
1958

The *Vim* crew
1958

Vim's sideways-bending boom
1958

for *Weatherly*, which he skippered, sails for this America's Cup were made of polyester, or "Dacron," as DuPont called its polyester.

Headstay sag and its effect on headsail shape received some of my attention. The headstay on a 12-Meter might sag 12 inches. To help straighten it, we put a tape in the jib and put a wire cable inside. With a block and tackle, we were able to straighten the luff of the sail. Actually, it worked well without creating a hard spot in the headsail. However, since you had to unhook all of this stuff before changing sails, we eventually gave it up.

We had the lightest-weight mainsails. *Columbia* had mainsails made of cloth that was 14 ounces per sailmaker's yard. As weight aloft matters so much, we had mainsails constructed of 12-ounce cloth and then went down to 11-ounce cloth. Not only did the cloth weigh less, but the sails were made with smaller reinforcing patches.

Also, on *Vim* we substituted wire genoa sheets for rope. The rope would foul the rigging, while the wire would slide around nicely. On the other hand, *Vim* was decidedly underwinched. There were two primary coffee grinders—a Paul Luke design—that were used for tacking headsails or sheeting spinnakers, but they were prone to breaking. Being undependable and having no backup, we developed a sheet stopper that would work on wire in preparation for a tack or if we needed to free a winch for a spinnaker set.

Vim was a good boat and much improved, and as the trials neared in the summer of 1958 we felt confident. In the July 7, 1958, issue of *Newsweek*, we learned just how good she was.

The weekly newsmagazine reported that *Vim* could sail within two degrees of the wind—which was about 33 degrees closer than she could actually point in ideal conditions. Wrote Alfred F. Loomis under his pseudonym "Spun Yarn" in *Yachting* magazine, "Such being the case, the New York YC can save itself a lot of trouble and expense by canceling the remaining trial races and selecting *Vim* to defend the Cup." *Newsweek* issued a retraction on July 28.

After its 21-year hiatus, the America's Cup was big news in 1958. *Life* magazine devoted numerous pages to it. The May 12, 1958, cover of *Sports Illustrated* featured a picture of the America's Cup. The "Top Sporting Event of 1958," is how the magazine billed it. By September, Red Smith, the dean of American sportswriters, would complain that the America's Cup was getting more coverage in newspapers and magazines than Major League Baseball's pennant race.

A third of the way through the summer, our crew realized that Don Matthews, the owner's son, wasn't skilled enough to be skipper for America's Cup competition. Crewmember Jakob Isbrandtsen, later the owner of the estimable *Running Tide*, had the unenviable task of telling John Matthews that his son should be replaced as skipper. Don was a reasonable sailor—he once won the Raven Nationals—and a good guy. He was the youngest son of John Matthews from his second marriage (navigator Dick Matthews was from the previous marriage). Of course, to his mother Don was the golden boy. Isbrandtsen, who was head of American Export Line and a customer of Matthews's, went to him and said, "Look, we can't go on the way we are. If we do, we're not going to make

Professor, Ted, and Bus Mosbacher
1958

The *Columbia* crew
1958

it. We need Bus Mosbacher to sail the boat." Matthews made the tough decision and promoted Bus over his son.

I knew Bus from sailing International One Designs, a most important class of its day. The class was created in 1936 by Cornelius "Corny" Shields Sr. (who would be sailing on *Columbia* in that America's Cup summer of 1958). There were IOD fleets on Long Island Sound, in Marblehead, at Southwest Harbor, Maine, and in Bermuda, where our IOD *Princess* had won in 1950, racing against Mosbacher and other top skippers like Bill Luders Jr., Bill Cox, Corny Shields, and Arthur Knapp Jr. Mosbacher would become a fixture in the America's Cup: After *Vim*, he would skipper *Weatherly*, the successful defender in 1962, and *Intrepid*, the successful defender in 1967. He would be commodore of the New York Yacht Club in 1984.

On the foredeck, we had Brad Noyes and Buddy Bombard, with Dick Bertram, a spinnaker expert who often sailed with Carleton Mitchell and would soon found Bertram Yachts. My roles were sail-trimmer and sailmaker. A "crew of owners," we were called. I wasn't sure if that was meant as a compliment or not.

On *Columbia*, Briggs Cunningham was the skipper. A true two-sport star, Cunningham was even better known as the driver, builder, and team leader of race cars in America and Europe. He finished second at the first Watkins Glen Grand Prix in 1948. The next year, Cunningham again finished second in a Ferrari. He built the touchstone Cunningham C4R racecar in 1951, which won the 1953 12 Hours of Sebring and a National Championship. A C4R placed third at the Le Mans 24 Hours race in France. The car, as well as "Mr. C.," as Cunningham was known, were important enough to appear on the cover of *Time* magazine in 1954. His legacy to the sport of sailing is the Cunningham, a line for adjusting the tension of a mainsail's luff.

Also on *Columbia* was Rod Stephens, known to friends as "Tarzan" for his frequent trips aloft, who worked the bow. His brother, Olin Stephens, the designer of both *Columbia* and *Vim*, was in the afterguard. Cornelius "Glit" Shields, son of the legendary Corny, was in the crew. An ailing Corny Shields, a 63-year-old stockbroker, who had recently suffered a massive heart attack, was there too, watching his son and the crew from *Columbia*'s tender *Chaperone*.

After three days of racing in the final trials *Weatherly*, skippered by Arthur Knapp Jr., and *Easterner*, skippered by Chandler Hovey, were excused. The latter boat hadn't won a race. This left *Vim* and *Columbia*.

That summer, Mosbacher had unleashed his "tail-chasing" technique of aggressive circling before the start, which has since become a match-racing standard. As he said, "We had a great advantage in 1958 in that nobody had really gotten involved in this ring-around-the-rosy business before in quite that sense. [Mike] Vanderbilt did something like that in the J-

boats, but we had the advantage of having a fairly new thing going for us; we had a superb crew to handle the boat in doing it; and we had to do it. We were slower [than *Columbia*], and so there was no choice about not doing it."

A contribution I suggested was the dip-pole jibe. It, too, would become a standard. There was no limit on foot length for 12-Meter spinnakers. For example, *Sceptre*, the challenger in 1958, had a spinnaker whose foot length exceeded her overall length. We concluded, however, that maximum-size spinnakers were slow. Nevertheless, the spinnakers on *Vim* were still large and unruly. The accepted methods for jibing them then were end-for-ending the spinnaker pole (which is still done on small boats) or using two poles (which was done on the largest boats). Neither was particularly suited to the match-racing environment.

With the dip-pole jibe, each clew of the spinnaker had a rope sheet and a wire guy, except in the lightest winds. On the order to "stand by to jibe," the unloaded wire guy was led forward to a man on the bow. The boat was squared to the wind, and the front end of the pole dropped to clear the headstay. At the same time, a tripping line opened the jaws, allowing the old guy to come loose. Once the pole cleared the headstay, the bowman would place the new guy in the jaws, being careful not to twist it. Simultaneously, the main would be jibed, the new guy tensioned, and the old sheet eased. Everything stayed under control.

There were refinements in the course of that summer. For example, we changed the end fitting of the spinnaker pole from aluminum, which would chafe on the wire guy, to stainless steel. Also, since the pole was never turned end-for-end, the end fitting was enlarged. This helped to release the old guy and to capture the new one more easily.

Vic Romagna, the legendary spinnaker expert on *Weatherly*, was completely undone when *Vim* initiated a jibing duel, using the dip-pole jibe. We gained on every downwind turn. *Weatherly* soon used the same system, but in this maneuver, *Vim* was ahead of the other boats that summer.

As August gave way to September, Corny Shields Sr. replaced Cunningham as starting and upwind helmsman on *Columbia*, despite his doctor's orders to remain off racing boats. As Carleton Mitchell wrote, "Now with Corny at the helm for the start and first windward leg, *Columbia* went superbly. It was as dramatic a moment as had ever occurred in any sport, a man risking his life for the things he loved best. The crew seemed revitalized." In truth, Cunningham was totally undone by Mosbacher's circling tactics before the start.

Vim and *Columbia* met on September 4, and the latter won in a breezy 15 knots by 4:21. The next day, in light winds, it

The *Vim* crew prepares for a mark rounding
1958

Vim trails _Columbia_, having chosen a spinnaker that was too large for the conditions
1958

was _Vim_ by 10 seconds. Two days later, we raced again, and the gun went to _Columbia_ by 2:22. It was now apparent that _Columbia_ was faster with the wind over eight knots; _Vim_ was at least competitive in lighter winds.

On _Vim_, we thought it was over. There were sullen handshakes all around. Nevertheless, the word from the committee boat was that the race tomorrow would be over a triangular course. Was it, we wondered, that Mike Vanderbilt, then age 74, had pressured the America's Cup Committee on which he served to give _Vim_ another chance? He certainly still loved his old boat. _Vim_ won this race on September 8 by 1:35. This gave each boat two wins and two losses, but the next day, the new boat won by 2:11.

Cunningham steered _Columbia_ in what proved to be the final race in a 20-mph northwesterly breeze. The new boat rounded the first mark with a huge minute-and-seven-second lead. We responded on _Vim_ on the downwind leg with a smaller chute and closed the gap. We rounded the mark inches ahead. On the weather leg, _Columbia_ seemed to be pointing higher and footing faster–a tough combination to beat. Before they rounded, however, Mosbacher initiated a tacking duel and regained the lead, only to relinquish it again at the mark. Behind by a boat length, our crew on _Vim_ responded with a better spinnaker set and retook the lead. This time, however, _Columbia_ opted for her smaller chute.

We had two choices: "Big Harry" or "Little Harry" the two red-topped spinnakers I had built, named for New York Yacht Club Commodore Henry "Harry" Sears, a most red-headed man. Having negotiated with the Royal Yacht Squadron to revive the America's Cup competition, Sears had quit the America's Cup Committee to head the *Columbia* syndicate. "It would have looked awfully damned silly to have sponsored a challenge and then have no boats to defend," he said.

The two spinnakers looked the same, and the foredeck crew mistakenly set "Big Harry" when the call was for the smaller sail. ("Big Harry" was a huge spinnaker–61 feet on the luff and 65 feet wide). That decided the race. *Columbia* won by 12 seconds and was selected for the defense. Twelve seconds!

Columbia went on to beat the British *Sceptre* easily, winning all four of the America's Cup races by an average margin of eight minutes.

Briggs Cunningham skippered the American defender in the America's Cup match. On the day he won the America's Cup, Cunningham's auto-racing team was racing at Watkins Glen, in upstate New York. During the raucous post-race festivities for *Columbia*, Cunningham–who was never one for parties–spotted a dockside telephone. He placed a call to the track to find out how his team had fared. He learned that one of his drivers, Eddie Crawford, had won the main event. With his mind on the auto race, Cunningham rejoined *Columbia*'s crew and friends, now even deeper in celebration for winning the first postwar America's Cup. An America's Cup fan approached him and gushed, "Briggs, that was a fine race!"

"That's what I just heard!" said Cunningham. "I wish I could've seen it."

The first *Robin*
1959

Chapter 4

Robin

"When the tried and true blue-water racers of the New York Yacht Club set out a fortnight ago for their annual series of races off the New England Coast, a lean, shy sailor out of Marblehead, Mass. tagged along with his new sloop to see what she could do. Last week the fleet was marveling at the record of the 40-ft. plump-breasted Robin *and young (32) Designer-Owner Fredrick Emmart Hood: four wins in seven races and an overall first-season record of eight wins in twelve races. Ted Hood's record was roughly equivalent to a rookie batting .425 in the majors. What made the feat even more outstanding was the fact that* Robin *was the first boat he had ever designed."*

– Time *magazine, August 17, 1959*

Despite what the magazine said, as I've recounted, my debut in design and boatbuilding actually began when I converted a rowboat to a sailboat at age 12. More elaborate was *Doohdet*, the sailboat I designed and built when I was 15. She was not *Blitzen*, the 55-foot Olin Stephens-designed cutter about which I was dreaming, but my father said, "Why don't you start with something a little smaller?" The result was the 12-foot sailboat described in chapter 1. I was inordinately proud of her; all the kids came around asking for rides.

When I returned home after 18 months in the Navy, I noticed *Doohdet* was gone; someone had stolen her.

I was quite upset, in truth. To drown my sorrows, I guess you might say, I went for an afternoon sail in an old 11-foot Dyer dinghy, a nice Phil Rhodes lapstrake design, not to be confused with the pram-type Dyer dhow so popular today as a trainer for kids. It was a fine March day for Marblehead, and I sailed upwind in a gentle and warm breeze until I found myself in the ocean. Suddenly a squall blew up. I was pretty far out, and it was blowing close to 25 knots. Then I noticed that no one else was out; it was so early in the season. I started running downwind for home, but the bow of the boat

Ted on the beach in front of the Eastern Yacht Club pier with his 11-foot Dyer dinghy
1947

kept trying to bury itself. The water, which splashed in, now felt very cold. I was forced to sit on the transom in an attempt to keep the bow out of the water. I couldn't head up either because of the likelihood of swamping.

Then, the mast broke, which actually was a relief. I hurriedly constructed a jury rig and put the boat on a reach for shore. There, I anchored the boat with a beautiful bronze Herreshoff anchor—funny how I remember that detail so clearly—and improved the jury rig sufficiently to nurse the dinghy around a point and upwind into the harbor.

Quixotic, the next boat I built, would have to wait until 1955. By that time, I had bought Little Harbor Boatyard in Marblehead as a site to build my sail loft. Nevertheless, I did inherit a boatyard and a few boatbuilders, headed by Ducky Stanley, the yard manager for the previous owner, who came to work for me after I bought the property. I kept the yard crew working, mostly doing repairs to boats in the yard, but they were certainly capable of building the occasional boat that came our way. *Quixotic*, a 5.5-Meter, was designed by Ray Hunt for my friend Don McNamara, John Collins, a sports writer for the *Boston Herald,* and me. Each of us anted up about $5,000. We hoped to qualify for the 1956 Olympics in her and almost did, finishing second, as I've described in chapter 3.

Quixotic showed a short fin keel, which was very fine at the leading edge, with a bulb that extended all the way back to the aft edge of the rudder. I said to Ray Hunt, "How do you expect us to build that?" "That's your problem!" he said.

We did build it, including integrating the bulb and the rudder via flaps, and built it to Lloyd's specifications at that. We

Ray Hunt
1957

**The *Quixotic* crew: Ted with Don McNamara (second from left) and
John Collins (far right) during the Olympic trials**
1956

were helped in this regard by Fenwick Williams, who did the
detail work for Ray Hunt. Hunt provided sketches, while
Williams, who lived in Marblehead, provided beautiful drawings that went to us and to Lloyd's.

McNamara, Collins, and I were happy with *Quixotic* and
had all but won the U.S. Olympic trials when, in the final race,
our mainsail dropped to the deck, along with our chances. I
mention this again because there were 13 5.5-Meters in those
trials, and they were as different in hull form as any yachts
could be. Yet, there was almost no difference in speed. To me,
that represents a very good measurement rule, one open to
many different solutions.

The idea that there could be very different approaches to
the design of comparable boats intrigued me greatly. With the
sailmaking business running well, I decided to venture into
hull design, too.

Design, build, sail, and sell: that's how I approached this
facet of the business. The model at least dates as far back as
the 1920s, when John G. Alden designed a series of
schooners that shared the name *Malabar*. His *Malabar IV*, for
example, won the 1923 Bermuda Race, with two other
*Malabar*s winning a total of three of the first five spots. Then
in 1932, *Malabar X* set the course record in the Newport-
Bermuda Race; she was immediately followed into the Onion
Patch by three other *Malabar*s that Alden would design, sail,
and sell.

Finisterre
1958

My boats were called *Robin*, or variations on that theme–a good name, I thought, for a man named Hood. Then there was the fact that my wife, Sue, wouldn't let me name any of our sons Robin. Robert was as close as I could get.

I painted them Robin's-egg gray-blue, too. The color and name actually came from Marblehead's famous Chandler Hovey, who had a Q-boat named *Robin* with a gray-blue hull that I had always admired as a kid when I raced on my father's R-boat in the mid-1930s.

My first *Robin* was a 40-footer, launched in 1958, when I was 32. I had been working on her design in my spare time since about 1955. She was influenced by *Finisterre*, designed by Olin Stephens for Carleton Mitchell. "Mitch" wanted a yacht with a centerboard, as he had cruised and raced extensively in the 56-foot centerboard yawl *Caribbee*, designed by Rhodes. As he told Olin Stephens, he wanted "the biggest little boat he could get." When the 38-foot *Finisterre* was launched in 1954, Stephens remarked, "I think you've got a fine cruising boat but don't expect to win many prizes."

At first she confirmed Olin's prediction with an average performance in the 1955 Southern Ocean Racing Conference (SORC). But then Mitch got her tuned up, and she began to fly. I won't claim it was my crosscut spinnaker that made the difference, but I'd like to think it helped the boat sail to its potential. With *Finisterre*, Carleton Mitchell won three consecutive Bermuda Races in 1956, 1958, and 1960, a record never duplicated.

While Mitchell's accomplishments with *Finisterre* are remarkable, I know that he benefited from atypical weather during those three Bermuda Races. Normally, the Bermuda Race is a windy close reach or beat, with spinnakers rarely coming out of the bag. He happened to hit three consecutive races in this biennial event with medium winds and plenty of downwind work for the shallow *Finisterre*.

If derivative of *Finisterre*, my *Robin* certainly wasn't a duplicate of her. Otherwise, why bother? This *Robin* was also influenced by the Nevins Yawl, the Block Island 40, and Bermuda 40. In fact, I made all the sails for the first Bermuda 40s, as I did for the Block Island 40s.

Comparing *Robin* to *Finisterre*, she was two feet longer overall, but showed the same waterline length. Thus, she had more overhang. Also, *Robin*'s centerboard was shaped like a high-aspect-ratio daggerboard rather than the low-aspect (barn-door-shaped) centerboard on *Finisterre*. *Robin*'s hull showed less draft than *Finisterre*. With the board up, my design *Robin* drew 3 1/2 feet; with it down, 11 feet; while *Finisterre* drew 8 feet.

Robin was beamier and had a mast that was six feet taller. This gave her sail plan a much higher aspect ratio. Like a deeper keel or centerboard, that is a boon to upwind speed. Also, the taller mast gave her more sail area, helpful in light air and when sailing off the wind. This *Robin* was, basically, a

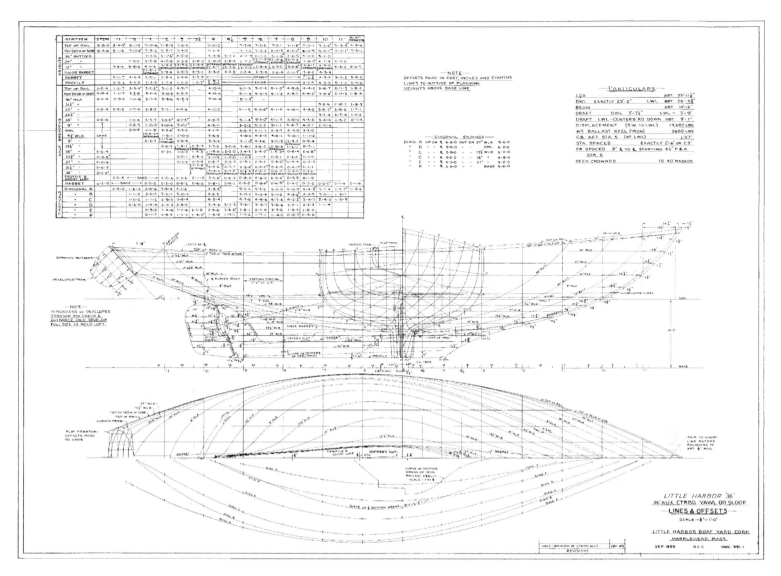

Lines of the *Robin Too*, typical of Ted's early designs
1959

heavy-weather hull with a light-air rig. To be precise, she weighed 21,000 pounds and flew 760 square feet of sail. Rather than a large weight being distributed in the keel, it was distributed in the hull, near the bottom of the boat. Only 25 percent (5,000 pounds) of the boat's weight was ballast.

We made her mast, a first for us. We had paid Bill Luders Jr. something like $1,200 for the mast for the 5.5-Meter *Quixotic*, which seemed outrageous to me. I decided that, from then on, I'd make my own.

For *Robin* we bought an extrusion, then cut it and tapered it, clamped it together, and welded it. Willy Fraser, a machinist and metal worker, built the mast. We used a drill and tap to add stainless tangs and sheaves. Forty-two years later, the mast is still in her. How do I know? I bought her back in 1994 or 95 for $4,000. Arnie Gay, who once owned this boat—he called her *Babe*—said, "Hey, Ted, I think I saw the old *Robin* in some yard south of Annapolis." I went and looked at her, did my own survey, and bought her. Like a lawyer who represents himself, surveying is, apparently, not my strong suit. The boat

Sue Hood christens the first *Robin*
1959

that cost me $36,000 to build in 1958, and $4,000 to buy back 37 years later, cost me $200,000 to rebuild in 1998. I still race this first *Robin*, and she can still win races.

She is of relatively heavy displacement, with a wide beam, and a centerboard at the bottom of a relatively shallow keel. This gave her shoal draft, an advantage for the cruising sailor, which is why Carleton Mitchell had reintroduced the concept in *Finisterre*.

The consensus was that centerboards, keel/centerboards, or daggerboards weren't efficient to windward. I've been told that Olin Stephens was unenthusiastic about putting a centerboard in *Finisterre* until Mitchell threatened to find another designer. My opinion, unchanged to this day, is that centerboards are better upwind, because they present a much more efficient wing. Keels need to be thick and heavy, both by measurement rules and for engineering reasons. They need to be bulky because they're carrying a load of lead. Asking one structure to do all of that makes for an inferior foil. One exception is the modern thin keel with bulb-ballast bottom, made possible by new high-strength materials.

The first *Robin* was made of wood and had an iron rather than lead keel. Iron was cheaper than lead, which appealed to me, and the old Cruising Club of America (CCA) Rule gave credit for iron ballast over lead. We coated the iron keel in epoxy. Forty-six years later, there is no rust there.

She was, as mentioned, only 25 percent ballast, while the typical keel-boat of this era was 35 to 40 percent ballast. Instead of ballast, I used beam—a lot of it near the waterline— to provide form stability with less weight.

Dan Lowell, who then worked for me, was the principal figure in building that boat. He came from a family that has been building lobsterboats in Maine for 75 years. This wasn't a big boat for him, but it was a big boat for the shed in which we built it. We had to move it from one shed to a new one and barely got it out of the first one to construct the deck. We caulked the seams with cotton; for putty we used epoxy and sawdust, which glued the seams. The sawdust keeps the epoxy soft, allowing some give.

Robin proved adept at round-the-buoys racing more than distance racing. Her first summer, 1959, *Robin* competed in the New York Yacht Club's Annual Cruise, which that year visited Marblehead. While not a member of the New York Yacht Club then, I was a member of Eastern Yacht Club, and Eastern Yacht Club yachts were invited to race. Several members of Eastern were members of New York and vice versa. *Robin* won the important Astor Cup. We competed with three couples as crew, and the women weren't that experienced, as I recall. The guys were good, however; especially when you

Ted's racing success dominated the press
1959

Blue Water Regatta Dominated by Hoods

By LEONARD M. FOWLE

...LEHEAD, Sept. 24—...as no stopping the ...the Blue Water Sail... opened the F...

followed by a five... weather leg t... Point...

Hood Takes Astor Cup With Newly-Built Robin

MARBLEHEAD—The five-week-old Robin, built, owned and skippered by Marblehead boatyard operator and sailmaker Ted Hood, Thursday won the coveted Astor Cup, highlight of the New York Yacht Club's annual cruise visit to Eastern Yacht Club.

Competing in cruising division four, Robin posted a five-m... corrected time margin... Noyes' new Tigo...

It was ... effo...

The fleet departs Fr... ing for Provincetown.
12-METER CLA...
1—Weatherly, Henry D. ... Mercer 2:5...
2—Easterner, Chandler ... Hovey 3:0...
CLASS I...
1—Nina, Decoursey ... Fales 3:0...
2—Caper, H ... Pratt 3:1...
3—S+... 3:1...

COURSE: Nev... Eastern Point ... Waste Lighted ... Second Leg to... Cl...
Pos.
1—Robin, Bruce...
2—Jennifer, R...
3—Double Tak...
4—Contessa, J...
5—Pandora, R...
6—White Wing...
7—Madd...

A 'Do-It-Yourself' Victory
...bin Wins Lipton Cup;
Rare Dead Heat for 2...

Marblehead Yachting

By ...LUTHER EVANS
...erald Sports Writer

...yacht race co-featured ...rare "dead heat" for ...place, Fred E. (Ted) ...of the New York Yacht ...Saturday won the 28... 28th annual Lipton Cup ...with his new do-it-your-

where he left off last February in winning the Nassau Cup — the Hood out-sailed 48 rivals — the biggest and finest fleet ever assembled for a circuit race.

Logging a corrected time of three hours, 23 minutes and 45 seconds in moderate to light north-northeast breezes, Robin finished with a comfor... ...of seven minutes...

boats that couldn't beat one another.

Tied at voyage's end with identical corrected times of three hours, 30 minutes and 48 seconds were:

Fun, 40-foot cutter co-skippered by Emil (Bus) Mosbacher and A. Lee Loomis of New York's Storm Trysail Club and;

Pirouette II, 39-foot sloop

MARBLEHEAD, Aug. 5 (P)—...Kane's Georjabelle by 30 seconds... The hard driven sailing craft on ...over Charles Pingree's Sonora, the New York Yacht club's an... which finished 3:40 ahead of nual cruise had a respite today ...Jacob Isbrandtsen's Windrose, of with no competition scheduled ...**CLOSEST FINISH** until Thursday's contest for the ...In the closest finish of th... Astor Cup off here. ...day, Larry Reybine's Crick... ...crossed the line only eight ...
The big cruising fleet, with 57 ...onds ahead of Fred Hibbo... competing under canvas, arrived ...Caprice. Commodore Geo... here last night. They raced the ...Hinman's Flagship Sagola... last 25 miles of a 50-mile trip ...in third, a mintue astern... from Mattapoisett in a light ...price.
...breeze. ...A. A. Hobart's yawl...
...ERLY AGAIN ...won in Class D, lea... ...brought his ...Matthews Cythlen at... ...home port by 53 seconds. Third... ...feat by ...White's Gum Drop w... ...seconds later than ...
...ST DEFEAT
...D results

Hood-Planned Robin Too Il... Nabs Halifax Time Trophy

Head Attraction
N.Y. Skippers Inspect Robin

By JOHN AHERN

MARBLEHEAD, Aug. 6—It was a day for seeing and this port's winding lanes, antique... and quaint houses got the full treatment from hundreds of competitors in town with the York fleet.

The ladies visited Abbott Hall and the galleries. The men traveled to Teddy Hood's yard for a look at Robin.

She's the 40-foot centerboarder that has been the hit of the cruise. She has won three races, taking the prized Corsair Cup, and she has finished fifth. Today she had to be rated up with the favorites in the Stor Cup regatta and there are yachtsmen here who say she won't be beat on the final two runs.

As boats go, she's not one of the pretty ones, not like the long, lovely Pleione or the graceful Sonora. On the contrary, Robin is a fat little lad...

But speed is her dish... competitor, who the... had the ultima... willing to ta... of the way... for all... ...esigns... John...

"Well, we just wan... see what we could do... boat," the 31-year-old... maker said. "We picke... the better points of a... boats and tried putting... together. That was four... ago and we finally go... done this year. We're... happy with her."

Robin is the ultima... centerboarders. She ha... entrance of a Finnisterr... the run of a Cape Cod ca... She's flat an... smooth an... stability...
"W...

...RD M. FOWLE
...sail-

with an elapsed time of 67:35:48, Lord Jim took the Halifax Tourist Bureau Cup.

...dered the Class A ...Avard Fuller's ...iogenes which ...vince of Nova ...by 8 minutes ...nds from Peter ...Magic Carpet, the ...Halifax race win... ...prize went to G. W. ...te's yawl White Mist.

rial Trophy for the schooner making the best corrected time seemed certain to go to DeCoursey Fales' famed Nina for the second time by a matter of 22 minutes over Lord Jim.

Gay Gull III in winning Class B by 48 minutes and 49 second... from Arthur Homer's yaw... Salmagal III earned the Bost...

YACHTS
Page Thirty-eight

Touche, Robin Win Edgartown Races

By JOHN AHERN

...vey's Carol. Phil Robertson's ...Amourette also swept the 210 ...The grasp, Impala ran a ...at the ...under the bluff on ... being... ...k Island and sa... ...les while t...

...ood's Sloop ...ton Leader

By LEONARD FOWLE
...June 27—...ward-win... gain startle...

...Skipper of R...

Marblehead Skipper Wins Nassau Race

...'s Robin Captures ...'s Astor Cup

...er's Touche the New... ...while the ... ...commodore ... ...t hun...

Robin's 1960 SORC crew.
From left to right: Vic Romagna, Ted Hood, Brad Noyes, Jakob Isbrandtsen, Bus Mosbacher, and Lee Loomis
1960

consider that the crew on a 40-footer today is 10 or more. Even *Time* magazine remarked at the unexpected success of this *Robin*. The newsmagazine described me as a "Marblehead Marvel." I had to smile at that.

This *Robin* won 10 of the 14 races she sailed that first season. The following winter, I trucked her to Florida to compete in three races of the SORC: Lipton Cup, Miami-Nassau, and Nassau Cup. Helping to pay her way were sailing friends: Bus Mosbacher, Lee Loomis, and Jakob Isbrandtsen. Also in the crew was Vic Romagna, the spinnaker trimmer on *Weatherly* in the 1958 America's Cup. He was considered the best spinnaker trimmer around. Along, too, was my friend Brad Noyes.

We won the Nassau Cup and the Lipton Cup, both of which were day races, but finished second in our class and sixth overall in the Miami-Nassau Race. *Robin* was good upwind, particularly when it was windy, and good off the wind. She wasn't much for reaching, however. I sold that *Robin* to Bus Mosbacher and Lee Loomis after the SORC. They called her *Fun*. They split the steering duties and would often argue about who was the better helmsman.

For the next year, 1960, I designed another 40-foot *Robin*, but I rigged this one as a yawl and gave her a little more draft than her predecessor. Also, rather than building her in Marblehead, we built her in Osaka, Japan, at International Marine. Actually, we built four yachts that year in Japan: two

The 36-foot *Robin Too II*, one of four boats that Ted had built in Japan
1961

Robin

of the 40-footers and two 36-footers to sell if anyone was interested. Fortunately, there was some interest.

One of the 36-footers was a keel-boat and the other a centerboard design, as I was interested in comparing the performance of keel versus centerboard. It was interesting to discover that the centerboard version was faster upwind and the keel version faster downwind.

The boats were built by two Americans: Don Jacobs and Alan Mott, GIs who had stayed in Japan after World War II. I knew of their work as we were outfitting two of their Eldredge-McInnis designed yawls in Marblehead. I asked them for a quote to build the two 40-footers and two 36-footers. It ended up being about half of what it would have cost if we constructed them in Marblehead: about $18,000 each for the 40-footers. That was without rigs and sails, but with a complete engine, cast-bronze hollow centerboard, and double-planked mahogany construction.

The aluminum mast and wood boom we built in Marblehead, made all the rigging, put on the lifelines and winches, and built the sails. In a week, they would be sailing away. I sold the 40-footers for $35,000 each, including eight racing sails.

The 40-footer I raced featured a stunted mainsail, about two-thirds on the luff. I had decided to test my suspicion that mainsails were not as effective as most sailors thought, so the luff of the main ended well below the top of the fore triangle or mast. Also, the CCA measurement rule favored boats with small mains, until the rule would be changed after this *Robin,* which was followed by the similarly appointed *Storm,* a Luders 40.

Her mainsail may have been small, but this *Robin* made up for it with big overlapping jibs. We used a genoa staysail and a spinnaker staysail, which boats don't seem to use any more. The mizzen was good all the time, but particularly in heavy air going to windward with reefed main. For balance and steering in rough seas, we had three mizzen staysails: windward, reaching, and spinnaker, which kept the crew busy.

We took the yawl south, again for the SORC, and won the Gulf Stream Trophy, which was for the best finishes in three races: Lipton Cup (which we won overall), Miami-Nassau, and Nassau Cup. That summer, we also took a first and second in the Edgartown Regatta at Martha's Vineyard and won three races during the New York Yacht Club's Annual Cruise, including the Astor Cup, again. I had joined the club three months earlier.

My crew was fairly constant during the years 1959-68. It included Jack Blodgett, Joe Parker, Paul Casey, and Dick McManus—all friends—and often their wives. I don't remember

Ted at the helm of the 47-foot, steel-hulled *Robin*
1964

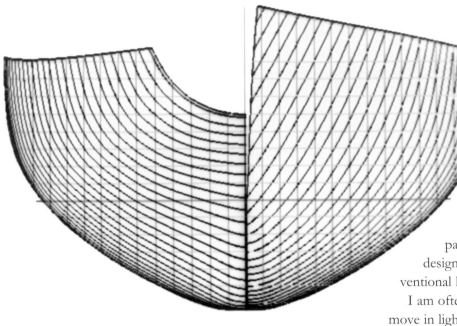

The "whale-bottom" or "delta" hull design in bow perspective (right) and stern view (left)
1972

worrying a lot about organization; you sail with people long enough, they know what to do and when. After 1968, when we won the Bermuda Race overall, I often sailed with people from the loft.

The next year, 1961, I designed and sailed *Robin Too II*, a 36-footer built in Japan. She was a fat keel-boat with a yawl rig. She finished first overall in the 1961 Marblehead-Halifax Race. She also won the Northern Ocean Racing Trophy (NORT)–the Stamford Yacht Club's blue-water sailing award, conceived in 1961 to induce participation in offshore yacht racing. We actually built a second boat that year; this one a centerboarder. Otherwise, the two were identical. The center-boarder was called *Robin II*, and my brother Bruce campaigned her. By comparing these two boats, I came to the conclusion that the centerboard version was better to windward, while the keel version was better off the wind. This was contrary to popular wisdom.

Already we were well down the road to what would become known as the "Hood style." The typical yacht we design is beamy for added stability through flotation, while allowing generous accommodations. The boats feature a high-aspect-ratio centerboard or daggerboard. This can take the form of a keel/centerboard or a pure centerboard or dagger-board shoal-draft yacht. In time, we called the pure center-board or daggerboard yacht "delta form." Either way, the boats show less heel angle than do keel-boats. Not all of our designs conformed to this–there were "horses for courses," like *Dynamite* or *American Promise*, discussed later–but most of them fit that description.

They are seakindly and good looking, too; the type of yacht in which I like to cruise and race. In time, they flew in the face of the light-displacement yachts and yacht designers. It was my mission–no, my pleasure–to prove such yachts were fast. It remains so in my eighth decade. Nevertheless, racing rules aren't helping in this regard.

How, I have often been asked, can a shallow-draft hull possibly have enough stability to perform in heavy winds? It is interesting to compare the typical Hood "whale-bottom" design, as they've been charac-terized, to a light-displacement keel-boat. The page to the right illustrates how the "whale-bottom" design achieves stability equal to or greater than a con-ventional keel design.

I am often asked, how can a heavier-displacement boat move in light air? There are three forms of resistance to a hull moving through the water: frictional, wave-making, and form. In light winds, when a boat is moving well below maxi-mum speed, the overriding component of resistance is the skin friction of the water along the hull surface. There we strive to shape our heavier-displacement hull in such a way that minimizes the wetted-surface area below the waterline. A rowing shell has a hull section that is completely circular because that shape provides the least wetted surface for a given displacement. While our designs accentuate hull depth and waterline beam for stability reasons, our rounded V sec-tions follow the same goal of maximizing displacement (at the same time allowing cruising amenities and increasing interior volume) with a minimum hull surface area.

Comparing a cross section of each hull, note how a shal-low-draft, heavy-displacement hull has a smaller chain-girth measurement. That is, the distance measured on an imaginary string running from the waterline to the bottom of the keel is shorter, meaning that when averaged out over the length of the hull, the wetted surface is comparable to a light-displace-ment hull. In this manner, a heavier-displacement hull can maintain fast straight-line speed in light air if the displace-ment is distributed properly. (The importance of form, or how you distribute the underwater volume of a hull, is dis-cussed in chapter 6 with *Dynamite*, a Two-Tonner designed for E. Llwyd Ecclestone who won the 1972 Canada's Cup.)

Of course, a heavier boat will not perform as well when short-tacking up a narrow channel because of the extra time needed to accelerate. When sailing downwind in heavy air, a lighter boat will certainly surf more easily, but how common is heavy downwind sailing? Typically, we sail in winds less than 25 knots. Under those conditions, people who favor our designs are looking to make a fast passage in safety and com-fort. That was what I look for in a yacht, though it was satis-fying, to be sure, that our yachts won their fair share of racing prizes.

The Delta Form Hull

"They are seakindly and good looking, too; the type of yacht in which I like to cruise and race. In time, they flew in the face of the light-displacement yachts and yacht designers. It was my mission—no, my pleasure—to prove such yachts were fast. It remains so in my eighth decade. Nevertheless, racing rules aren't helping in this regard."

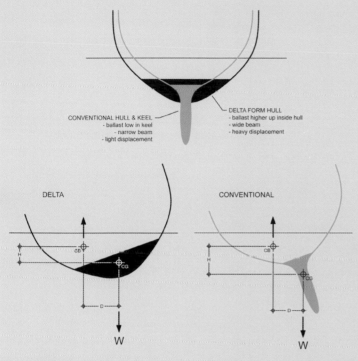

CONVENTIONAL HULL & KEEL
- ballast low in keel
- narrow beam
- light displacement

DELTA FORM HULL
- ballast higher up inside hull
- wide beam
- heavy displacement

DELTA

CONVENTIONAL

The illustration below highlights a side benefit to the Hood delta hull design—much more hull volume is available within which to place accommodations, equipment, and storage, making for a much more comfortable and useful yacht.

On the left is a typical conventional hull cross section showing area available for accommodations and storage. At right is a cross section of a delta hull, showing a larger area for accommodations, storage, and tankage.

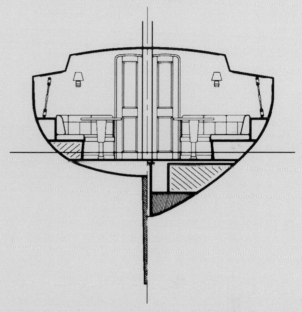

The illustrations above show the method by which Hood's delta form hull gains stability versus conventional keel-boats. The stability of all vessels comes from the righting moment created by the distance (D) between the vessel's center of gravity (CG) and center of buoyancy (CB) times the overall weight of the vessel (W).

$$Stability = D \times W$$

Conventional keel-boats rely on placing ballast low in the vessel (in the keel) to increase D. Hood's designs rely on beam to increase D, as well as heavier vessel weight (W). For the same length of boat, a Hood design will often have a larger D and W than a conventional keel-boat of the same size, therefore higher stability.

Due to this increased stability, Hood designs also could carry more sail area. In addition, the smaller vertical distance between CG and CB (H) created a smaller pitching moment, resulting in Hood designs being very comfortable yachts at sea.

Shown below is the main salon of a delta-hull yacht, in this case a Little Harbor 53. The large volume available for accommodations is evident. Also, the heavy displacement Hood hull design is very forgiving of construction weight, thus the weight of all this woodwork does not undermine the performance of the Hood-designed yachts.

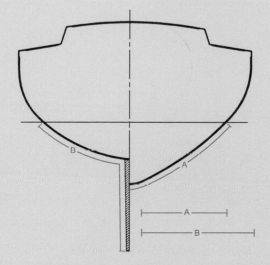

At left is a comparison of the "chain girth" measurements of a conventional hull (on the left) and a delta hull (on the right). The Delta hull's shorter girth measurement is an indication of its lower wetted surface.

**Following the success of
his 45-foot *Robin*, Ted
had Frans Maas build the
46-foot *Robin*, shown
here on the New York
Yacht Club Cruise**
1963

Early in 1962, I took delivery of a 45-foot centerboarder of my design built of steel by Frans Maas at his Maas Yacht Builders in Breskens, the Netherlands. This began an association with this Dutch boatbuilder that lasted until 1974. The 45-footer had a plywood deck with teak overlaid, which made it very "yachty" looking to my eye. It also had twin centerboards. The forward one was 10 feet deep and the aft one 4 feet. (With the boards up, the boat drew 4 feet.) The intention was to pull the forward one up when off the wind. The back one might be raised, too, if steering wasn't a problem when off the wind. As it turned out, this arrangement was too complicated. To house the twin centerboards, we used a long trunk that created drag, even when closed by flaps. Eventually, we concluded that one deep centerboard is better than two shallow ones, and we changed the boat's arrangement.

I sailed the new boat from Marblehead to Norfolk the week after Thanksgiving, to get her partway to Florida for the SORC. There was snow and ice on deck, a miserable passage. I was distracted, too, as around the same time I started design work on a 12-Meter, eventually called *Nefertiti*.

Nevertheless, I managed to sneak away to do that SORC. In the 403-mile St. Petersburg-Ft. Lauderdale Race, then the signature contest of the SORC, we were doing very well, until rounding the tip of Florida, at Key West. Then it was a most uncomfortable beat north with a boisterous northeast wind blowing against the northeast-flowing Gulf Stream. While off watch and below decks, I sensed a change in the motion of the boat. Things had settled down. Hurrying back on deck I asked, "What the Hell's going on?" The crew was mostly from Marblehead, and someone said they had tacked close to shore to get out of the rough seas of the Gulf Stream. I shouted "Tack!" To avoid the chop, they'd opted out of the strong, beneficial push of the Gulf Stream. Fortunately, we got back on track and won that Lauderdale race overall.

We also won the Miami-Cat Cay Race overall. That race went from Miami north to Ft. Lauderdale, then east across the Gulf Stream to Cat Cay in the Bahamas, a beautiful little island, as I recall it, with a good marina and nice homes.

We finished first in class but second overall in the SORC that year. It pleased me greatly that my designs were proving themselves in competition, even—or especially—if in rig and hull form they defied much of the prevailing logic of boat design.

Nefertiti **on the wind with her small heavy-weather genoa**
1962

Chapter 5

Nefertiti

Bus Mosbacher said, "I was very fortunate because the three times I was involved in the America's Cup [Vim 1958, Weatherly 1962 and Intrepid 1967], Ted Hood made virtually all the sails we used. Other sailmakers did make sails, and we tried them, but in those days I don't think there was anyone close to Ted. I guess I can give you a good example of how great an effort he made in our behalf: In the summer of '62, in the final trials, Columbia and Easterner were eliminated, and the final-final trials came down to Nefertiti–the boat Ted designed, built and sailed and Weatherly–the boat I was sailing. We had one lay day after the other two boats were defeated and before the two of us were to go at each other, and Ted spent a couple of hours on Weatherly with me working on our spinnakers. And I guess there was great trust, too, because I gave Ted our spinnakers, and he took them to the loft that night and brought them both back the next morning to use in racing against him. And they were improved!"

– Nautical Quarterly, *Volume 1*

The Marblehead-to-Halifax Ocean Race of 1961 was a good one for me. As I mentioned, we won the 360-nautical-mile race overall aboard *Robin Too II*, the 36-foot yawl I had designed.

It proved a good race, too, for *Lord Jim*, a striking old gaff-rigged schooner belonging to Evan Ross Anderson, the commodore of the Boston Yacht Club. I had built the sails for her for this race. Anderson's goal for the Marblehead-Halifax Race was to beat another schooner, the famous *Niña*, then owned by DeCoursey Fales, former commodore of the New York Yacht Club. It was to be a battle of the schooners, a battle of the commodores.

In 1928 *Niña*, designed by Starling Burgess for Paul Hammond, had won the transatlantic race to Spain.[1] After

---

[1] Source material on *Niña* is "*Niña*–A Great Reckoning in a Little Room," *Nautical Quarterly,* Winter 1980.

The staysail schooner *Niña* off the wind
1961

that, she won Britain's Fastnet Race, skippered by the famous American yachtsman C. Sherman Hoyt. The British were not pleased by this Yankee yacht and her Yankee yachtsmen. Said the Royal Ocean Racing Club, *Niña* was designed to "cheat" the rule. Today, as has long been the way, any designer takes a long, hard gaze at the racing rule before committing pencil to paper. Designers ponder: Are there "soft spots" that can be exploited? Race organizers may not like it, but this is the way designs, and rules, are improved.

In *Niña's* case, the British yachtsmen believed her staysail schooner rig was questionable, her hull was too lightly built, and her lack of interior bulkheads was a further flaunting of normal safe practice. They wished to ban her from ever competing in the Fastnet Race again, citing safety issues. In her defense Sherman Hoyt reminded them that she had won a transatlantic race and crossed the stormy Bay of Biscay simply to reach the start of the Fastnet Race, proving herself a tough ocean racer even before winning that difficult ocean race. And she's still sailing more than 75 years later.

Lord Jim was designed in 1936 by John G. Alden, known fondly as "John o' Boston," and built by the Lawley yard in Neponset, Massachusetts. She was a schooner, a dated rig in the eyes of the Cruising Club of America Rule that was in effect at the time. The rule had much more to say about sloops and yawls. Commodore Anderson, head of the industrial consulting firm Anderson-Nichols in Boston, invited me and my friend Don McNamara to lunch to discuss *Lord Jim* and the Marblehead-to-Halifax Ocean Race.

To improve her speed, I suggested that he increase the area between the masts and increase the size of the fore triangle. For the area between the masts, I proposed we build a huge, overlapping genoa, nicknamed a "gollywobbler," which was basically unmeasured sail area and a very useful sail when reaching. A longer, more efficient fore triangle, however, would require a more rugged and taller mast, as I pointed out. Anderson, an engineer, liked the idea, so we designed and built a new foremast—nothing fancy about it, it was simply an aluminum tube. We also built a masthead spinnaker and a large masthead jib for *Lord Jim*. The new rig likely proved helpful, as *Lord Jim* beat *Niña* in the Marblehead-Halifax Race.

In the flush of success after the race, the question arose on *Lord Jim*, "What should this crew do next?" Don McNamara, who sailed aboard her in the Halifax Race, suggested the America's Cup. The next Cup was scheduled for 1962, when a defender from the New York Yacht Club would meet the Australian 12-Meter *Gretel*, the first Australian challenger to the America's Cup.

Boston-area yacht designers, if less-so Boston yachts, have written some important chapters in the history of the America's Cup. The Boston yacht designer Edward Burgess drew three successful defenders: *Puritan* (1885), *Mayflower* (1886), and *Volunteer* (1887). His *Puritan*, the defender in 1885,

Ross Anderson at *Nefertiti*'s launch
1962

Ted inspects
***Nefertiti*'s masthead**
1962

The mast is stepped
1962

was designed for a syndicate of 10 Boston yachtsmen, most notably General Charles J. Paine and J. Malcolm Forbes, both members of the New York Yacht Club.

Then there was Burgess's son Starling, who designed an equal number of successful defenders: *Enterprise* (1930), *Rainbow* (1934), and *Ranger* (1937) during the J-Class era.

The most unlikely Boston connection to the America's Cup was Thomas W. Lawson, who wished to campaign his aptly named *Independence* in the America's Cup competition of 1901. One problem: he wasn't a member of the New York Yacht Club, the defending club. The yacht club saw a way around that technicality and proposed nominally chartering *Independence* to a member. But Lawson was not one to compromise. He wanted an argument. As he wrote in an extraordinary book, *The Lawson History of the America's Cup: A Record of Fifty Years*, "No ship belonging to any American other than a member of a certain yacht club–their own–would be permitted to defend the nation's trophy."

Though not a legitimate entry, Lawson's *Independence* sailed eight races in 1901: six against defense candidates *Columbia* and *Constitution*–both Nathanael Herreshoff designs–and two matches against *Columbia*, the eventual defender. Under the command of Captain Hank Haff, a two-time winner of the America's Cup, she lost all of them. One observer described *Independence* as "going at steamship speed and giving an exhibition of heeling such as we have never before witnessed."

***Nefertiti* ready to launch at Lower Graves Yacht Yard, Marblehead**
1962

Ted at the helm
1962

Lawson, a stock-market speculator who had made his first million in 1888, when he was 31, died penniless in 1925.

This was not a model we wished to emulate. Before committing to the America's Cup of 1962, Anderson formed a syndicate that included most notably Robert Purcell, president of International Basic Economy Corporation. He came aboard as a minority partner. By Thanksgiving of 1961, the pieces were in place. The new Boston/Marblehead 12-Meter would be named *Nefertiti*, which was Mrs. Purcell's decision. Nefertiti was an Egyptian Queen, whose name means "a beautiful woman has arrived."

Around this time, Don McNamara suggested he and I co-skipper the boat. An old friend from Marblehead, McNamara had been an usher at my wedding. When he had gone into the army, he had loaned me his International 210, *Bantry*, named for Bantry Bay in County Cork, Ireland. I had made sails for this boat.

The plan was that McNamara would steer the boat downwind, while I would steer her upwind. Despite our friendship, we were an unlikely duo. John Rousmaniere much later characterized the relationship this way: "Hood taciturn and technically minded, and McNamara emotionally extravagant and perpetually charging up San Juan Hill."

And I would design the boat. I knew little about the International Rule, to which the 12-Meter class was designed. I had only designed ocean racers to the Cruising Club of America Rule, and only five of them at that. So there was much to learn and little time. That said, I had been very involved with *Vim* in the 1958 America's Cup in sails, rig, boom, ballast, and sail-handling techniques, including the dip-pole jibe that we pioneered.

Time was precious as the 1962 America's Cup was but six months away. Nevertheless, I wasn't interested in a me-too design. I decided to try something a little different: a lighter and wider boat than all previous 12s. As in my ocean designs, I expected the greater beam to provide some stability even if the hull were lighter, with less ballast than usual.

To the model-testing tank I went, which was also a first for me. The tank was at Stevens Institute of Technology in Hoboken, New Jersey. The 200-foot-long tank had been built in the 1930s, and the hull-forms of such notable performers as the "Super J" *Ranger* had been perfected there. To help me, I hired Britton Chance Jr., who was about 24 at the time. His father, Dr. Britton Chance, had won a gold medal in the 1952 Olympics in the 5.5-Meter class. The junior Chance had had some experience in the tank.[2]

It was an around-the-clock effort. We spent nights doing model changes with putty in the shop next to the tank. The next day we would put the model in the tank. I traveled back

2 Later, Britton Chance Jr. designed *Chancegger*, a 12-Meter for Baron Marcel Bich of France, redesigned Olin Stephens's famous *Intrepid* that defended the America's Cup in 1970 for the second time, and designed *Mariner*, a challenger in 1974.

Nefertiti's crew
1962

and forth, balancing design and my sailmaking business. Chance and I became regulars on the Eastern Airlines Shuttle, commuting between New York and Boston. We started with two models, one of which was quickly rejected. To the one that looked more promising, we made 26 further variations. It cost about $1,000 a run, a fortune it seemed to me.

The 12-Meter rule is based on "horse trading." Things that make you go fast must be balanced by things that make you go slow, at least in the eyes of the rule. For example, a yacht with extra sail area, which makes you fast, might be forced to balance the equation by being heavier, which generally makes the boat slower.

Nefertiti ended up being the lightest 12-Meter in 1962. We got stability from the beam, which was two feet wider than the others, rather than from ballast. The conventional 12s reduced wetted surface by building to the minimum 11-feet, 10fi-inch specification. The "broad-hipped" *Nefertiti* might appear to have more wetted surface, but actually her cross-sectional area was less. There was more area high, less low. So while there may have been more wetted surface, there was less frontal resistance—a net gain, I believe. In addition, we took a penalty by making the hull fuller at the girths, both aft and forward, to gain sailing length with a shorter measured water-line. Tank tests said move the rudder aft and make the keel longer. And while wetted surface kept going up, it kept saying, "Better, better, better." I worried, however, about wetted-surface drag. How would the yacht perform in light air?

Nefertiti showing her broad transom
1962

Once tank testing had settled _Nefertiti_'s beamier-than-normal hull shape, I opted for a bigger-than-normal fore triangle. This made sense, as the rule measured 85 percent of the sail in the fore triangle and 100 percent of the main. Ultimately, _Nefertiti_ showed a J measurement–the distance from the mast to the headstay–of 26 feet. On our competitors _Columbia_ and _Weatherly_, the J measurement was about 22^1/$_2$ feet. Another reason for a wider boat was to trim this oversized sail effectively. (This is shown clearly in the photo above.)

Lower Graves Yacht Yard in Marblehead began building the boat of oak and mahogany in early 1962.[3] I'd worked there as a kid, during World War II, building wooden landing craft. They discovered that I was a pretty good woodworker. I made 56 cents an hour–a good wage in those days. We chose Graves because it was local, and this was a Boston/Marblehead effort. As important, the yard had the time to build the yacht to our very tight schedule.

McNamara and I would walk over to Lower Graves and watch _Nefertiti_ take shape, piece by piece, or stick by stick.

Hood Sails built the aluminum mast with the minimum weight and the maximum taper. The rule governing the America's Cup then specified a minimum height to the mast's center of gravity. We hit it spot on–normally lead is added later to counterbalance miscalculations, but extra weight aloft

3 It wasn't until 1974 that America's Cup 12-Meter yachts like _Courageous, Mariner,_ and _Southern Cross_ were built in aluminum and, in 1986, fiberglass: _Kiwi Magic._

slows the boat. We charged $7,500 for the mast, which included streamlined rod rigging, making about $800 profit on it, which was pretty good back then.

Nefertiti's rig was unusual. For the tangs, we used high-tensile steel rather than heavier stainless steel. We had only one set of running backstays, not two. On the mast, the runner tangs were well below the headstay, while the jumper strut was well above the headstay (usually they are at the same height). By offsetting the jumper struts from the tangs, the mast could be more easily bent to complement sail shape. Off the wind, or upwind in very light air, you want a fuller main. Under normal upwind conditions you want the option to flatten the main and headsail. You could adjust the bend of *Nefertiti*'s mast—really adjust it—with the permanent backstay. Also, you could jibe the boat using the permanent backstay alone, without having to fiddle with runners. The mast worked well and lasted for nearly 40 years, until 2001. It was lost while *Nefertiti* was in transit aboard a ship, not when sailing, so it was sad to learn of the loss of such a beautiful spar. It cost $100,000 to replace that mast in 2001—that's more than 12 times the original cost.

Nefertiti was launched on May 19, 1962, before a huge crowd in Marblehead. It was 96 days "from the woodpile to the water," as Don McNamara put it. We put the mast in her before the launching and went sailing the next day.

We were the new guys on the block, with the only new boat. Besides *Nefertiti*, another defense candidate was

Nefertiti, on a reach, leads Columbia
1962

Don McNamara (third from left) with crew
1962

Weatherly, designed for the 1958 competition by Philip Rhodes and redesigned by Bill Luders Jr. for 1962. *Weatherly* was tender in 1958, so Luders unceremoniously chopped two feet off her stern and added the comparable weight—about 2,000 pounds—to the keel. He also increased inside ballast and added a new keel. At least as important, Bus Mosbacher was added to the crew to be *Weatherly's* skipper.

Mosbacher had made a name for himself with *Vim* in 1958, despite losing to the eventual defender, *Columbia*. In 1961, there had been a scrimmage of some of the 12-Meter yachts from 1958: *Columbia*, *Weatherly*, and *Easterner*, which had never won a trials race. At the helm of *Easterner*, Mosbacher proved his feel for 12-Meters by making her competitive with *Weatherly* and *Columbia*.

For 1962, *Columbia*, the defender from 1958, was back; she was now owned by the Shields brothers: Paul and Cornelius, investment bankers from New York. *Columbia* was skippered by Cornelius "Glit" Shields, the 28-year-old son of the legendary "Cornie" Shields, later the driving force behind the Shields class. Glit had crewed on *Columbia* in her successful defense of the America's Cup in 1958. The Sparkman & Stephens-designed boat featured a new keel in 1962.

Also making an encore was *Easterner*, designed by C. Raymond Hunt, for Chandler Hovey Sr. of Boston, a commodore of the Eastern Yacht Club whose America's Cup involvement had begun with the J-boats. He was a member of the *Yankee* syndicate in 1930 and managed the same syndicate in 1934. He campaigned *Rainbow* against *Ranger* in 1937 and also owned *Weetamoe*, the first American J-Class yacht.

Easterner's helmsman for the 1962 trials was George O'Day, an Olympic gold-medalist in the 5.5-Meter class in 1960. In the spirit of "Corinthian" sailing, a number of Hoveys manned *Easterner*. And while she was occasionally very fast—as Mosbacher had demonstrated the year before—"The trouble was that her owners never quite knew why," according to *Life* magazine.

The crew of *Nefertiti* was relatively inexperienced. The only veterans of the America's Cup were my friend Bradley Noyes and me. We had sailed together on *Vim*, and I invited him to join the afterguard of *Nefertiti*.

At Don McNamara's insistence, everyone in the crew had a number on his back—an idea that dates to the J-Class era, I believe, and Commodore Harold "Mike" Vanderbilt, the ultimate organizational man. Practicing complex maneuvers like tacking, jibing, and spinnaker setting and dropping was done under the watchful eye of a videotape camera aboard *King Tut*, our tender, or even from a helicopter. This was likely the first time I saw videotape. Each night, McNamara would review the tapes with the crew, analyzing performance. I think he found it more interesting than I did. Besides, at night, I had sails to recut, not just for our boat, but for all of them.

The America's Cup was different in 1962 than it is today,

Brad Noyes
1962

when budgets are said to be in excess of $100 million. The entire cost of the *Nefertiti* program, including the boat, tender, sails, and the feeding and sheltering of the crew—no one was paid in those days—was $450,000. That's not a typo!

That said, we lived well in a Newport mansion overlooking the ocean, near Bailey's Beach. Campaigns then lasted weeks, not years. Between trials, you'd go back to work at your "day job." We ate as a group at the mansion, or else at a restaurant across from the Viking Hotel. In a way, it was glamorous, but I don't remember enjoying that aspect of the Cup as much as some others did—all my time-off was spent working on sails.

The "Preliminary Trials," scheduled to start June 4, 1962, were canceled by the New York Yacht Club due to the fact that "the contestants were not available."

In the first race of the "Observation Trials" on July 2, we easily beat the 1958 defender, *Columbia*, a good omen. Then we easily beat *Easterner*.

In the next race, Mosbacher on *Weatherly* beat me at the start. It wasn't pretty. This was followed by a most unfortunate spinnaker set. McNamara charged to the foredeck as if "up San Juan Hill" to help clear the sail from the headstay. On the way back, he noticed two winch-grinders sipping drinks. As he later wrote in his book, *White Sails, Black Clouds*: "That made my day. Systematically and silently, I kicked the cans over the side. We had a rigid rule: no one left the deck without permission."

Don's reaction, I thought, was out of proportion to the "crime." Can you imagine today a football lineman being denied a drink during a break in the action? Besides, there was no room for extra crew on the foredeck to help with the fouled spinnaker. Even if there were, their weight—grinders are the football linemen of the America's Cup—would have sunk the bow, further slowing the boat.

That wasn't the end of it, however. Don kicked them off the boat, but not before we spent an hour after the race, working on spinnaker drills. One of the crew-members he dismissed was his brother; the other was the owner's son. Then consider that we had actually won the race. This was only the third race, and already we were in crisis.

The round ended with *Nefertiti* leading with a record of 11-1. It was an auspicious start. Our only loss was to *Weatherly* on July 11, which finished second with six victories. We beat her in three of four matches.

After, *Nefertiti* was damaged at the dock when her mooring lines parted. Sabotage was suspected, and guards were posted to protect the yachts.

The New York Yacht Club was formed on July 30, 1844, on board the yacht *Gimcrack* in New York Harbor. John Cox Stevens, its first commodore, then announced a cruise to Newport for the nine member yachts, to commence in three days. The Annual Cruise—somewhat misnamed as it is more racing than cruising—has become a fixture of the club ever

Weather rail
1962

Nefertiti showing her power on the wind
1962

since. In the summer of 1962, all four of the America's Cup defense candidates, as well as *Vim*, joined 55 other yachts from the New York Yacht Club's fleet in the Annual Cruise.[4] It went from New London, Connecticut, to Padanaram, Massachusetts, with stops at Block Island, Newport, Mattapoisett, Hadley's Harbor, and Marion.

The Cruise, which proved to be rather windy, did not go well for us: not the racing, not even the navigation. At one point, we ran aground at Marion, in Buzzards Bay. It made little difference that the yacht was being steered at that moment by Robert Purcell, the syndicate co-head. It took our tender an hour to haul us off the mud. *Weatherly* won the important Queen's Cup, beating us boat-for-boat by 35 seconds.

As the Cruise ended, Don McNamara was wound tight. He had a sarcastic way of speaking that the crew found wearing. He seemed to rub people the wrong way. Syndicate head Ross Anderson suggested he take a few weeks off to calm down. McNamara stormed off the boat, never to return. His brother and the owner's son returned to *Nefertiti* as winch-grinders, and I was named skipper. At first I thought my position was temporary, until Don returned.

But Don was gone, and he blamed me for what had happened. We didn't speak for years after that. This was sad for me as we had been good friends; as I said, he had been an usher at my wedding. Many years later, we renewed our friendship, but we never spoke about that summer on *Nefertiti*.

The "Final Trials" began on August 15. I was now the sole skipper of *Nefertiti*. Nevertheless, there was my day job to consider. There were no exclusives in those days in the America's Cup, and I had my sails on all the defense candidates. I even had sails on the challenger, *Gretel*, one of which would play an important role in the Cup match that lay ahead. At day's end, I would find myself working on our sails, as well as on those for *Weatherly*, *Columbia*, and *Easterner*. My crew on *Nefertiti* was not thrilled by this, believing it was helping the "enemy." I didn't see it that way. I told them, "If we can't beat *Weatherly* with our sails, we don't deserve to be the defender."

I built two new spinnakers for *Nefertiti*. One of them was 65 feet wide and 62 feet on the luff, so it was wider than it was tall. *Nefertiti* was flying that spinnaker when she was pictured on the cover of *Newsweek* magazine. It described *Nefertiti* as "glamorous," "exciting," and "intriguing because she is guided by the only man ever to design, skipper and

4 Sir Frank Packer's Australian team–the challenger in 1962–had chartered *Vim* for 1962 as a trial horse for their new *Gretel*.

5 This quote from *Newsweek*, while complimentary, is not exactly true, as the famous Nathanael Greene Herreshoff designed the hull and made sails for *Constitution*, a defense candidate in the 1901 America's Cup. Herreshoff also built her and steered her, but was not the official skipper.

Nefertiti's huge Hood spinnaker
1962

Nefertiti

Nefertiti crosses _Weatherly_
1962

make the sails for an America's Cup boat–Frederick Emmart (Ted) Hood."[5]

By August 21, *Weatherly* had five wins in this round, *Nefertiti*, four. We had split our two matches. That day the New York Yacht Club announced, "By order of the America's Cup Committee, only *Weatherly* and *Nefertiti* [are to continue] competition in the Final Trial Races."

The die was cast at this point. We knew *Nefertiti* was faster in heavy winds. Twelve knots seemed to be the dividing line. What would the remainder of the series bring?

The answer: light winds, as a high-pressure system gripped Narragansett Bay, which was not uncommon for Newport in August. We lost three straight races to *Weatherly*, in 10 knots, 7 knots, and 11 knots, respectively. The America's Cup Committee named *Weatherly* the defender, and the curtain dropped on *Nefertiti*, but not before we visited *Weatherly* aboard *King Tut* and gave her three cheers.

I told the *New York Times*: "I guess we weren't a good enough all-around boat. The selection committee could do nothing else. I think *Nefertiti* would have done better in higher winds than we had, but not that much better."

Some felt that three races between the final two yachts was a quick decision. Writing in *The History of the New York Yacht Club*, John Parkinson Jr. explained, "The America's Cup Committee is a power unto itself, beyond which there is no appeal."

The decision had come down to the final race. We knew our performance during the Annual Cruise had not been inspiring. The boat had sailed very well, especially in strong winds, but she and her crew remained something of an unknown quantity, and the committee went with a predictable boat and crew in whom it had confidence.

In the end, abundant wetted surface proved the fatal flaw for *Nefertiti*. The test tank of 1961-62 included a formula to calculate wetted-surface drag, but it proved to be the wrong formula. Had we not gone to the tank at all, who knows how *Nefertiti* might have fared?

So *Weatherly* met *Gretel* in the 1962 America's Cup. The races began before a huge spectator fleet, reported to be 2,000 boats. The first race had to be delayed to organize the spectator fleet. The Australians were already very popular in Newport. Among the spectators were President and Mrs. John F. Kennedy aboard the U.S. Navy destroyer *Joseph P. Kennedy Jr.*, named for the president's brother killed in World War II.

Gretel was led by Jock Sturrock, who wasn't named skipper until the eleventh hour. American newspapers speculated that the naming of a skipper was delayed to keep the spotlight on Sir Frank Packer, syndicate head, who seemed to relish the attention. *Gretel* was designed by Alan Payne and proved to be a fast boat—faster, I believe, than the defender—but her sails and crew were not as good.

Then there was a spinnaker I had designed for John Matthews, the owner of *Vim*. Matthews, you will recall, had chartered *Vim* to the Australians, who used her as a trial horse for *Gretel*. He asked for the best all-around spinnaker I could build. It was to be all white, with no numbers on it. Why he bought it I didn't know. Perhaps he purchased it, I then wondered, to augment the old Hood sails that were on *Vim*.

Weatherly won the first race by 3:04. The second race was sailed in 25 knots of wind—certainly not *Weatherly*'s weather. At the second mark, *Weatherly* was protecting a thin 14-second lead. It was then that *Gretel*, flying that spinnaker of mine, caught a huge wave and surfed past *Weatherly*. The crew reported a speed of 20 knots, but I doubt it was quite that high. The challenger from Australia would go on to win the second race by 47 seconds. This was only the sixth race a challenger had won in the then-111-year history of the America's Cup, and the first race won by a challenger since

***Nefertiti* heads home**
1962

1934. It said something about the Australians, too, and their future in this event.

Had the visitors from Down Under chosen to race the next day, when it was again windy, they might have won the third race, too, but they called for a lay day. Normalcy returned to Newport weather, and *Weatherly* won the next three races in light winds.

I have written here about "exclusives" in the America's Cup. In addition to flying my spinnaker, *Gretel* had been tested at the same Stevens Institute of Technology tank as the American crop of yachts, and five of the seven winches aboard had been replaced with American designs.

After that series, the New York Yacht Club passed a country-of-origin rule reserving American sails, gear, test tanks, and designers for American defenders. The America's Cup, the club reasoned, is supposed to be a "friendly competition between foreign nations," as reads its underlying Deed of Gift. In other words, it is not just a sailboat race, but a design contest, pitting one nation's sailors, designers, boatbuilders, and sailmakers against another nation's sailors, designers, boatbuilders, and sailmakers. This issue continued to play a role at least through the 2003 America's Cup in New Zealand, where designers and sailors had to establish residency in the country for which they wished to work two years prior to the event.

A footnote: *Nefertiti* made an encore appearance in 1964 to answer a challenge from the Royal Thames Yacht Club in

With her white Hood spinnaker, *Gretel* charges ahead of *Weatherly* in race two
1962

**_Nefertiti_ and _Constellation_–note _Constellation_'s bendy boom,
used to flatten her mainsail**
1964

England. Ross Anderson, her owner, signed me on again as
skipper.

Nefertiti, unchanged from 1962, was again off the pace, as
the star of that summer proved to be the new 12-Meter
Constellation, designed by Sparkman & Stephens, which would
meet the British challenger *Sovereign* in the 1964 America's
Cup series. I made sails for *Constellation*, too. The final score in
the 1964 America's Cup was 4-0, to the defender.

Ted examines a test-tank model
1995

Chapter 6

The Designer

For me, there have been 39 *Robin*s. Figuring out how to make them go fast has been a pleasure. I would try a keel or centerboard version, a sloop or a yawl. I would race them, take from them what ideas I could, sell them, and then use the proceeds to help build another one. Many years there were more than one: I would build one for the summer up north and start another to ship south for the next winter's SORC.

Sometimes the best ideas would find their way into my Little Harbor line of sailboats, from 40 to 75 feet, or in the production yachts we designed for others like Bristol, Tartan, Wauquiez, Hinckley, and Hatteras. When we owned Ericson Yachts in California, I kept a 46-footer called *Robin West*, designed by Bruce King, out there. Both the 39- and 46-foot Ericsons were good roomy, flush-deck yachts that won races. All told, there have been nearly 1,100 copies of Hood-designed production boats.

Indigo was a 47-foot Little Harbor, built for Scrubby Wellman, who owned a fancy gentlemen's club in Nassau. He wanted to race the boat in the 1968 transatlantic race. We had Maas build a couple of 47-footers to the same design; I kept the first one, which had an extra-tall rig. They were centerboard yachts, but the centerboard could move forward and back, not just pivot like a centerboard, to change the balance of the yacht.

For example, if the center of effort (CE) in the sails lines up with the center of lateral resistance (CLR) in the hull, a boat steers straight. Or if the CE is behind the CLR, weather helm is increased. Some weather helm–three to five degrees–is beneficial, up to a point. Lastly, if the CE is ahead of CLR, lee helm is produced, which is most undesirable. By moving

Indigo
1967

The 52-foot *Robin* beating out of St. Petersburg
1967

the centerboard forward or back, you could change the balance of the yacht.

For the transatlantic race, Wellman wanted a special head, mounted just inside the companionway. This would keep the crew in need still engaged or, at least, closer to the action and would, presumably, keep the main head cleaner and the boat dryer. He wanted the head as small as it could be, and we built it in the lobby of his club in Nassau, where he tried it on for size. It was quite a sight.

Wellman was in ill health when he left on the transatlantic race and told the crew, should he not make it, to simply bury him at sea. He did make it, and *Indigo* won the transatlantic race in 1968, between Bermuda and Travemunde, Germany, beating 31 other yachts.

Around 1967, Dick Carter, a dinghy sailor, came to Hood Sailmakers as an efficiency expert, a job he had been doing for his family's business. He analyzed the sailmaking business to see how we could do things in a more efficient manner.

This emphasis on efficiency led to our building sails with the computer, a first, I imagine, for the industry. No one had computers in those days, so we would phone into a mainframe computer offsite. The computer would respond with the panel layout–the orientation and broadseaming of the panels that comprised the sail–and tell us how to cut the panels out of the rolls of cloth with the least waste. But the telephone had trouble talking to the computer, or vice versa, and the finished sails often did not match the plan. However, we couldn't determine that until the sail was stitched together and laid out on the floor. Finally, we gave up on the computer. That was $75,000 down the drain. Sometimes it is not good being the first.

Dick Carter proved to be a genius at advertising. A group of us would go to lunch and chat, and he'd come up with an advertisement. His advertisements told a story; for example, "the British are coming," a reference to an America's Cup series in which our sails would play a role. Or a story about the SORC would end with the words, "By the way, the winner had Hood sails." People seemed to like the ads and would look for them in the yachting magazines.

Like me, Dick Carter was interested in yacht design. He would often wander down to the design office to talk to me about boats.

For 1967, I had my *Robin*, a One-Tonner, built of steel in the Breskens, Holland by Frans Maas, with whom I had begun building boats in 1961. Carter had his design, *Tina*, built there, too. In those days, the Royal Ocean Racing Club favored boats featuring heavy construction, so steel seemed appropriate. Both yachts featured trim tabs, separate spade rudders, and fin keels. This was the same summer as *Intrepid*'s debut with those same and much ballyhooed features, but, in fact, the Cal 40, designed by Bill Lapworth, had come out with a separate spade rudder and fin keel three years earlier, in 1964.

Carter's *Tina* won the 1967 One Ton Cup; my *Robin* was second. "One-two for Frans Maas, builder, and Hood sails," is how Carter might have put it.

For 1967, we built a 52-foot *Robin*. Actually, she was supposed to be a 50-footer, but Maas by mistake added two inches to each of the 12 stations. We never realized we owned a larger boat until we put the mast in her and found things didn't fit. I didn't complain because it was a bigger boat and a better boat and a better-looking boat. The yacht slept nine in four separate cabins. She was another daggerboard-type centerboard yacht; her draft was a thin 4 feet 3 inches. Stability came primarily from 6½ tons of lead poured into the bilges; and, of course, by way of her hull shape. Her record that first summer was undistinguished.

The next outing for the 52-foot *Robin* was the 1967 St. Petersburg-Ft. Lauderdale Race. Off Miami and nearing the finish, we were tacking to stay in the Gulf Stream. The wind was from the north-northeast and measured a steady 40 knots. Then the mast came tumbling down; fortunately no one was hurt. About an hour later, we were passed by higher-rated *Figaro IV*, which had won the SORC overall in 1965, and were asked if we needed help. We didn't, and she sailed on to win the race.

That mast had a groove in the bottom to let the wires exit, and the groove opened up. With that, the mast slid aft at the butt and fell. We were able to salvage the streamlined elliptical rod rigging, running rigging, spreaders, and other mast fittings. We had enough of an extrusion back in Marblehead to build another mast and have it shipped down. *Robin* had a new mast in a week.

That summer, this *Robin* won the New York Yacht Club's Cygnet Cup. The trophy, awarded to the winner of the club's first regatta in 1845, is given at the discretion of the Race Committee to the "outstanding performance of any yacht enrolled and taking part in the Annual Cruise."

The next year, 1968, I decided to enter this *Robin* in the Newport-Bermuda Race. This would be my debut in the classic East Coast ocean race in which so many sailors have proven themselves since 1906.

One would have to look twice to realize that the Bermuda Race *Robin* was the same one I'd campaigned in the SORC the previous year. Now she was rigged as a yawl rather than a sloop, just to try something different. We chopped three feet off the boom, added a second mast, and then used three mizzen staysails: a spinnaker staysail, regular mizzen staysail, and a windward staysail. The yawl proved better.

Below, I had replaced her ambitious but unsuccessful centerboard with a daggerboard that penetrated the deck. The old centerboard had a trim tab to help give more lift to windward, but it required extra structure to support the trim tab and to allow one to raise and lower it. The centerboard was about six inches thick, which I had concluded was too wide. The

The 52-foot Robin re-rigged as a yawl for the Bermuda Race
1968

Ted's *Robins*

"My boats were called Robin, or variations on that theme–a good name, I thought, for a man named Hood. Then there was the fact that my wife, Sue, wouldn't let me name any of my sons Robin. Robert was as close as I could get.

I painted them Robin's-egg gray-blue, too. The color and name also came from Marblehead's famous Chandler Hovey, who had a Q-boat named Robin with a gray-blue hull that I always admired as a kid when I raced on my father's R-boat in the mid 'thirties.

For me, there have been 39 Robins. Figuring out how to make them go fast has been a pleasure. Many years there were more than one: I would build one for the summer up north and start another to ship south for the next winter's SORC."

A sampling of *Robin*s

The first *Robin*
40'–built at Little Harbor, Marblehead
1959

Robin Too II
36'–one of 4 boats built in Osaka, Japan
1961

Robin
36'–Japan
1962

Robin
46'–Frans Maas
1963

Robin
47'–Maas
1964

Robin
36'–Maas
1966

Robin
52'–Maas
1967

Robin
50'–Maas
1969

Robin
54'–Maas
1971

Robin
36'–Maas
1973

Robin
36'–Little Harbor
1974

Robin
75'–Little Harbor, Taiwan
1985

Blue Robin
48'–Little Harbor, Taiwan
1997

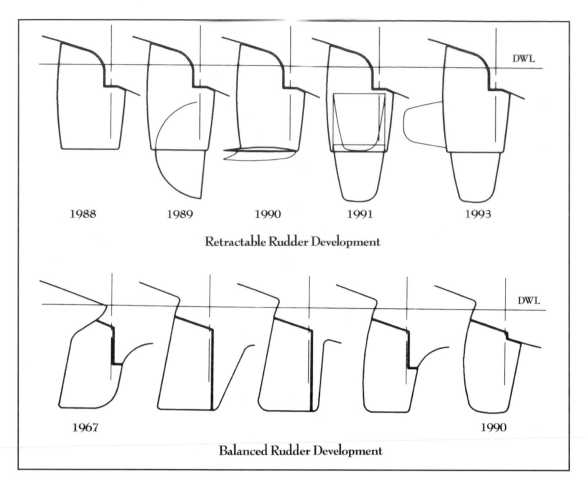

1988   1989   1990   1991   1993   DWL

Retractable Rudder Development

1967   1990   DWL

Balanced Rudder Development

Rudder design development
1967 - 1993

daggerboard replacement was about three inches thick.

I had also changed *Robin*'s rudder. In her earlier manifestation, she had a barn-door rudder with a trim tab on it. A little wheel would move the rudder's trim tab. I had found that the trim tab created more resistance than assistance, so we opted for an improved rudder shape without a trim tab. The new rudder was slightly balanced.

A balanced rudder is designed so that a portion of the total rudder area–approximately 10-15 percent–is ahead of the rudder post. As the rudder is turned, the flow of water assists the helmsman in steering. The rudder on an airplane is similarly balanced.

Over the years, we continued to experiment with rudder shapes and with retractable tabs to increase the rudder's effectiveness under different sailing conditions. The progression of ideas is suggested in the diagrams above.

For the 1968 Bermuda Race, I asked Bob Bavier, whom I knew from IOD racing and the America's Cup, to be my navigator. Then I asked noted weatherman Don Kent from Boston, who at this writing still does the weather on Cape Cod, if he would sail with us in the race. He said, "I know nothing about that, but there's this guy Joe Chase in the office who knows a lot more about offshore weather than I do. He's done some sailing, too." So Joe Chase came with us, and I

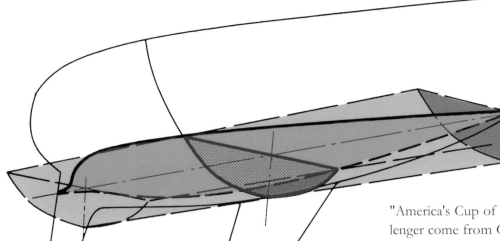

Prismatic Coefficient (PC): the blue shape shown above has a PC of 1; the shape in green, similar to *Dynamite*'s hull shape, has a PC of around .5

1972

think he helped some, but he didn't know anything about the Gulf Stream, which is a big factor in the Bermuda Race. That wide stream of warm water can set you east at two or three knots per hour as you cross it on the way to Bermuda, and the weather along the Gulf Stream is often unstable. Since the 1960s, oceanographers and Bermuda Race sailors have learned about the warm core eddies or meanders that sometimes spin off the Gulf Stream. Now, a crucial part of Bermuda Race strategy is to hitch a ride on a Gulf Stream meander toward Bermuda. Satellite imagery helps ocean navigators pinpoint such meanders.

We had light air for the first couple of days. I remember passing the Russian fishing and processing fleet at night, all lit up like a city working around the clock.

We were hard on the wind on port tack. Then the wind went southwest and headed us. We tacked onto starboard and were lifted onto the layline to Bermuda. We finished with New York Yacht Club Commodore Irving Pratt's *Caper*, a 56-footer that owed us five hours. He seemed unhappy to see us. I was proud to come away from my first Bermuda Race with an overall win. Our tactics had been good, and we had a good boat and a good crew.

Around the same time, I sold a 53-foot one-off glass centerboard yawl I owned to Frank Zorniger, who ran a large automobile dealership in the Midwest. I raced aboard this *Revener* on Lake Michigan in the Chicago-Mackinac Race of 1970 with Brad Noyes and E. Llwyd Ecclestone. Before the race, I asked the owner if he had a storm trysail, a special storm sail that runs up a dedicated track on the back of the mast, like a mainsail, but is loose-footed. He said they weren't

needed on the Lakes. In that race, it blew 60 knots on the nose. Less than half the fleet finished; *Charisma*, a large Islander, was badly damaged. Storm trysail or not, we finished the race and did fairly well, as I recall.

The Canada's Cup is known as the "America's Cup of the Great Lakes." A defender and challenger come from Canada and the U.S. for a match-racing series. It has been in play since 1896, the same year the modern Olympics debuted. E. Llwyd Ecclestone, for whom we had designed *Bikini II*, was interested in competing in the 1972 edition of this regatta. He approached us for a design, and the result was *Dynamite*, rated as a Two Tonner under the then fledgling International Offshore Rule (IOR).

We did some tank testing for this design at the Stevens Institute of Technology in Hoboken. I don't believe we got much useful data out of the tank. I went with my gut feelings on the hull shape, as is my way. *Dynamite* ended up as a keel boat. The keel was raked aft, similar to what C&C was doing at the time.

In shape, *Dynamite* had fine ends and was full in the middle. This shape gave her a low "prismatic coefficient," to use the technical term, to complement her tall rig for light air, low-speed sailing.

Prismatic coefficient (PC) defines how displacement is distributed along a hull, or how fine or full are the ends. Typical sailboats have a range of .45 to .55, with a maximum theoretical number of 1.00 possible only for a submerged cylinder, with equal distribution of volume along the entire length (a barge, for example). A powerboat designed for high speeds has a light-displacement hull with relatively fuller ends and a PC in the .70 range. However, when this boat is operated at speeds below planing, a large wave develops, and the boat operates far less efficiently because of the increased drag until it gets up on a plane. A boat like *Dynamite*, with a low PC—fine in the ends and full in the middle—was aimed at light winds.

Compare her to a light-displacement vessel with a relatively higher prismatic coefficient. That boat can plane or surf downwind much more easily in a stiff breeze, but at lower boat speeds in light to moderate wind, the lighter boat with the higher PC develops more resistance.

Maas built *Dynamite*. I believe she was the last boat he ever did build for us. We had started with him in about 1961, after building eight boats in Japan, and left Maas in 1972. All of a sudden, his prices started going up and up. I said, "Frans, you don't want my business anymore? How come the prices keep going up?"

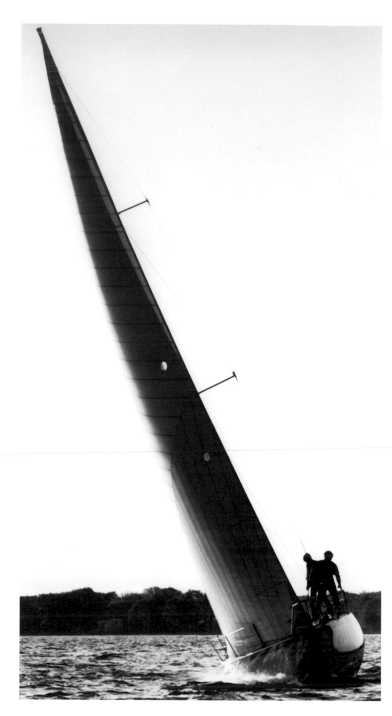

Dynamite, Canada's Cup winner
1972

He replied, "Social benefits in this country are now equal to wages."

Dynamite had an Airex-foam core and a cold-molded wood deck. She ended up being 40 feet overall—30 feet on the water—showed a beam of 12 feet, and had a draft of 7 feet.

She also featured one of our new grooved headstay devices. It was not an entirely new idea, however, as I remember Manfred Curry, in his 1925 book _Aerodynamics of Sails and Racing Tactics_, showing a boat with a wooden foil around the headstay with a luff groove facing aft.

I had been thinking about the turbulence created by the hanks and irregular tension on the leading edge of the headsail. I couldn't see why the equivalent of a sail track couldn't be devised for the jib. The headstay device for _Dynamite_ came from stainless-steel bar stock, which ran through an eight-stage rolling mill to shape it like a C. We wanted to trademark the name "C-Stay," but we learned you couldn't trademark a name that was descriptive, so we thought of Sea-Stay, which we could and did trademark.

Dynamite also likely had the first hydraulic backstay ever used. Robbie Doyle, a talented small-boat sailor who worked for Hood in Marblehead, eventually becoming vice president, sailed aboard the boat as the Hood representative and soon enough tactician. He was a firm believer in adjusting the backstay in small boats to complement sail shape. In a conversation with Dieter Empacher, a yacht designer who worked at Hood, and me, Doyle said we needed to figure out a way to do that on _Dynamite_. First they looked at a block and tackle, but this was a 40-foot yacht, not a dinghy. Next, it was suggested it be done hydraulically. That idea was scoffed at, until I said, "Why not?" After _Dynamite_, a hydraulic backstay became a standard for race boats.

The Canada's Cup of 1972 matched the challenger _Dynamite_, of Bayview Yacht Club in Detroit, with the defender _Mirage_, of the Royal Canadian Yacht Club in Toronto, a C&C design.

In light air in Toronto, _Dynamite_ won the first two course races. During the long-distance race, the wind died with _Dynamite_ ahead. _Mirage_ got the new breeze first and won the race, receiving the important two points for the distance race, meaning the score was tied. Then _Dynamite_ won the rubber match in light winds.

The 1972 series put the Canada's Cup on the map. I designed three Two Tonners for the 1975 series, to be sailed in Detroit, none of which proved the winner. I built one of these 40-foot keel-boats for myself, too, that I used to win my class in the 1975 SORC. This was after we left Maas but before we began building boats in Taiwan. We were building these race boats at my yard in Marblehead.

That boat made the U.S.'s Admiral's Cup team—then the "World Series" of ocean racing—in England. To get the boat over there, friends Lee Van Gemert, Phil Stegall, Walter

Greene, and George Kiskadian, who was ill with cancer, decided to race her in the 1975 transatlantic race, with Lee as skipper. They took along two of my sons, Rick, 18, and Ted, 16. This 40-foot *Robin*, with a tall rig aimed at light air, was the smallest boat in the transatlantic race.

My father had a 40-foot trawler, and we followed them at the beginning of the race, from Newport to Woods Hole. It was light air that first day. We went to Hadley's Harbor for the night, as they continued on. The next morning we woke up to a strong nor'easter. Nevertheless, we took the trawler across Buzzards Bay and had no easy time getting to the Cape Cod Canal. It got so bad that we had to leave the boat in the Canal for three days until the storm blew itself out.

Offshore, it was being described as a hurricane, and several transatlantic racing boats dropped out. I wasn't particularly worried because it was, I knew, a good boat and a very good crew. My wife, Sue, however, was terribly worried. In time, we learned from *Kialoa*, the maxi boat in the race that was also functioning as the contact boat, that they had heard from *Robin*. That was a relief.

Robin went on to win the 1975 transatlantic race and was the top scorer on the U.S. team in the Admiral's Cup, but the U.S. team didn't fare very well in that series. Sadly, cancer claimed George Kiskadian a couple of months after this transatlantic race.

Ted checks sails on *Courageous,* with Bob Bavier at the helm
1974

Chapter 7

America's Cup Trials 1974

"A worker and a perfectionist, Hood is a man who cares little for the limelight. After
Courageous's clinching victory over Intrepid*, most of the syndicate boats made a bee-line*
for shore to start celebrating. Hood stayed out another hour to test heavy-weather sails
which Courageous *might be needing if it blows up this coming week."*

– Dave Philips in the Providence Journal

T he 1974 America's Cup had actually been scheduled for 1973. The 1973 series was postponed by the New York Yacht Club for a year to allow Lloyd's Register of Shipping to come up with scantlings for aluminum 12-Meters. Prior to that, they'd only been built of wood.

Originally, there were seven "foreign" challengers, an unheard-of number in those days. Multiple challengers had only become a reality in the previous Cup in 1970. The delay, however, coincided with an economic recession. There was, you might recall, the Arab-Israeli War in 1973 and then an oil embargo. This reduced the field of seven challengers to two: Baron Marcel Bich of France, manufacturer of the popular ballpoint (Bic) pen and razors, who was making his second appearance; and Alan Bond, a land-developer from Western Australia, making his debut.

Defense candidate *Courageous* was close to being stillborn. Her original syndicate, formed in 1970, included William J. Strawbridge, F. Briggs Dalzell, and J. Burr Bartram Jr. These three had fielded the impressive *Intrepid*, the successful defender in 1967, when designed by Olin Stephens, and *Intrepid* again in 1970, when redesigned by Britton Chance.

In January 1974, the *New York Times* reported that *Courageous'* syndicate had given up. With that, Bill Ficker, to be *Courageous'* skipper—he had skippered *Intrepid* in 1970 —announced he, too, wouldn't participate due to business conflicts. Ficker's crew opted out, too.

Nevertheless, Minneford Yacht Yard in City Island, New York, kept building the yacht. Maybe, they reasoned, if they

Courageous in the lift revealing Olin Stephens's latest thinking
1974

stopped, the yacht would never be ready in time. Then Robert McCullough, who would become commodore of the New York Yacht Club the next year, stepped in and saved _Courageous_. He found backers for her and recruited crew from his East Coast friends.

In 1974, _Courageous_ and the impending America's Cup against Australia or France were far from my mind. Strawbridge, who originally headed the _Courageous_ syndicate, asked me the year before to sail aboard what was to be the seventh 12-Meter designed by Olin Stephens of Sparkman & Stephens. I declined, however; I told him I just could not take the entire summer off to sail on the boat.

The America's Cup was getting to be a full-summer commitment. Now, of course, it is a full-time, even lifetime, job. Prior Cups had been a week here, a week there. I had a business to run and other aspects of the sport in which I remained interested, like ocean racing.

The America's Cup actually seemed to hurt my sailmaking business, as customers assumed I would be too busy to give them the attention they deserved. This wasn't true. Hood Sailmakers wasn't a one-man band then, if it ever was, but this was a hard perception to shake. In 1974, I had 17 lofts in America, Australia, England, Italy, and South America, and many able managers and employees, including Lee Van

Gemert, Robbie Doyle, and Charlie Hamlin. At this point, I had sold Hood Sailmakers to Charles Leighton and his CML Industries (NordicTrack, Boston Whaler, Carroll Reed, Kelty Backpacks, etc.), but continued to work there under a management agreement, or earn-out (see chapter 9).

Then, I wasn't that impressed with the design of *Courageous*. The deck layout appeared awkward and even dangerous to me. The deck of that yacht was riddled with openings in an effort to save weight. Also, the bow had less freeboard than the stern, in an effort to lengthen the headstay. Aft, *Courageous* was busy, with two steering wheels side by side, each with a trim-tab wheel inside of it. To accommodate a mainsail with a long leech or, perhaps, in the interest of an end-plate effect—to keep the airflow from escaping from the high-pressure windward side of the sail to the low-pressure leeward side—the boom was so low to the deck that the genoa tailers had to duck their heads in the middle of a tack. The boom practically touched the top of the two wheels, which made jibing scary for the helmsman.

So having said no to my direct participation in the America's Cup, I chose to sail the One Ton Cup in England, an event I'd enjoyed in the past. Not to be minimized, I'd also found any number of loft managers at various One Ton Cups, for example, Chris Bouzaid (New Zealand and Australia), Ed Botterell (Canada), and R. Bunty King (England). I would compete there in my new One-Tonner *Robin*, a light-displacement aluminum sloop built by Palmer Johnson in Wisconsin. The new skipper for *Courageous* would be Robert N. Bavier Jr., age 55, the influential publisher of *Yachting* magazine. In 1964

Bob McCullough (left) and Olin Stephens observe a *Courageous* design test-tank run
1974

Robbie Doyle
1974

Bavier had come to the rescue of *Constellation*, replacing Eric Ridder, her original skipper. This transfer was handled in a quiet, gentlemanly fashion.

With Bavier at the helm in 1964, *Constellation* had managed to beat *American Eagle*, another potential and very potent defender. *Constellation* was also helped, I believe, by opting to use Hood sails exclusively. She then easily beat *Sovereign*, the challenger from Britain.

The birth of *Mariner*, on the other hand, was straightforward, at least in the beginning. She represented a new generation at the America's Cup: Ted Turner, Dennis Conner, Britton Chance, and Robbie Doyle.

Ted Turner was then 34. He came to the helm of an America's Cup yacht because of the two Southern Ocean Racing Conference (SORC) series he won, the first in the Cal 40 *Vamp* in 1964. That was where I first met him. He won his second SORC in 1970 in the 12-Meter *American Eagle*. With the latter boat, an America's Cup 12-Meter turned into a successful ocean racer, he had also won the World Ocean Racing Championship in 1970. He was named the 1970 Yachtsman of the Year, as a result.

Dennis Conner, who would be Turner's tactician on *Mariner*, was then 32. A San Diego sailor, he had won the Star Worlds in 1971 and the Congressional Cup in 1973. Conner met and beat Turner at a Congressional Cup, which was America's foremost match-racing series, held in Long Beach, California.

Britton Chance Jr., *Mariner*'s designer, was then 34. He had

Mariner's radical underbody
1974

George Hinman, Briggs Cunningham, and Ted Turner
1974

assisted me in the tank testing for *Nefertiti* in 1962. As mentioned, for the 1970 America's Cup series, Chance had redesigned Olin Stephens's *Intrepid*, which beat *Gretel II*, the Australian challenger, 4-1. Not everyone thought he had improved the speed of *Intrepid*, however. The defender was lucky to beat *Gretel II*, a faster boat. It is interesting to note that *Gretel* was faster than *Weatherly* in 1962 and *Gretel II* was thought to be faster than *Intrepid* in 1970. Both *Gretel*s were designed by Alan Payne, an Australian.

Chance also designed the 12-Meter *Chancegger* for Baron Marcel Bich of France. Being an American, Chance wasn't eligible to design an America's Cup boat for a French syndicate, but this boat influenced the design of Bich's *France I*, which would be making an encore appearance in the 1974 America's Cup.

Other key players on the *Mariner* team included Robbie Doyle, who worked for me at Hood Sailmakers. A young graduate of Harvard University, Doyle lived in Marblehead, like me, and we were members of the same clubs. He joined me in the sailmaking business, eventually becoming a vice president. Later, he would establish Doyle Sails. Robbie would be the sail-trimmer on *Mariner*.

Mariner's syndicate head was George R. Hinman, a former commodore of the New York Yacht Club, who had sailed *American Eagle*, a trial horse in 1967. Commodore Hinman would also skipper *Mariner*'s trial horse, *Valiant*, a boat that also had a shot at selection as the Cup defender.

Olin Stephens, Bob Bavier, and Ted Hood
1974

Hinman was the polar opposite of Ted Turner. He was older, calm, collected, and quiet. Turner, as the world would learn, was always talking. Six years later, he would start his CNN and become a billionaire through its later merger with AOL Time Warner. Ted Turner was *Time* magazine's Man of the Year in 1991. Then as now, one never knew what he would say next.

He was a good sport, a character, always making people laugh. In one One-Ton series in the thick fog off Marblehead, Turner was lost—we all were—searching for a mark that was supposed to be lighted but wasn't. I could hear him yelling, "Ted Hood! Where the Hell are you?" I don't know if he thought I possessed some special local knowledge, but the curtain of fog looked pretty much the same to me as it probably did to him.

Britton Chance would later say he wasn't comfortable with Turner as skipper, so he opted for a radical design in the hopes of garnering some extra speed. His focus was on the waves that surround a hull. At hull speed, or top speed, a displacement boat has a bow and stern wave. The length of the waterline determines the distance between these waves and, thus, top-end speed. The longer the waterline the farther you separate the bow and stern waves, and the faster the hull speed. This is reflected in the formula for hull speed of a displacement yacht: 1.34 x waterline length.

When a boat first parts the water, the bow wave rises, like snow before a snowplow. Then, as the hull gets wider, the flow around it accelerates, like wind around a sail or over an

Gerry Driscoll
1974

airplane wing. Where the hull narrows again, the pressure is suddenly released, and the quarter or stern wave forms.

Chance attempted to trick the ocean into thinking that *Mariner* was a longer boat on the water than she actually was. He kept the back end of the boat artificially full and then chopped it off abruptly in a bold horizontal and vertical stroke, where the rule dictated. Would the ocean be fooled?

An unknown quantity was *Intrepid*, to be skippered by Gerry Driscoll, a San Diego boatbuilder and Star world champion. *Intrepid's* tactician was Bill Buchan, of Seattle, who also won the Star worlds in 1961 and 1970. Buchan would win them again in 1985 and an Olympic gold medal in 1984. *Intrepid* was primarily a West Coast effort.

Olin Stephens was most fond of *Intrepid* when he designed her in 1967, describing the yacht as "a breakthrough–probably the most forward step in the 12-Meter class." As designed, *Intrepid* had a trim tab, a second rudder on the trailing edge of the keel (something never seen before on a 12-Meter yacht), winches below deck to keep weight low, and a spade rudder separate from the fin keel. Stephens was never happy with the Chance redesign of *Intrepid*, and the 1974 *Intrepid* syndicate gave him the opportunity to redesign her. A few years ago, Olin admitted to me that *Intrepid* in 1974 had just about the same lines as *Courageous*. The top of *Intrepid's* mast was made from titanium, an exotic material that was "grandfathered" in for the 1974 version of *Intrepid*.

Stephens had two designs in the competition: the new, aluminum *Courageous* and the old, wooden *Intrepid*. If *Intrepid* proved successful, she would be the first yacht to defend the America's Cup three times. The syndicate's motto was "Knock on wood." Its message and West Coast origins inspired a lot of people who never had any interest in the America's Cup before. It was refreshing to see that.

Intrepid also had John Marshall, head of North Sails East in Connecticut, and the right-hand man of company-founder Lowell North. For some, North Sails versus Hood Sailmakers would become a subplot of this America's Cup.

While I certainly wanted to see our sails do well, I don't remember being that concerned about the commercial battle. I have always been able to separate my love of the sport from the business of sailing.

If not expecting to sail aboard *Courageous*, I made most of her sails, at least in the beginning. She also had some Hard sails, if memory serves me right. Wally Ross was a principal at Hard Sails. Very skilled in advertising, the business that I believe he came from to sailmaking, I feared Hard Sails in those days more than North because of its effective advertising.

Of interest, perhaps, was the price of a 12-Meter mainsail in that era. I charged $4,200 for a 12-Meter mainsail, beginning in 1958 with *Vim*, and made a tidy profit on it. Sixteen years later, in 1974, I still charged $4,200, without making

such a tidy profit. These were Dacron sails, although the 1974 America's Cup saw the timid introduction of Kevlar mains. I had a Kevlar mainsail on my *Robin* in the 1974 SORC, with strong and expensive Kevlar in the fill and Dacron in the warp. This Kevlar sail ripped in the final race, the Nassau Cup. Today, a carbon-fiber mainsail for an America's Cup Class yacht costs $75,000.

I went aboard *Courageous* in early June off City Island, New York, to check on the sails. It wasn't a good first impression. I was ferried out to the yacht that at this point was under tow. The crew was bailing frantically. The wind against the tide had generated an awful chop; when under tow, the boat, skippered by Bob Bavier, had buried its bow in a wave and nearly gone under as water poured through the deck openings. They nearly lost *Courageous* that day. (A similar episode would happen later in the summer. The next time the America's Cup world assembled in 1977, such openings would be disallowed.) At that moment, I was glad I had chosen to sail in the One-Ton Cup rather than the America's Cup. To that end, I loaded my One-Tonner *Robin* on a freighter bound for England.

The new 12-Meters *Mariner* and *Courageous* met in the New York Yacht Club's Annual Regatta on Long Island Sound in early June. *Courageous* soundly defeated *Mariner* in both races, one of which was by an astounding eight minutes in a 16-mile race. Already questions were being asked about *Mariner's* design.

The preliminary trials to name a defender were held at Newport in the final week of June. The old *Intrepid* posted the best record: 5-2. This was not that surprising as the yacht had been sailing for five months in California before coming to Newport. The new yachts, *Courageous* and *Mariner*, were practically fresh out of the box.

The head start aside, *Intrepid* had split her four races with *Courageous*. *Mariner* beat no one but her stablemate, *Valiant*. Turner and his tactician Dennis Conner had to be discouraged at this point. At the end of the preliminary trials, both *Mariner* and *Valiant* would return to Derecktor's boatyard in Mamaroneck, New York, to be rebuilt.

Both yachts had truncated sterns. This seemed odd, as the *Mariner* stern was so radical that one wondered why they both shared this design feature. It was akin to putting "all your eggs" in one very odd-shaped basket. Had they not altered *Valiant's* 1970 America's Cup shape, they might have known far earlier that *Mariner* was slow. And they might have had the time to fix her.

As June ended, the disharmony within the *Mariner* syndicate had grown public: Commodore Hinman complained he never agreed to the changes that Chance made to *Valiant*. He ordered that *Valiant* be returned to her 1970 form. Chance blamed Turner's lack of skill for *Mariner's* lack of success. Turner blamed Chance for a poor design. Some of the heated exchanges between Turner and Chance became infamous.

Valiant, Mariner's trial horse
1974

Still, I was on the outside looking in until the freighter that was to carry my One-Tonner to Europe developed propeller troubles and had to return to port and be hauled out. *Robin* was left high and dry as deck cargo, and I was more on the loose that summer of 1974 than I had anticipated.

When the trials began again two weeks later, on July 13, there was *Valiant*, returned to her 1970 shape–which, in truth, was no great shape–but no *Mariner*. Chance, the newspapers said, was still working at the Davidson Laboratory Test Tank at Stevens Institute of Technology on a modified "fastback" concept. Lesser modifications had been made to *Courageous*, which had ballast removed in a trade for more sail area, and to *Intrepid*, which had her rudder moved aft several inches, to help her steering.

Intrepid won the second round, too. Her cumulative score through two rounds was 12-5, *Courageous*'s 11-6. In the first race between *Intrepid* and *Courageous*, the boats tacked 53 times on the first weather leg and a total of 105 times during the race. It reminded observers of the pitched battles in 1958 between *Columbia* and *Vim*, on which I had sailed. That year, too, it was a new Olin Stephens design and an old Olin Stephens design in the spotlight.

With *Mariner* missing in action in July, *Valiant*'s record was 1-12. *Valiant*'s sole win came against *Intrepid*. In that race, Commodore Hinman had relinquished her helm to Turner and his tactician Dennis Conner.

The victory was the result of a very aggressive but legal luff. As Conner would write in an America's Cup book, written with my co-author, Michael Levitt, "Why Driscoll didn't anticipate this [luff], I don't know. What did he expect us to do roll over and die? The collision resulted in a substantial hole in *Intrepid*'s hide. The wound in *Intrepid* was repaired but not so in Driscoll. As if we were outlaws, he gave us a wide berth from then on. He probably figured we were crazy."

I sailed the New York Yacht Club's Annual Cruise on another *Robin* of mine. Members of the *Courageous* syndicate, including syndicate head Bob McCullough, visited the boat and asked me if I'd go aboard *Courageous* and see what I could do to help out. I said that I would.

By August 10, I was sailing on the boat full-time as "sail-trimmer." It was a little awkward due to the fact that 12-Meters raced in the America's Cup with an 11-member crew, and I was an extra. The *Courageous* syndicate received permission from the New York Yacht Club's America's Cup Committee to race with an extra hand, which didn't please the *Intrepid* crew.

Nevertheless, I was comfortable with Bob Bavier, her skipper, and liked him. He had navigated for me in a few ocean races under conditions that quickly reveal a person's strengths and weaknesses. One was a heavy-weather Miami-Nassau Race, on my Little Harbor 50, during an SORC. Bob was steady, but an extra crew-member we had picked up on the dock got so seasick that he wanted to jump overboard. This isn't an exaggeration; we had to tie him down to keep him from doing that. During that race, a new jib that had never been out of the bag was swept off the foredeck by the seas. In the 1968 Newport-Bermuda Race, with Bavier navigating for us, we won the race overall. In the 1970 Bermuda Race, Bavier, again navigating for us, missed the island. Can't win them all.

Just about the same time I joined *Courageous*, the syndicate ordered North sails, believing that they might account for *Intrepid*'s edge over the other three boats with Hood sails. Some people were struck by the sight of me trimming these North sails. It wasn't hard to do. Again, I've always tried to separate the business from the sport, and I was interested in seeing these North sails close up. I felt sure I could learn something. These North sails were heavy, while I worked hard to keep sails as light as they could safely be. I didn't particularly like the shape either, because the draft was aft, and they were full. That was North's idea at the time.

The Final Trials began August 15. *Mariner* was back, but with a new and conventional stern and a new skipper: Dennis Conner. Ted Turner was now driving the trial horse *Valiant*, some said because he was so talkative he couldn't concentrate fully. In view of his demotion, Turner told his crew that anyone who quit out of sympathy for him would never sail with him again. It was a class act.

Below decks on *Mariner*; Dennis Conner and Ted Turner can be seen in the cockpit
1974

Neither boat was improved, and on August 20, after *Courageous* beat *Mariner* by more than 8 minutes and *Intrepid* bested *Valiant* by more than 10 minutes, the syndicate was excused. The news was delivered by New York Yacht Club Commodore Henry Sturgis Morgan, the 74-year-old grandson of Commodore J. Pierpont Morgan, who had bought the land on which the club's 44th Street clubhouse stands.

Commodore Morgan put his hand on Commodore Hinman's shoulder and said, "Sorry, old chap."

Then there were two: *Intrepid* and *Courageous*. Around this time Dennis Conner, fresh from the helm of *Mariner*, joined us in the cockpit of *Courageous*, to be starting helmsman. Commodore McCullough welcomed Conner to *Courageous* with this instruction: "Young man, I don't want you to feel as though we're putting any undue pressure on you. I don't want you to feel as though you have to dominate *Intrepid* at the start. Just as long as you're comfortably ahead..."

The plan was for Conner to start the boat, I would steer her upwind, and Bavier downwind. For a number of reasons that was a crowded cockpit.

The New York Yacht Club America's Cup Committee ran a selection process whose rules were only known to itself. It ran as many races as it wanted, only being required to name a defender by a certain date. *Intrepid* won the first race of these head-to-head battles, but then *Courageous* won the next four. The decision for the New York Yacht Club's America's Cup Committee seemed clear: *Courageous* would defend. However, *Intrepid* rebounded by winning three straight races. *Intrepid* was clearly better in heavier winds, *Courageous* better in light. The score was tied at four on August 29.

The next day's race was cancelled at the third mark, as storm clouds gathered. That was a good decision, as the winds gusted to 40 knots while we were being towed in.

Before the race was cancelled, however, Bavier lost a sizable lead, following a good start by Conner, when *Courageous* hoisted the wrong spinnaker. *Intrepid* sailed around us, despite the pleas of the crew to change to a heavier sail.

The next morning I reported to the boat and was told by Commodore McCullough that I was skipper. I was shocked that my old friend Bob Bavier would no longer be in the cockpit. I said, "What about Bob?"

McCullough said, "He's just taking some time off."

Bavier explained it this way in the *New York Times*: "Since we have apparently arrived at a stalemate, I want to do everything possible to ensure *Courageous*'s success."

The *Times* article, written by William Wallace, concluded: "Hood will need all his coolness to bail out *Courageous*. He said he would be making all the decisions."

So history repeated itself. Bob Bavier, who replaced Eric Ridder on *Constellation* in 1964 was, himself, replaced in 1974 by me. And two lay days, due to lack of wind, gave me time to think about things.

If the *Intrepid* crew seemed muted by the changes in personnel on *Courageous*–particularly the elevation of Conner–Alan Bond, the Australian syndicate head for *Southern Cross*, wasn't. He issued a press release, claiming, "We are extremely apprehensive and concerned to learn of Conner's appointment specifically in the role of starting helmsman." The release cited Conner's Congressional Cup match-racing reputation as "an aggressive helmsman" and raised the specter of unsportsmanlike "fouling and striking tactics," which Bond claimed would be dangerous and "degrading to the dignity and prestige of the America's Cup as one of the world's most important sporting events." Bond pointed to the three protests lodged by *Intrepid* against *Courageous* for tactics that Dennis used in starts and concluded with a warning that "there is a definite element of danger to the safety of the crew and boats by the adoption of rodeo tactics afloat."

Bond's remarks were strange for a number of reasons. First, he had not yet beaten the French. Second, we had yet to beat *Intrepid*. Perhaps most important, the remarks gave us a small measure of confidence that we sorely needed, and they might well have shaken the confidence of *Intrepid*. How would you, a crew-member on *Intrepid*, like to read that warning in the *New York Times* along with your morning coffee? Now Alan Bond was saying what Gerry Driscoll, *Intrepid*'s skipper, was probably thinking: Dennis Conner is someone to be feared at the start.

With the canceled races, we used the time to practice maneuvers in a number of short-course races. I said, "Everyone knows their job. Now we're going to go out and practice." The legs were three-quarters of a mile long, and I asked them to do everything twice as fast: set the chute, take it down, jibe, round-up, tack. The crew of *Courageous* said they learned more in those two days of practice than they had during the entire summer.

On September 2, Labor Day, with the score tied, we sailed the final race against *Intrepid*. The wind was gusting over 25 knots. We sailed this day in such conditions because time had run out. The rules required that a defender be named by this day to meet the Australian challenger, *Southern Cross*. The Australians had beaten the Baron Bich-led *France* in the challenger elimination series 4-0.

We had raced with North sails as well as Hood sails through August. For the final race, I decided that we would go with a Hood mainsail and headsail. The mainsail was seven years old, having been used on *Intrepid* in two previous Cups. It was also a light-air sail (6.8-ounce cloth); in fact, I believe it was the lightest 12-Meter mainsail ever made. It was short on the foot, however, which I liked in such marginal conditions.

Courageous on the wind
1974

America's Cup Trials 1974

Intrepid (left) and *Courageous* battle it out on an upwind leg, with *Intrepid*'s wide-panel North sails contrasting with *Courageous*'s narrow-panel Hood sails
1974

Also, being so light, it added less weight aloft, meaning less heel, which is so important in such conditions.

Commodore McCullough, the syndicate head, was puzzled by my choice. He could see the distinctive brown thread and smaller panels that distinguished the Hood sails from the North sails. Using the radio, McCullough asked, "Don't you think we ought to be getting the North sails on?" There would be three more radio exchanges to that effect, each more insistent. Finally, I told Halsey Herreshoff, our navigator, who was working the radio, "You tell Bob, as long as I am skipper I will choose the sails."

At the starting line, I waved Conner off. I told him I would start *Courageous*. He had no experience starting a 12-Meter in such strong winds, and I thought I could do a better job. He seemed to understand and accepted the change.

We won the start, although *Intrepid*'s Gerry Driscoll might well have crossed us on port tack and crossed the line first. However, *Intrepid* tacked beneath and ahead of us, and both boats sailed off on a long starboard tack. It was rainy and misty, with limited visibility. When Herreshoff said we were getting near the layline, we tacked early and left *Intrepid* on starboard. By tacking early to port, it would mean that we would make our final approach to the mark on starboard tack, with rights, while *Intrepid* would be vulnerable on port. Then, too, she might overstand, which, as it turned out, she did.

When *Intrepid* tacked to port, she broke a lower runner.

Fortunately for her, it was not on the side that held up the mast. Thus, they rounded the mark 42 seconds behind us.

The next leg was a reach, but steering was marginal in the windy conditions. I sailed high of the course and waited to see whether *Intrepid* would hoist a spinnaker or not. She did. As the spinnaker filled, *Intrepid* heeled ominously. Then the spinnaker collapsed and she fought to regain her feet. The sail filled again and exploded. That added a few precious seconds to our lead.

A jibe set at the end of the second weather leg was the distinguishing call. After hoisting the spinnaker, we didn't drop our jib, but used both headsails to sail directly to the leeward mark. In this much wind, the shortest time to the mark proved to be a straight line–rare geometry in downwind sailing. Also, sometimes two headsails are better than one. (One saw the same thing in race two of the 2003 America's Cup, when *Alinghi* from Switzerland flew a staysail with her spinnaker on the final leeward leg to pass *New Zealand*, sailing under spinnaker alone.)

The light-air mainsail survived, and we won the defense trials in strong winds–*Intrepid*'s strong suit–by 1:47.

After the gun, many of the yachts hurried home to partake in the victory celebration. Not *Courageous*. I kept the crew out for another hour, testing heavy-weather sails. You don't get these conditions every day at Newport, and, I believed, the party could wait just a while longer. Also, it was time for us to shift gears, to focus on the Australians, who we would meet in the twenty-second defense. The *Courageous* crew seemed not to mind.

When we got back to the dock, Commodore McCullough said to me, "It's a good thing you won," referring to my choice of sails. "You'd have been in big trouble if you lost."

Shortly thereafter, Commodore Morgan stepped on the *Courageous* dock from the New York Yacht Club's launch *Navette*, shook my hand, and said, "I'm happy to tell you that you have been selected to defend the America's Cup."

Then I was tossed into the water, as was former skipper Bob Bavier, navigator Halsey Herreshoff, and tactician Jack Sutphen, who got off the boat when Conner joined it, and finally Dennis Conner and the rest of the crew. The only one to escape the dunking was Commodore McCullough, who departed the scene as soon as the horseplay started.

Sharing in the celebration was the red-shirted *Intrepid* crew, and Ted Turner and Commodore Hinman from *Mariner-Valiant*. Their presence was special. Eustace "Sonny" Vynne, head of the *Intrepid* syndicate, said to a still-dry Commodore McCullough, "I think we made *Courageous* a little bit faster, and if we did, we accomplished something."

Commodore McCullough said, "You made us a lot faster, and also a lot grayer."

After four America's Cup campaigns, Ted finally tastes victory
1974

Chapter 8

A Successful Defense

"So now Courageous, *a new tin bucket from the Bronx sailed by a brand new skipper from Marblehead, Mass., stands elected as the defender of the America's Cup. Picking the latest baby of naval architect Olin Stephens, over her wood-hulled predecessor,* Intrepid, *was no easy task for the New York Yacht Club's selection committee…. In the 123 years that the trophy has reposed on these shores, candidates for the role of defender had never been so evenly matched. This gave the selection committee its most difficult job since 1876."*

– Red Smith, writing in his column in the New York Times

I took the Australians on *Southern Cross* seriously in 1974. I knew the boat's designer, Bob Miller, who would take the name Ben Lexcen two years later. As Ben Lexcen, he would design *Australia II* for Alan Bond, which won the 1983 America's Cup.

I had tried to hire Miller, a World Champion in the Flying Dutchman class, to run Hood Sails in Australia after the death of Joe Pierce, who had opened the franchise for us. Despite having worked as a sailmaker at Miller & Whitworth–his sails would be on *Southern Cross*–Miller was more interested in yacht design than sailmaking. I could understand that.

Others took the Australians seriously, too. In the *New York Times*, Steve Cady wrote about Australian Syndicate Head Alan Bond. "'Bondy,' thinks the New York Yacht Club, is simply the wrong kind of person to be challenging for a trophy as sacred as the America's Cup. His money is new, made on penny and dollar stocks and later on land speculation, and his manners are terrible. Brash when he arrived here, he is now being described as boorish and uncouth. Worst of all, he appears to have come up with an extremely fast 12-Meter."

Alan Bond, who was 36–the youngest challenger ever when he came to Newport with *Southern Cross*–was actually born in England, not Australia, and raised in Ealing, outside London. When Alan was 13, his father moved the family to Fremantle, Western Australia, in hopes his health would improve in the drier climate. At age 14, Bond quit school and

Southern Cross leads Courageous at a start
1974

got a job as an apprentice sign painter. Soon, he started his own company that painted signs and did remodeling. That led to property development.

Alan Bond made his first million dollars at age 29, from developments on the outskirts of Perth, including Kardinya and Yanchep Sun City. He plastered the name of Yanchep Sun City–"home of the Twelves"–on the transom of *Southern Cross* until his Royal Perth Yacht Club objected. Finally, after much posturing, he changed it to "Fremantle," which is the port of Perth.

Bond outraged the New York Yacht Club by saying: "Anyone who considers racing for the America's Cup isn't a business proposition is a bloody fool. There can be no other justification for spending $6 million on the Australian challenge unless the return is going to involve something more than just an ornate silver pitcher."

Alan Bond's *Southern Cross* beat the French 4-0 in the 1974 challenger trials. In two America's Cup series, the French had yet to win a race. The Miller design was skippered by Jim Hardy, *Gretel II*'s popular skipper from 1970. In the course of that summer, Hardy, a wine merchant, had replaced John Cuneo, an optometrist and an Olympic gold-medalist in the Dragon Class.

It was a long, long week between the end of the defense trials and the start of the America's Cup. During that period, Alan Bond protested the deck layout of *Courageous*. While this matter was being litigated, *Courageous* syndicate member Joe

Alan Bond
1974

Ben Lexcen
1974

Bartram apprehended John Cuneo, the reserve helmsman of *Southern Cross*, and another crew-member late one night aboard *Courageous*, armed with tape measures. This was reminiscent of 1970, when Bond and Ben Miller stole aboard *Valiant* and were ordered away by Vic Romagna, a crew-member. The *New York Times* headlined its story: "Aussie Spies Steal Aboard *Courageous*."

The first race for the America's Cup was on September 10. The wind from the southwest was 11 knots when we started, 7 when we finished, and visibility was limited. That would play a role in the drama. Due to the fog, the race committee delayed the start until 2:30.

As anticipated by Alan Bond–perhaps, because it was anticipated by Alan Bond–Dennis Conner was making a lot of noise at the start. While that isn't my style, I recognized its tactical advantage against this opponent.

Courageous won the start by three seconds and tacked to port to cover the Australians. Then it was a long port tack to the layline. Who was faster, I couldn't say at this point: We seemed to be footing faster, the Australians, to leeward on our starboard side, pointing higher.

A wind shift to the right benefited them since they were on our right. *Southern Cross* tacked first for the mark. She seemed about to cross us, but we tacked ahead, in the safe leeward position. By pointing higher, the Australian boat was

Aggressive maneuvers during a start sequence
1974

rolling over us. Now the question was: Where is the mark? If we'd both overstood, we were ahead. If not, they were.

Then we got a glimpse of the mark, about 12 degrees below us, meaning we were ahead. However, in the limited visibility we wondered: Did the Australians know this? Quietly we eased sheets and sailed slightly below the close-hauled course, as the Australians continued to point. Obviously, they hadn't seen the mark. When they were about five boat lengths to weather of us–wasted distance since the mark was below us–we unambiguously eased sheets and close-reached to the mark. *Courageous* rounded it with a 34-second lead, which ballooned to 4:54 at the finish. This had more to do with the fact that the wind died at the end of the race, which finished at 6:22 p.m.

The truth is, the Australians could easily have won that race–they had the speed to do that–but tactically, they seemed unsound, at least this day. We had had a summer of tough racing with a very keen and skilled opponent: *Intrepid*. Interestingly, at the post-race press conference Alan Bond called Dennis Conner a "cowboy" who used "rodeo tactics."

While Dennis Conner and I are very different in temperament, I appreciated his presence in the afterguard of *Courageous*. We certainly needed someone in that role. Not only was he good at starting the boat, but he seemed to have planted himself in the Australians' collective psyche. They seemed afraid of him, which can be an advantage in match-racing. I was also pleased to have Halsey Herreshoff there as navigator, as he was certainly the most experienced and most successful navigator in the 12-Meter era.

The second race was interesting, too. First, it was postponed a day, due to a lack of wind. At the start, we followed *Southern Cross* into the spectator fleet with about seven minutes to go until the gun. *Southern Cross* took one side of a privileged vessel; we took the other. Then, the Australian boat tacked to port, probably expecting us to follow. However, we didn't tack but held the starboard tack with all rights.

This time, Dennis Conner wasn't yelling, I was. "Starboard! Starboard!" I repeated. Recognizing, he couldn't cross us, Hardy in desperation tried to tack, but it was too late. We had to alter course to avoid a collision. Up went our protest flag, followed a few moments later by one on the Australian boat.

While I was sure we would win the protest, there was still a race to sail. The Australians took the start by a thin second. *Southern Cross* was ahead and to windward of us. This time, I squeezed the Australian boat up, forcing her to tack. We tacked to cover, but *Southern Cross* had gained on us, likely the beneficiary of a wind shift, to the right. She tacked and crossed ahead of us. The Australians now led in race two of the America's Cup. However, after crossing us, she didn't tack to realize the gain. That is the most fundamental maneuver in match racing. As the boats split, we got a wind shift. And the wind continued to shift in our favor. We won the race by 1:11.

We couldn't withdraw the protest, however; not the least of reasons being that the Australians were also protesting us, for sailing lower than the close-hauled course in an attempt to cause a collision. This was years before on-the-water umpires in the America's Cup, and a protest hearing awaited us that evening. Dennis Conner, as tactician, represented us there. He faced not Jim Hardy, or anyone on the Australian boat, but Alan Bond's attorney. This was likely the moment when attorneys and rules advisors became an integral part of the America's Cup scene.

This was the first America's Cup conducted with the benefit of an international jury: Dr. Beppe Croce, of Italy, president of the International Yacht Racing Union, Arthur Barron, of England, and Livius A. Sherwood, of Canada. They ruled that "*Southern Cross* complied with the obligations laid upon her by Rule 14," dismissing our protest on her. They also ruled that "*Southern Cross* did not establish to the satisfaction of the International Jury that *Courageous* bore away from her closehauled course, while on starboard tack or that at any time *Southern Cross* had to bear away to keep clear of *Courageous*," dismissing her protest on us.

Frankly, I was surprised by that, as there's nothing so basic as port-starboard, but you can't win one race twice. To understand this decision, or lack of one, one has to look no further than race two in the 1970 America's Cup between *Intrepid* and *Gretel II*, skippered by the same Jim Hardy. In this race, Hardy turned the starting duties over to Martin Visser to see if he could do any better. Bill Ficker, the American skipper of *Intrepid*, aware that he was sailing a slower boat, took a chance. He attempted to squeeze between the committee boat and the Australian challenger. The Australians headed up to block *Intrepid*'s way.

Just after the starting signal, *Gretel II* smashed into *Intrepid*'s port side. This appeared to be a clear-cut violation of the racing rules that said a yacht cannot sail above a close-hauled course after the starting signal has been made. *Gretel II* ended up passing *Intrepid* in this race and winning it. Nevertheless, the Australians were disqualified by the New York Yacht Club's Race Committee that then heard such protests.

"*Gretel* Robbed" screamed the next morning's headline in an Australian newspaper. Said *Gretel II* syndicate head Sir Frank Packer, an Australian skipper "protesting to the New York Yacht Club committee is like a man complaining to his mother-in-law about his wife."

Responding to the weight of public opinion in 1974, the New York Yacht Club considered resailing the race. Bob Bavier, publisher of *Yachting* and head of the North American Yacht Racing Union (US Sailing's predecessor), was asked if it would be appropriate to do this. This former winning

Courageous leads Southern Cross
1974

Ted celebrates with daughter Nancy and son Bob
1974

America's Cup skipper, who would also skipper this same *Courageous* through much of 1974, was clear: "The Australians deserved to win on the race course," he said. "They simply don't know the rules."

This sentiment was echoed by John Bertrand, a young sailor on the Australian boat, making his America's Cup debut in 1970 (in 1983, he would skipper *Australia II*, the first challenger to win the America's Cup)." I remember what it was like. I was holding the genoa, and I was the one who had to let it go because we were going above closehauled, and it was back-winding. Then, when we crossed the finish line, Bill Fesq, the navigator, got out the rule book and read the relevant passage. Among the crew there was a thunderous, stunned silence as the full significance became apparent. Our afterguard did not know the rules."

It took three tries to get race three into the record books. For this race, Bond fired the navigator, fired tactician Hugh Treharne, and brought former skipper John Cuneo back aboard as tactician.

With fog shrouding the course, the race committee canceled the race on September 13. The next day, *Southern Cross* won the start by all of eight seconds. As the weather boat, *Southern Cross* kept trying to sail lower for speed. But, we chose to emphasize pointing, rather than footing. Five minutes after the start, we forced the Australian challenger to tack. We were now ahead. Nevertheless, the yachts didn't finish the race before the time limit expired.

Finally, the third race was completed on September 16. In the tussle at the start, both boats were over the line at the gun. We got back first and led by 16 seconds at the start and 5:27 at the finish.

Race four was sailed the next day in southwest winds of 12 knots. Bond sailed aboard his *Southern Cross* in this race, grinding winches. One minute before the start, both *Courageous* and *Southern Cross* headed away from the line. We were to leeward and ahead. We had to wait for *Southern Cross* to tack for the line. She was slow to come out of the tack, and we sailed around her. We won the start by 20 seconds and the fourth race by 7:19. The America's Cup was safe for a while.

The traditional dunking awaited us at the end of a successful defense. I was pushed in first, followed by tactician Dennis Conner. Someone caught Commodore McCullough, the syndicate head who had rescued *Courageous* at the eleventh hour, and pushed him in, too. Even Olin Stephens, her designer, found himself swimming.

I had defended the America's Cup, something I had been trying to do since 1958, when I first sailed aboard *Vim*, or maybe since 1937, when I was 10 years old, and my friends and I snuck aboard the J-Class yachts when they visited Marblehead.

Nevertheless, I didn't feel like a hero. Maybe it was the fact that I only skippered *Courageous* in five races: the final race of the trials and the four races of the America's Cup. Or perhaps because I hadn't designed the yacht, I didn't feel a special sense of accomplishment. I don't know why, but I didn't.

That year, I was named Yachtsman of the Year, because of the America's Cup and the Southern Ocean Racing Conference that we won. It was a surprising year when you consider how different it would have been if the freighter carrying my One-Tonner had actually arrived in England.

Ted inspects the cloth of a test sail
1974

Chapter 9
Success, Growth & Changes

"All of a sudden this guy Joe Pearce has started Hood Sails in Sydney, and all of a sudden a couple of Hood sails show up in Auckland. As the largest sailmaker in New Zealand I decided that to protect my turf, I had to beat the boats that had Hood sails. So I built Rainbow II *and took her to the One Ton Cup. But before that, I decided to take a business trip to America. Went to visit Sparkman & Stephens, and that's where I bought the plans for this boat. Then I went to Marblehead and knocked on Ted Hood's door. I met this fellow Lee Van Gemert and said I want to meet Mr. Hood. Ted Hood took me through the loft. I'll always remember that. That's what I was there for."*

– Chris Bouzaid

When I was young I often said, "Look, if I can be a sailmaker for the rest of my life, make $12,000 a year, run a sail loft, sail, and work on boats, I'll be happy." By the end of the 1960s, I was still interested in sailmaking but I also had developed interests in boatbuilding, yacht design, and sail-handling devices.

Early success in sailmaking came to be noticed by a larger world. Hood sails were on the 12-Meter *Weatherly*, the successful defender in the 1962 America's Cup. *Weatherly* beat *Gretel*, which also used a few of our sails—most notably that spinnaker from *Vim*. Similarly Hood sails were on *Constellation*, the 1964 America's Cup defender. Around this time, *Yachting* magazine described me as "Sailmaker to the Twelves." Hood sails would be used on *Intrepid*, the 1967 and 1970 defender, and on *Courageous,* the 1974 and 1977 defender. On the surface at least, such recognition was good for business, but, in truth, business suffered during an America's Cup summer when people concluded I was too busy.

The erroneous perception that Hood Sails was a one-man band was one reason I decided to expand the business, first to Australia in 1964. Joe Pearce, an Australian, was *Gretel*'s sailmaker in 1962. We became what I thought of as "sailmaking friends" during that America's Cup. He ran a loft in Sydney called Joe Pearce Sails, I believe. Pearce opened a Hood Sails loft in Australia. Not only would he make sails for offshore boats, but he could make Hood sails for America's Cup yachts if and when Australia challenged again. This seemed an obvious answer to the prohibitions established by the New York Yacht Club in its "country of origin" rules.

The association with Pearce paid dividends almost immediately. In the 1964 America's Cup, I was skippering my design, *Nefertiti,* and making her sails as well as making sails for *Constellation,* *American Eagle,* and *Easterner.* Joe Pearce helped with *Constellation*'s sails, along with Lee Van Gemert, a newly hired salesman at the Marblehead loft, but an engineer and good sailor. *Constellation* was the successful defender that year.

The next loft we opened was in 1967 in Lymington, England, and was headed by R. Bunty King–someone I met during a One Ton Cup in Copenhagen the previous year. King literally would write the book on spinnakers; his book was titled *Spinnakers.* I spent a lot of time in England, designing and overseeing the construction of the loft building, work which I enjoyed a great deal, and training the sailmakers. That loft is still there, although Hood Sails is no longer mine and hasn't been for years.

Ed Botterell, Chris Bouzaid, and Bunty King with Ted
1970s

On the strength of the English loft, and further expansion in Europe, we began manufacturing polyester sailcloth at a high-tech facility in Ireland, which is still operating. In Marblehead we'd used Prince water-jets to help weave lightweight spinnaker cloth; a jet of water would shoot the yarn across, rather than employing an old-fashioned shuttle, but it wasn't appropriate for the weaving of heavy Dacron cloth. To do this in Ireland, which provided tax breaks for those willing to set up manufacturing facilities, we matched heavy-duty Draper looms to the Prince water-jets. Not only was this much faster but you could weave the material tighter.

Unfortunately, Joe Pearce died at a young age. Eventually, we formed a partnership with the energetic and entrepreneurial Chris Bouzaid in a New Zealand loft, who had once visited me in Marblehead. Bouzaid, considered the father of New Zealand yachting, would take over Australia, too, again in a partnership arrangement. Next, came Ed Botterell, who opened a Canadian loft in Ottawa in 1968. I met Botterell in 1967 in Le Havre, France, at the One Ton Cup, an event I enjoyed, and got reacquainted with Bouzaid at the One Ton Cup the next year in Heligoland, a group of islands in the North Sea off the coast of Germany.

In that One Ton Cup in Heligoland, we got lost in the distance race. By the time we made it back, the rest of the fleet was happily racing Optimists. The one that Chris Bouzaid was sailing had tipped over; we passed him a line to give him a tow. We could have towed him to the main island where we were racing and staying, but nearby was a separate little island with an airstrip on it. And a nudist colony. We chose to tow him to that island. We enjoyed watching the relatively overdressed Bouzaid thread his way carefully through the nudists to get to the ferry dock. If overdressed, he had no wallet and, thus, no money. He had to pawn his watch to get back across to the main island. We had a good laugh over that. You couldn't help but like Chris Bouzaid.

The New Zealand Sports Hall of Fame describes Chris Bouzaid this way: "One of the yachtsmen who set the course for New Zealand to gain such international renown in ocean racing. He first attempted to win the One Ton Cup, devised as an everyman's America's Cup, in 1968 and after finishing second to the German yacht *Optimist,* crewed for the Germans in the 1968-69 Sydney-Hobart Race. Thus armed with sail and other tactical information, Bouzaid and his yacht *Rainbow II* took on *Optimist* again in the One Ton Cup off Germany in 1969, and this time he was successful, firmly putting New Zealand on the international yachting map. Bouzaid won the cup again in 1972 and had two seconds as well. He also captained the New Zealand Admiral's Cup challenge in 1975 and helmed in the 1979 contest, the year the Fastnet race claimed 18 lives."

A Hood Sails loft was started in Nice, France, by Royston Comport, who was sailing with me in Heligoland; he soon relocated the loft to Italy. In time there were lofts in Buenos Aires and Japan. In the 1970s, we also expanded throughout the United States. This established Hood as the first worldwide sailmaker; the closest thing before us was Ratsey with its two lofts: in England and in America.

My expectation was that these would be sales and service

An International Organization

"If my formal training was limited, my hands-on experience in sailmaking was more extensive. With, perhaps, the impulsiveness of youth, I decided to let the marketplace decide if I were a sailmaker or not."

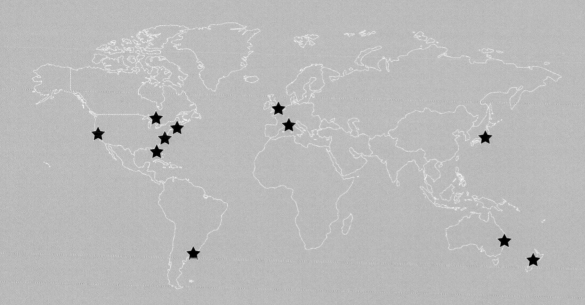

By the 1970s, Hood Sailmakers had lofts in the USA, Canada, Argentina, England, France, Australia, New Zealand, and Japan.

The expansion of the Hood Sailmakers organization was mainly due to the fact that people wanted to work with and around Ted Hood, the man they had heard so much about.

Ted was often approached by someone he had met on the race course about coming to work for him, sometimes with the intent of opening a Hood loft in an area where one did not yet exist. Ted usually said *"Sure, why not."*

Thus, Ted was sort of a Pied Piper of sailmakers, and soon he had a group of disciples worldwide.

To foster communication between the various lofts, annual seminars took place at the mother loft in Marblehead. These were stimulating events, where many ideas were exchanged and flourished.

Above: Ted makes a point to the group on the loft floor

Left: Seminar participants discuss the cut of a spinnaker

Chris Bouzaid
1982

Ed Botterell
2004

lofts, and that they would secure finished sails from us in Marblehead, but it didn't always—often—work that way. These were creative and energetic guys, who wanted to run satellite lofts, and that's the way the business evolved in most cases. They'd come to the Marblehead loft for a time to learn how we did things the Hood way. By that I mean sailmaking; we kept cloth manufacturing a family secret, as I've said.

This was long before there were facsimile machines, email, and web sites, and communications was via letters, often stuffed with photographs of sails, telephone calls, occasional visits, which I enjoyed, and yearly seminars. I considered these seminars, staged in Marblehead, important to keep the company marching in the same direction, always difficult in an expanding business with lofts around the world.

The seminars would last for four days. We'd teach what cloth to use for low-aspect-ratio genoas and for high-aspect-ratio mains; how to taper the seams in a sail—that is, broad-seaming; and about spinnaker design. We'd go out and fly spinnakers on a pole and measure projected area. Projected area is key in downwind sails. This was the reason for being of the crosscut spinnaker, which I patented. We would take spinnakers or triangular sails aboard boats and measure the effects of varying sail trim. With a wind gauge we'd measure velocity on the weather and leeward side of sails and in the slot; then we'd change sail shape through halyard tension, changing the leads, bending or straightening the mast. The effects could be measured in wind velocity. You always want maximum velocity on the lee side of sails or in the slot between the main and jib.

Sailmaking was changing in the mid-1970s, however. North Sails, started by Lowell North in San Diego, was becoming a force in the marketplace. Rather than weaving Dacron sailcloth tight, as we did, on proprietary looms, North and most of the other sailmakers purchased sailcloth from the same suppliers that used plastics to tighten the weave. The sails would often break down after a few uses; my father would often say that no one wanted disposable sails. What he didn't see—none of us did—that durability and value were becoming less important than one or two wins.

Also, in time the plastics would become better. And laminates of Mylar, Kevlar, and Carbon, etc.—glued to polyester—were just on the horizon. It would be a sailmaking revolution of the same magnitude as when Dacron replaced cotton in the early 1950s. This cloth revolution was my opening in sailmaking then.

Such competition—as well as rapid expansion—used up our cash reserves, however, and in 1971, I sold Hood Sailmakers to CML, of Acton, Massachusetts, but continued to run the company. It was a five-year earn-out deal, as was CML's way, which gave me some cash upfront but promised considerably more if and when we continued to be profitable. CML was headed by Charles Leighton and G. Robert Tod, both

Harvard Business School alumni. I knew Leighton from the 1956 Mallory Cup Trials for Massachusetts Bay.

CML owned or would own such growth companies as NordicTrack, Boston Whaler, and Carroll Reed (women's fashion clothing), and the Nature Company. CML provided some management expertise. Hood Sails benefited, I believe, from Harvard MBAs like John Stang who became general manager–which freed me up to pursue new ideas–Charlie Hamlin, sales manager, and Howard Zimmerman, who ran Marblehead Manufacturing–our sailcloth arm. Hood Sails was even a Harvard Business School Case Study.

When under CML we formalized mast making, headstay devices, rigging, etc. under the name Hood Yacht Systems. We'd been building masts since the first *Robin* in 1959. Art Fraser, who ran Little Harbor Boatyard in Marblehead, helped to build that boat, along with Dan Lowell. Fraser later married Gayle Griffiths, my best secretary. Art Fraser's brother Willy was a machinist and metal worker, who built the mast for that first *Robin*. The first mast is still in her 46 years later. He built most of our masts until he died young of a heart condition.

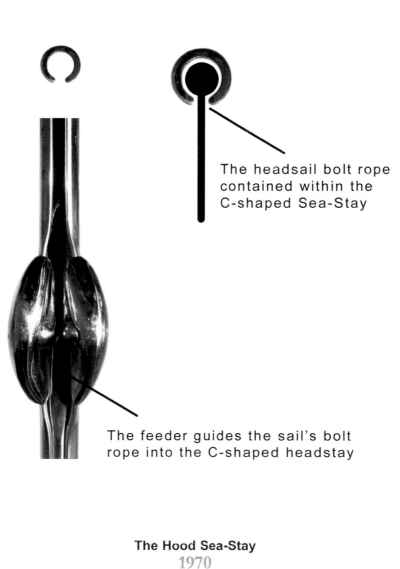

The headsail bolt rope contained within the C-shaped Sea-Stay

The feeder guides the sail's bolt rope into the C-shaped headstay

The Hood Sea-Stay
1970

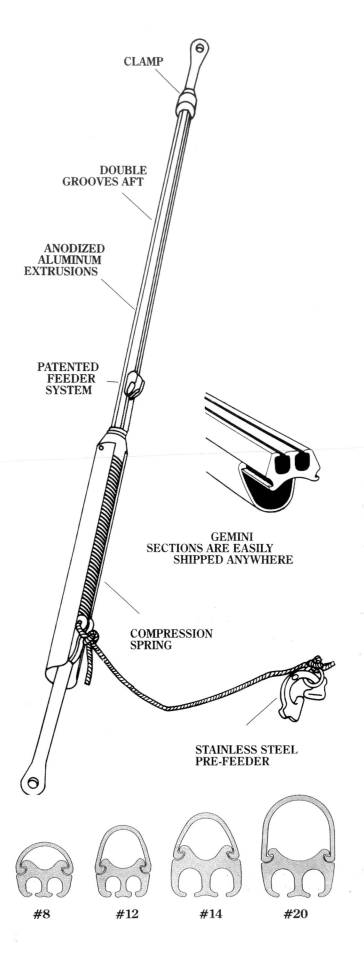

CLAMP

DOUBLE
GROOVES AFT

ANODIZED
ALUMINUM
EXTRUSIONS

PATENTED
FEEDER
SYSTEM

GEMINI
SECTIONS ARE EASILY
SHIPPED ANYWHERE

COMPRESSION
SPRING

STAINLESS STEEL
PRE-FEEDER

#8   #12   #14   #20

The Gemini head foil system–model #12 was used on the America's Cup 12-Meters
1973

We named the business Hood Yacht Systems and moved it to the Pequot Mills building in nearby Salem, where Gary Uhring was its first manager. My son Rick, after graduating from Brown University and MIT with engineering degrees, worked there; Rick eventually ran that division.

Hood Yacht Systems created a grooved headstay, the Sea-Stay. The Sea-Stay, made of stainless steel, offered continuous luff support, gave the sail an aerodynamically cleaner leading edge, and eliminated the hanks normally used to attach a headsail to the headstay. It proved extremely popular.

This was tried on a One-Tonner of mine, then an Ericson 39 that I raced, and on *Dynamite*, the yacht of my design that won the 1972 Canada's Cup for E. Llwyd Ecclestone. Because The Sea-Stay eliminated the need for hanks, people thought I was nuts; they said, without hanks you'll lose the sail over the side. They pointed out all kinds of problems, but after about a year of trials, which included the development of a pre-feeder to get the sail started in the track, and turtles (long, narrow, zippered sacks to store the sail when on deck), we got it to work.

A short time later we developed an aluminum extrusion that fit over the normal headstay as an alternative to the more expensive Sea-Stay. It had two grooves facing aft, which ended the need for bare-headed headsail changes. The "new" sail would be raised in the groove next to the other, and then the "old" sail would be dropped. This we did successfully later on in what we called the Gemini. It was used by the 12-Meter yachts in the 1974 America's Cup, including on *Courageous*, the winner, on which I ended up as skipper.

The design of the Gemini was interesting. The small grooves on the device were matched to small $1/8$-inch firm rope on the luffs of headsails. Built to such close tolerances, they almost never failed and offered much less windage than the Twinstay, for example, produced by a competitor who once worked for me. Also, the Twinstay was the headstay, so it was under tension and also had to twist for sail changes–the combination of tensile and twisting loads caused some of them to fail.

There was a cruising version, too, called the SeaFurl. For reefing and furling, we employed double swivels, which we patented. As such, the best known users of the technology, like Harken, who was the largest, paid Hood Yacht Systems a royalty. The Harken brothers, Olaf and Peter, were good guys who–partly because they had many patents of their own–honored patents.

Due to the success of the Sea-Stay, we became one of the biggest shippers from Logan Airport in Boston to England and the rest of Europe. Each of the Sea-Stays had to be man-

At right, details of the Stoway Mast
1986

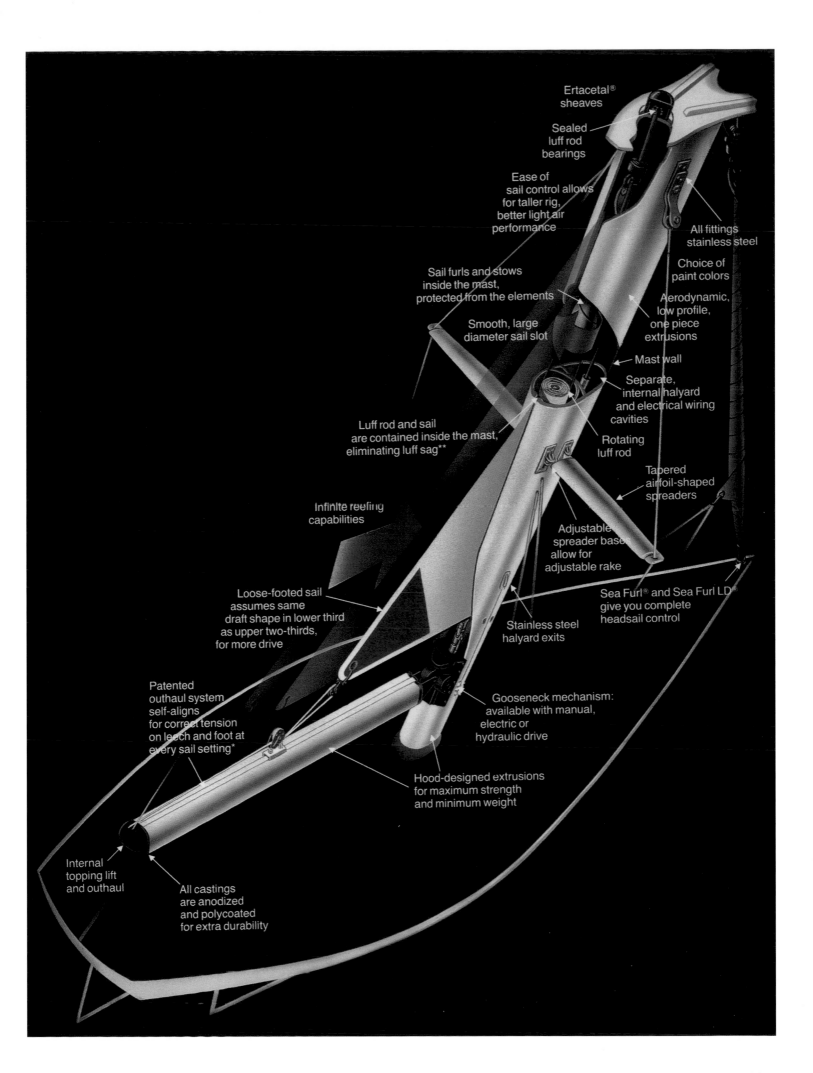

Ertacetal® sheaves

Sealed luff rod bearings

Ease of sail control allows for taller rig, better light air performance

All fittings stainless steel

Choice of paint colors

Sail furls and stows inside the mast, protected from the elements

Aerodynamic, low profile, one piece extrusions

Smooth, large diameter sail slot

Mast wall

Separate, internal halyard and electrical wiring cavities

Luff rod and sail are contained inside the mast, eliminating luff sag**

Rotating luff rod

Tapered airfoil-shaped spreaders

Infinite reefing capabilities

Adjustable spreader bases allow for adjustable rake

Loose-footed sail assumes same draft shape in lower third as upper two-thirds, for more drive

Sea Furl® and Sea Furl LD® give you complete headsail control

Stainless steel halyard exits

Patented outhaul system self-aligns for correct tension on leech and foot at every sail setting*

Gooseneck mechanism: available with manual, electric or hydraulic drive

Hood-designed extrusions for maximum strength and minimum weight

Internal topping lift and outhaul

All castings are anodized and polycoated for extra durability ufactured separately, but they would coil nicely into five- or six-foot rolls. They would fit in the holds of airplanes. Today, hanks have all but disappeared in favor of grooved foils, which are now produced in different forms by other manufacturing concerns.

Beginning in 1977, Hood Yacht Systems started offering the Stoway mast. Here, the loose-footed batten-less mainsail winds up inside a dedicated mast. When not sailing, the mast acts as a sail cover. The mainsail can be easily set, furled, and—most importantly—reefed by one person, by either pulling on the outhaul or furling it inside the mast. I had purchased an exclusive license of the self-furling mast idea from a Maine inventor, Patrick Jackson, who had no interest in developing or manufacturing it.

The salient design feature of the Stoway mast is that the aluminum wand inside the mast, which the sail wraps around, is bigger than the slot in the mast. It could sag within the mast up to three inches. That meant the wand wasn't under tension, and thus, the sail ran smoothly in or out. This is what Jackson had patented. It took a lot of development to make that basic idea work, but it was worth it, and the use of internal-furling masts became widespread. With this product, we had little success enforcing our patents, partly because our main competitors were in Europe.

At the height, in about 1982, we sold about 100 Stoway masts a year, bringing in $2 million, and about 3,000 SeaFurls and Geminis, bringing in $4 million, for a total of $6 million.

Ted with Chris Bouzaid
1970s

One of the smartest things that Hood Sails did during its time with CML was to buy Ericson Yachts in Southern California. A production boatbuilder, Ericson was probably best known for the Ericson 39 and 46. They were good, fast, flush-decked boats—designed by Bruce King. We bought the company for around $2 million, sold the buildings for about the same amount of money, and Ericson made a good profit in its first year under Hood.

Per Hoel became an important advisor to Hood Sails. He was Norwegian, but he also spoke Swedish as well as English. He came to the U.S. when working for a large drug company. He started an automobile dealership and did very well at it. Then he began importing 30-foot sailboats into this country as a hobby. I got to know him, as we outfitted his boats in our yard. In time, he became a director of my company.

Through him, we nearly bought Hallberg, a noted boat manufacturer in Kungsviken on the island of Orust in Sweden. I had a deal to buy the Hallberg property and business—Harry Hallberg was unable to work anymore due to an injury. However, Charlie Leighton, who owned CML, said, "I don't want you buying it. It's competition for what we're doing." That was a shame. The land and marina alone were worth more than what we would have paid for it. Rassy came along and bought it; it continues today under the name Hallberg-Rassy.

Ericson helped considerably in my five-year earn-out with CML. According to its formula, I now owned the majority of the parent company, which the management of CML had not planned on. In 1976, CML offered me a cash payment and Hood Sailmakers back debt-free, in exchange for my CML stock, which seemed like a good deal, and I accepted. In hindsight, I would have done much better financially by keeping the CML stock, as CML went on to do very well.

A short time later, in 1977, Per helped convince me to sell a portion of Hood Sailmakers to its management: Chris Bouzaid, who by this time ran the Australian and New Zealand lofts, and Robbie Doyle, a vice president of Hood who worked in Marblehead. Doyle, a college sailing all-American, had graduated from Harvard University, before joining us at Hood. In 1972, he was tactician aboard *Dynamite*, the Canada's Cup winner, and in 1977, he helped Ted Turner win the America's Cup on *Courageous*.

One reason for selling Hood Sails again was competition from North Sails. As resin sails got better, as made by North and others, Hood got more vulnerable. This was also a time when my heart was more into boatbuilding, yacht design, and Hood Yacht Systems than sailmaking.

Eventually Robbie declined to be a partner, although he continued working for Hood for a few more years—before leaving to establish Doyle Sails—and Bouzaid purchased a portion of Hood Sails by merging his New Zealand company into it. This arrangement continued until 1982, when Hood Sails was sold again, this time to Jack Setton, a Frenchman, who owned Pioneer Electronics. He had approached Chris Bouzaid and me about adding Stoway masts to a radical 60-foot yacht he created called *Pioneer*—a light displacement sloop that had three 300-hp outboards on it, which could power at 17 knots!

Setton put a lot of money into Hood Sails and had any number of fresh ideas. He wanted us to build the fabric wings for ultra-light airplanes, which was difficult because there were so many liability issues. Nevertheless, we did make a lot of sailboard sails, which was pretty successful. Setton had unbelievable energy. He had an office in the Lyme Street headquarters in Marblehead that included a restaurant, where everyone in the company ate. He had a real Formula-1 racecar sitting in his office for a display.

After Setton bought the company, Harken, which had been paying Hood a royalty, came out with its own headsail-furling system and, because of better distribution, cut SeaFurl's sales from $4 million to $2 million. Around the same time, Robbie Doyle left Hood and started his own sail-making concern. Within one or two years, the sales of the Hood-Marblehead loft dropped from around $4 million to $2 million. The net effect was a negative $4 million in revenue. At the same time, Setton was spending like crazy on marketing and other overhead. In 1986, I bought Hood Yacht Systems back from him. I liked the company, and my son Rick enjoyed managing it, which he had been doing under Jack Setton.

Later in 1986 Setton sold Hood Sails–this time to Tim Woodhouse, who ran the Hood franchise in Detroit. My involvement with Hood Sails, which I started in 1950, in the bedroom and living room of my parents' house, ceased then. While saddened by this, it gave me the time to truly pursue other interests.

Ted Hood, designer, sailmaker, and skipper of Independence
1977

Chapter 10

America's Cup 1977

"But then the new boat is always the star at first, and rightfully so. And it was easy to forget that over the long winter of 1976-77 Ted Hood had masterminded the design modifications of Courageous, after a consultation with her original designer, Olin Stephens, that made her not only a legal 12 Meter but, by general consensus, a faster one."

– Roger Vaughan in Ted Turner: The Man Behind the Mouth

1974 was a very good year. We won the SORC with *Robin*, a boat of my design. We also built her, made the sails for her, and built the mast. That year, too, we won the America's Cup on *Courageous* while using Hood sails. As a result I was named Yachtsman of the Year.

Afterwards, the *Courageous* syndicate asked me to campaign this yacht in the next America's Cup, scheduled for 1977. I said I would if we could do it right: have two yachts, two crews, and two skippers, both helping each other. Either skipper, I felt sure, should have an equal chance to defend the America's Cup. This seemed to me to be in the best interests of the syndicate and the best way to get good crews.

Such a sentiment may seem naïve today when you consider that there haven't been defense trials since the 1995 America's Cup—the last Cup in San Diego. You need only look to the New Zealand defense of the America's Cup in 2003 to see how fatal a flaw that is. If the Kiwis had the benefit of full-fledge trials that featured real racing rather than intramurals, they might have discovered they had problems before the final Cup match.

I didn't fear competition, I welcomed it. I felt certain all of us would improve under competitive pressure. Helping the other defense efforts–whether working on their sails or loaning them sails if one boat or another was eliminated–is how we did things in the old days. My goal, according to the syndicate, which consisted of Lee Loomis, Perry Bass, Burr Bartram, William Strawbridge, and Charlie Adams–many of whom were involved with *Courageous* in 1974- was to defend the America's Cup. I took that seriously.

Lee Loomis
1977

When considering who would skipper the second boat, three or four potential skippers came to mind. One was Dennis Conner, who sailed with me in the 1974 America's Cup. Another was Bill Ficker, who had skippered *Intrepid* to victory in the 1970 America's Cup. An architect from California, Ficker had been offered the helm of *Courageous* in 1974, but as that syndicate foundered financially before righting itself, he opted out. A third potential skipper for us in 1977 was Ted Turner, who had been fired from the helm of *Mariner* in the previous Cup.

Eventually, we chose Turner. Maybe he wasn't the best sailor or best organizer, but he is a gifted leader. I felt certain he would organize a good team. Besides, after 1974, he had much to prove. History indicated, and would prove, that if given a proven design, Turner would sail the heck out of it. He had done that with *Vamp X*, a Cal 40 that won the 1966 SORC; *American Eagle* that won the World Ocean Racing Championship in 1970; *Lightnin'*, an S&S-designed One-Tonner, that had a banner year in 1973; my *Robin*, in which he won the One Ton North Americans; and, later, *Dora IV*, which he called *Tenacious*, that won the deadly Fastnet Race of 1979 in England.

Turner and I are polar opposites. He is called "the mouth of the South." I have been called "the quietest man to defend the America's Cup" by the America's Cup Hall of Fame. Nevertheless, we got on well.

With Turner, however, comes the need for a strong manager. He has great instincts for succeeding, but he is so full of spontaneous ideas and has such a volatile temper that I couldn't focus on the details if I had to react to him. I wasn't going to handle Turner, so I turned to Alfred Lee Loomis Jr., whom I'd known and sailed with since the 1950s, to manage both boats, *Independence* and *Courageous*, and both skippers, Turner and myself. After I'd made sails for his *Good News*, a 65-foot yawl, Lee brought me to the attention of John Matthews who owned *Vim*, with the result that I entered America's Cup competition and my then-fledgling sailmaking company became widely known. A couple of years later, Loomis and Bus Mosbacher bought my first ocean-racing design, *Robin*, which they called *Fun*. I liked Lee and had great trust in him.

With *Courageous* in house, we set out to build a second yacht to my design. The new boat would be called *Independence* and be aimed at light air. *Courageous* had proven herself in heavier winds.

Before designing *Independence*, however, we took a long look at *Courageous*, trying to figure out how to improve her. The Sparkman & Stephens yacht had some peculiarities, like a pinched stern with an odd reverse chine. It was a tortuous curve. If it satisfied the measurer, the water often has a different opinion of such things—think *Mariner*.

When weighing and measuring *Courageous*, we discovered a surprising thing. The yacht that won the 1974 America's Cup

Ted Turner
1977

wasn't what she was purported to be. *Courageous* was in essence too light for her waterline length. To put it in the context of the rule, she was probably a 12.03-Meter.

The assumption behind the measurement rule is that the longer the waterline length—which increases speed—the heavier you must make the boat, which decreases speed. Specifically, for every foot of waterline, you have to add about 3,500 pounds of displacement or ballast. You can also, of course, diminish sail area, which affects rating.

In *Courageous*'s case, it amounted to a 1,200-pound discrepancy. I phoned Olin Stephens, whose firm did the design. Olin didn't do the work himself, but he seemed embarrassed by the mistake.

To make her a legal 12-Meter, we cut off 2.5 inches at the bow by rounding the section. That was enough to satisfy the measurer and, maybe, it even contributed to speed.

To make the boat we would call *Independence* better in light winds, we turned to the test tank, despite my uneasy relationship with tank testing in the past. We ended up by making *Independence* shorter than *Courageous* on the waterline by about a foot, but giving her a larger mainsail, which was about two feet longer on the boom. The test-tank indicated that the exaggerated mainsail would be faster in light winds, but the test tank data placed more emphasis on the efficacy of mainsails than I ever did. I should have trusted my instincts here.

My *Nefertiti* (1962) was the widest 12-Meter ever. I used beam for stability—a theme of mine. She was 13 feet wide, versus 11 for the typical 12-Meter. As the International Rule penalizes excessive girth, we took a fairly steep penalty for this. *Independence* showed some exaggerated beam aft, too, which was similarly penalized.

The keel on *Independence* showed more lateral plane than that on *Courageous*. With *Courageous* in 1974, once you got her moving, you could pinch for a minute and a half. Besides the wider stern, *Independence* had a shorter waterline and was a lighter boat.

The deck on *Courageous* in 1977 was completely rebuilt to match that of *Independence*, her stablemate, and a change in the rules. Jeff Neuberth, a crew-member on *Independence*, took the lead in this, as no one had liked the layout on *Courageous* in her first iteration. The rule change brought the coffee-grinder winches and grinders back on deck. They'd been in the basement—a leaky basement—from 1967 (*Intrepid*) to 1974 (*Courageous*). Not only was this unpleasant for the crews, but it gave the yachts a mechanized look; they appeared to be on automatic pilot.

We launched the new boat, *Independence*, in the late summer of 1976. Both yachts belonged to the U.S. Merchant Marine Academy, Kings Point, to give contributors a tax deduction.

We sailed both *Courageous* and *Independence* in Marblehead until two days before Christmas that year. There were icicles forming on the clews of the jibs. Ted Turner was there only

***Independence* in her lift undergoing maintenance**
1977

Independence sailing off of Newport with Brenton Reef Tower in the background
1977

rarely; he doesn't have the attention span for testing. With Turner otherwise engaged, I used a variety of skippers on *Courageous*. Often it was Lee Van Gemert, who worked for me at the loft–I really appreciated Lee's help.

In testing, you line up so neither boat enjoys an advantage. Then you test an idea, like a new keel, sail, or traveler position. The test ends when one boat or the other gets ahead. Then you tack, line up, and test it again. You do that about eight times, to be sure the difference is real, not the result of a wind shift or something else. The surface wind is always shifting, changing in circles, in sailing. If the windward boat enjoys a lift that boat gains the advantage. If the leeward boat enjoys a header, that boat benefits. It's just geometry, so repetition reduces the variables.

One thing we tested was to put a Scheel keel on *Courageous*. The Scheel keel, with a bulb on the bottom, was made of fiberglass and foam. This should not be confused with the wings on the keel of *Australia II* that came about in 1983. There the wings were made of lead, which contributed to stability. Also, when the Australian boat heeled, the wings extended the draft. A 12-Meter is stingy when it comes to draft; the typical 12-Meter of this period showed about nine feet, two inches of draft, not much for a 70-foot boat. With keels or sails, a high-aspect ratio–tall and thin like a wing–is fastest to windward.

We concluded that the Scheel keel helped upwind speed slightly, but hurt downwind speed due to an increase in wetted-surface drag and frontal-area resistance, so it was a wash.

The Australians encountered the same problem in 1983: good upwind speed, bad downwind. They, however, focused on getting better speed downwind by developing better-shaped spinnakers. As created by Tom Schnackenberg, a young New Zealander, they were small-girth sails. How good were they? Few remember that the 1983 America's Cup was won downwind, where the drag of the winged keel is suspect, as was the Scheel keel to a lesser degree.

I made a mistake, I think, by not testing the Scheel keel further. We could have gotten more stability and lift with less weight and, perhaps, gained in other areas, as the Australians did in 1983.

Another thing we experimented with in 1976 was a Mylar jib that Hood Sails built for Chuck Kirsch's ocean-racer, *Scaramouche*. The fore triangle of this 54-foot masthead sloop, designed by German Frers, was the same size as the fore triangle on a 12-Meter. The sail was sandwich construction, with two layers of 3.4-ounce polyester on the outside and a layer of 2-ounce Mylar hidden on the inside. It added up to 9-ounce cloth—the weight of cloth in a 36-by-28$^{1}/_{2}$-inch section, or the "sailmaker's yard." However, the weaving of the fine, lightweight polyester was difficult and expensive.

By the end of our testing in the fall of 1976, *Courageous* seemed faster than our new *Independence*. If concerned, I wasn't about to abandon ship.

I've often been asked: Why didn't I take *Courageous* and give *Independence* to Turner? First, at some point I had said to him, "You take *Courageous*, which is a proven design, and I'll take the new design," and I wasn't going to go back on my word. Then, older boats are often faster in the early stages of the America's Cup trials, as it takes time to figure out the settings that make a new boat go fast. The old *Intrepid*, launched in 1967, was faster than this same *Courageous* almost through the last days of the trials in 1974. That's one reason I was asked to take command of this boat. Our old *Vim* in 1958 was faster than the three new 12-Meters almost to the last day of the trials. Finally, I had confidence we'd find some extra speed; there are many, many links in the chain of the America's Cup.

I've also been asked why I didn't change *Independence* if I knew she was slower by the end of 1976? Since she wasn't that much slower, I concluded that little things might add up. I frankly didn't know what to do to improve her. I wasn't interested in change for change's sake—taking a shot in the dark. You can make the boat slower as easily as making it faster. Then, there was no "a-ha!" flaw to which I could easily point, except, perhaps, the exaggerated size of the mainsail. To my way of thinking, jibs are more efficient than mains. The 12-Meter rule formula is calculated at 85 percent of the jib and 100 percent of the main. I believe it should be the opposite, but we were locked into this configuration by the hull shape.

Independence (left) leaves the dock as ***Courageous*** (right) prepares to depart
1977

The *Independence* crew included two of Ted's sons–Rick (top) and Ted
1977

I felt confident that we still had a chance, and having two boats helping each other and pushing each other, both would improve. In the America's Cup, as I've said, the fastest boat doesn't always win.

In 1977, there wasn't unlimited money to rectify problems, as there seems to be today. These were yacht designs, not space shots. Our budget for the two-boat, two-year 1977 America's Cup campaign, was $1.5 million!

The year 1977 started well for Turner. He won the 1977 Congressional Cup in his seventh attempt. Sailed at the Long Beach Yacht Club, this was basically the U.S. match-racing championship. Turner beat Lowell North, head of North Sails, who would skipper *Enterprise* in the 1977 America's Cup defense trials, as well as Pelle Peterson, who would skipper the Swedish-challenger *Sverige* in that country's debut, and Noel Robbins, who would skipper Alan Bond's *Australia*. That Congressional Cup was a who's who of the America's Cup, and it showed, at the very least, that Turner had righted himself following the dark days of *Mariner*.

One of the really nice things for me in 1977 was the fact that in the crew of *Independence* were two of my sons, Ted and Rick, at 18 and 20 years old. They were both attending Brown University; both had raced aboard my Two-Tonner *Robin* in 1975, winning the transatlantic race in the smallest boat, despite a hurricane.

For me, sailing has always been a family affair, and it pleased me to be joined by my two sons at this level of the game. My father, who had put me in a basket and taken me sailing when I was one month old, had really enjoyed seeing me win the America's Cup in 1974. My youngest son, Bob, had been a crew on the tender in 1974. That was nice, too.

According to the press, the storyline for 1977 was to be Hood against North or Hood Sails against North Sails. And in some ways that's how it played out, but in an odd way, as Turner took aim at Lowell North. If Turner gained strength by fighting such battles, Lowell North certainly lost his way. Ultimately, it wasn't flattering to either sailmaker or either sail-making organization.

In this Cup series, "exclusives" would be an issue, specifically sails. In the bygone days, I'd service most of the defenders in the America's Cup, including the one on which I was sailing. Servicing competing boats understandably upset my crew, but I had a business to run; something I never forgot. In 1977, to avoid such a conflict, I placed my able lieutenant Robbie Doyle on *Courageous*, to sail and make sails for Turner. Doyle and Turner seemed to get on well.

Nevertheless, Turner wanted the option to buy North sails, as well as Hood sails. Syndicate-head Lee Loomis said he could do that, but not to expect the syndicate, with which I was associated, to pay for North sails. If Turner put any money in the syndicate, as it has been written, I'm not aware of it. He may have bought a couple of sails toward the end.

Independence
1977

America's Cup 1977

Frankly, I appreciated Loomis's loyalty.

Turner complained that summer that I was Loomis's favorite, the "fair-haired boy." I know that Lee Loomis wanted me to win, but he behaved fairly, I believe. First, we gave Turner the better boat. Then, when we got a new sail he did, too. You have to understand that Loomis and Turner were two strong-minded guys. Most important, Turner seemed to gain strength by positioning himself as the underdog.

North Sails had made a big push in the 1974 America's Cup with *Intrepid*; North's John Marshall had sailed aboard the boat as mainsail-trimmer. They'd come close to shaking my hold on America's Cup sails–my sails had been on every America's Cup defender since 1962–but finally it was not to be, as I used my sails to win the 1974 defense trials and then the America's Cup. It wasn't just that they were mine, but I thought their design was better. The mainsail was old–it was first used on *Intrepid*, the Cup defender in 1967 and again in 1970. It was light, too, for the heavy winds, being 6.7-oz. cloth. For 1977, Lowell North used North sails exclusively on *Enterprise*.

At some point the previous year, Turner and North found themselves at the same regatta, the One Ton Cup, in Europe. Turner shouted over to North on another boat, "Lowell, you're going to sell me some sails, aren't you?" "Sure, Ted," Lowell responded. Be careful how you dismiss Turner.

In the America's Cup summer of 1977, Lowell North's *Enterprise* proudly displayed a Mylar light-air headsail, a first in this competition, or so the world thought. Since the dawning of the 12-Meter era, sails in the America's Cup had been Dacron, or polyester, with the occasional Kevlar sail used in 1974, but never very successfully. North's Mylar jib was pure (100-percent) Mylar film–nothing subtle about it, it was even the familiar green color of plastic garbage bags. Although the press dubbed them "garbage-bag sails," Mylar sails, when combined with polyester or Kevlar, would prove to be lower stretch and lighter in weight–always desirable characteristics in a sail.

The Mylar sail was paid for by the *Enterprise* group, and it wouldn't allow North to sell such sails to the competition, like Ted Turner. Turner made good use of this. At one point he told Walter Cronkite, filming a segment for television's popular *60 Minutes*, that Lowell North was a "lying son-of-a-bitch" for not selling him North Mylar sails, as he had promised. At a party, the two squared off after Turner threatened to ruin North, "even if it takes the rest of my life." It was close to ending in a fistfight.

Turner's outrage was all the more interesting when you consider that he had Mylar sails aboard *Courageous*, made by

Enterprise* crosses ahead of *Courageous
1977

Independence crosses *Courageous*–note the large mainsail on *Independence*–a mistake
1977

***Independence* heads for home**
1977

Hood. However, rather than being garbage-bag green, the Mylar sails on *Courageous* were encased by polyester, so the shiny Mylar, which came in any number of colors—we chose white—didn't show through. These were similar to the Mylar jib on *Scaramouche* that we had tested in 1976. I have no idea if Turner knew about these Hood Mylar sails or not.

Turner was unstoppable in June, sailing to a record in the preliminary trials of 7-1. His only loss was to *Enterprise*, which was basically a cleaned-up *Courageous*. We didn't win a race that round. In the Observation Trials, in July, we faired a little better going 5-7. However, it was very hard to get an edge, some traction, because every time we got a new sail, so, too, did *Courageous*. *Courageous* was 7-6 in that round, as was *Enterprise*. Nevertheless, we beat *Enterprise* four of six times that July.

On August 18 we'd split two races with North on *Enterprise*. Stormy weather caused the racing to be canceled from August 21 through 24. It was during this time that we learned that Lowell North was off the boat. He hadn't been covering the opposition. He seemed more interested in testing than in racing. North almost missed a start of a trials race while off testing sails. He'd become distant from the crew, once jibing the boat without telling them. These were the stories that were told when North was replaced by Malin Burnham, his tactician.

My *Independence* was excused a few days later, on August 29. We had lost the two preceding races to Burnham and Turner. Delivering the news as part of the New York Yacht Club's America's Cup Committee were Robert Bavier, whom I replaced as skipper in the previous America's Cup, and Commodore George R. Hinman, who had given Turner command of *Mariner* in 1974.

I was disappointed to learn in Roger Vaughan's book, *Ted Turner: The Man Behind the Mouth*, that after the defense trials, but before the America's Cup, Turner took it upon himself to go to the Merchant Marine Academy at Kings Point, which owned *Courageous*, to secure her for the next America's Cup, in 1980. He never asked or even told the syndicate that he was going to do this.[1]

On August 30, Turner beat *Enterprise*, and Turner and *Courageous* were named the defender. His only loss that round was to us on August 20. Not wishing to take anything away from Turner, or *Courageous*, he got better because of us, I believe, and we certainly got better because of him. In fact, at the end of the day, *Independence* was tied with *Enterprise*, a faster boat.

Also, one could fairly conclude that *Courageous* was the best 12-Meter ever, at least until the winged keels first sprouted in 1983. Olin Stephens, her original designer, could not improve on her. His offering in 1977 was *Enterprise*—similar in speed to our *Independence*.

---

1 Turner sailed *Courageous* in the 1980 Defense Trials; however, he lost to Dennis Conner sailing *Freedom*.

Turner beat the Australians on *Australia* 4-0, using Hood sails, in the 23rd defense of the America's Cup. An interesting thing was that, despite the score, the racing was close. Looking at this another way, *Courageous* in her 1974 form–or *Independence* or *Enterprise*, which ended up tied for second place at the end–might have even lost the America's Cup.

I did what I set out to do: have this syndicate successfully defend the America's Cup. Yet it wasn't the way I would have preferred. One of my disappointments in sailing is that I never really designed a winning America's Cup yacht. Frankly, it hurt to fail this time, especially since my sons Ted and Rick were so intimately involved. Being young, they were likely more disappointed than I was. I knew very well how hard this game can be.

My father was more disappointed than all of us. He had so enjoyed 1974. He had been involved in the America's Cup since my debut in 1958 with *Vim*, and he was an integral part of my sailmaking business. In 1977, he believed I should have won. Such is the pride of a parent–certainly this parent. He died in 1982, at age 82, of prostate cancer, after fighting the disease for five years.

Twenty-seven years later, as I write this, my enthusiasm for the 12-Meter class hasn't diminished. It hasn't been the America's Cup boat since 1987, but I would love to design and build another 12-Meter, based on what I have learned. I readily admit that I'm not a fan of the International America's Cup design introduced in the 1990s. In 1995, an Australian IACC yacht was lost, and in 2000 another such yacht was nearly lost after folding in half at the deck. Then there were the Kiwis' troubles in this regard in 2003. They nearly sank in the first race and lost their mast in another. Losing or nearly losing yachts is not good–it could be tragic–and it suggests the design is not up to the conditions it must face. For this and other reasons, the current America's Cup Class Rule is not a good one in my estimation.

The year 1977 would be the last time my sails were used in defending the America's Cup, as Dennis Conner used North sails in 1980 with *Freedom*. Perhaps that mattered less to me than it might have, as by then I was beginning to move in other directions.

Little Harbor 42
1986

Chapter 11

The Boatbuilder

"It takes three things to sail around the world alone," [Dodge] Morgan told the crowd that had gathered to greet and cheer him at dockside, shortly after he had taken a bite of a ceremonial cheeseburger, his favorite meal, which had been served to him on a silver-colored platter by David Hillier, owner of the nearby White Horse Tavern. "A good boat, an iron will and luck. To do so in record time takes a great boat, an iron will and extraordinary luck. And, my friends, here is a great boat."

– E. M. Swift, Sports Illustrated, *April 21, 1986*

P er Hoel, a friend and business associate, knew Dodge Morgan and introduced him to me in 1985. Morgan had invented a handheld radar in his garage. He built a unit that hung around one's neck. It was intended for use on boats, but a similar version was used by police, clocking speeders. Before that, Morgan had sailed and lived aboard *Coaster*, a 30-foot, 30-year-old Murray Peterson-designed gaff-headed schooner, eventually sailing her, mostly solo, to Alaska, by way of Hawaii. Per was an advisor to Dodge and his company, Controlonics Corporation.

Dodge Morgan had a dream. He wanted to sail alone around the world and set a world record in doing it. His design brief was to "accomplish a solo, nonstop, easterly circumnavigation by sail in 180 to 220 days." The record for a nonstop solo circumnavigation in that direction was then 313 days; it belonged to Robin Knox-Johnston, who accomplished the feat in 1969 in the 32-foot *Suhaili* in the Golden Globe Race, with an average speed of 3.6 knots. Going in the other direction–the harder westerly direction due to bucking the prevailing winds and currents–the record for a nonstop solo circumnavigation belonged to Chay Blythe who in 1971 did it in the 59-foot *British Steel* in 292 days, an average speed of 3.85 knots. One other record of the time should probably be mentioned: In the 1982-83 BOC Challenge, which included four stops for its solo sailors, Philippe Jeantot circumnavigated in the 56-foot *Crédit Agricole* in 159 days, a 7-knot average.

Morgan ended up talking to a couple of other designers, including Guy Ribadeau Dumas–the designer of *Crédit Agricole*, who proposed an extremely light and Spartan design–and German Frers before Per got us together.

Dodge would describe the first meeting this way in his book, *The Voyage of American Promise*: "Our first meeting on this project was prelude. Per talked. Ted grunted. I listened or delivered short sermons. And we got on together just fine."

I thought we got on famously. *American Promise*, the boat we designed and built, ended up being much heavier than the other designs he'd considered. I explained to Dodge that you can't accomplish anything if you don't finish. Nevertheless, he had heard disparaging comments about our designs being so heavy they would never make it around the world in less than 200 days.

American Promise ended up being about 60 feet overall. She was about 60 feet on the water, as well. *American Promise* was a keel-boat, too, with a shaped Scheel keel on the bottom. Forward of the main rudder was a rudder in a centerboard trunk that could be lowered to steer the boat if the main rudder broke. The centerboard/emergency rudder was surrounded by two skegs, port and starboard, to aid in tracking.

Dodge was in a hurry, so we built the boat in fiberglass at our yard in Marblehead. One design feature was a doghouse;

HOOD STOWAY® MAST SETS THE RECORD.

"My Hood Stoway, more than anything else, allowed me to sail at maximum efficiency all the time."

Dodge Morgan

Dodge Morgan in an advertisement for the Stoway Mast
1987

he could steer the boat from a nice pilothouse, if he chose. To make sure, the pilothouse "fit," Paul Wolter, the professional captain on *Palawan*, which belonged to Tom Watson, the chair of IBM, built a mockup of it out of plywood and cardboard. As time grew short, the pilothouse and deck ended up being constructed by Walter Greene in his Maine boatyard. Greene was a noted single-handed sailor, who often sailed with me.

To make sure that Dodge could complete the voyage, the boat had redundancy in its systems: two generators, two mainsails, two jibs.

To allow one man to match the mainsail to the wind, we specified a Stoway mast, which Hood Yacht Systems had been building since 1977. Recall, the loose-footed battenless mainsail winds up inside a dedicated mast. When not sailing, the mast acts as a sail cover. The mainsail can be easily set, furled, and most importantly reefed or unreefed by one man, by either pulling on the outhaul or furling it inside the mast.

Although these internal furling masts were mechanically reliable, they had a tendency to develop a whistle, or flute noise, as the wind blew across the sail slot in heavy-downwind sailing. As much of Dodge's voyage was likely to be downwind, we put plastic tubing around the edge of the slot so it wouldn't act like a reed. After that, all Hood Stoway masts were finished this way.

Morgan used two of our SeaFurls, one for the headsail and one for a staysail.

The boat was launched on time in 1985, but the voyage got off to a rocky start. Before leaving Maine, *American Promise* blew off her mooring in the midst of a hurricane and ended up hard on the rocks, which chewed up her keel. Then, after departing Maine in a celebration of family, friends, and well-wishers, Morgan was forced into Bermuda, due to trouble with his self-steering gear, which was untested. He had to fix the device and nurse his wounded pride back to health before departing Bermuda on November 12, 1985, but not before he had to borrow $20 to top off his fuel tanks. Morgan fell off the boat during a storm in the Southern Ocean, but his lifeline kept him attached, and the boat luffed up, allowing him to climb back aboard.

He arrived back in Bermuda on April 11, 1986, in 150 days, to set the record for a solo circumnavigation in either direction by all of 142 days. This was even 9 days faster than Philippe Jeantot did in *Crédit Agricole* with fours stops. Morgan's average speed was 7.16 knots.

Later Dodge told me that if he were to do it again in similar weather, he could knock another 15 days off the time. He had been very conservative on the voyage. Morgan was not a big-boat sailor. He didn't know the boat; in fact, he had never sailed that type of yacht before. Upon the completion of the voyage, he donated *American Promise* to the U. S. Naval Academy.

American Promise at the end of her journey.
1986

Ted with Per Hoel
1986

Ted inspects a Little Harbor, under construction in Taiwan, with Bruce Livingston
1986

LITTLE HARBOR YARD

After initial production in Kaohsiung on the island's southwest coast, The Little Harbor Yard was located on the northern-most point of Taiwan
1986

He must have been happy with us because, later, he purchased a Little Harbor 52, *Wings of Time*. He told *Yachting* magazine, which featured the boat on its cover, "Going to keep [this boat] until I'm drooling in my lap in my 80s."

As mentioned, we built Dodge Morgan's first boat in Marblehead, due to time constraints. But there were other considerations as well. I first built boats in Japan and then in Holland at the Maas Yard. After I found Maas to be too expensive in the early 1970s, I did a few boats in Maine and some in our own Marblehead yard, like several Two Tonners for the 1974 Canada's Cup. These were stripped down racing boats—nothing fancy about their interiors.

In 1979, we made a major decision—to start building boats in Taiwan. The day my wife, Sue, and I were on the plane, heading to Taiwan to complete the deal, President Carter broke off diplomatic relations with the Republic of China —that is, Taiwan. Arriving there, I didn't notice much of a change. Business is business to the Taiwanese capitalist.

To me, at least, Taiwan seemed an obvious choice to build boats. The Taiwanese seemed to be building good boats, if to lousy designs. They didn't know a good design from an inferior one, but they could sure build them. That said, it was very hard to market Taiwanese boats to western customers, at least in the beginning.

We started building our Little Harbor yachts at Lien Hwa Industrial Corp., in Kaohsiung. This was a new yard started by a wealthy Chinese businessman. He was a big importer of gases and welding materials and a large exporter of rice and importer of wheat. The Taiwanese government would practically give you the land if you built a factory there and employed a certain number of people.

Bob Riemans, who worked for Frans Maas, our Dutch boatbuilder, came to work for me at Lien Hwa. He stayed for a year and a half, but his wife didn't enjoy living in this country. We gave Lien Hwa ten orders for the Little Harbor 38, two orders for the 75, and two orders for the 62. They built and paid for the tooling and built the yachts. The first 75 we built there sold for $470,000. It included electric winches and an electric Stoway mast.

Mike Mitchell represented our interests at Lien Hwa after Riemans left. He was followed by Bruce Livingston, a Rhode Island native. Livingston became a key player for us in boatbuilding in Taiwan.

Later on we left Lien Hwa and moved to Alexander Marine, also in Kaohsiung. There we built Little Harbor 44s and 50s. Little Harbor gradually became known as a top quality brand. Our Little Harbor 50 sold then for $500,000. They are selling used today—20 years later—for considerably more.

Finally, at the urging of Bruce Livingston, we moved away from subcontracting the building of our yachts to these yards, and set up our own boatbuilding operation—this time on the northern end of the island. We were the first U.S. company to do this—our yachts reached an even higher level of quality.

The last 75 we built was for Bill Koch. Actually, it ended up larger than that, because when the yacht was two-thirds completed, he decided to add five feet to the stern. While waiting for this boat, Koch wanted to do some ocean racing, so we bought back Frank Zorniger's Little Harbor 53, *Revener*, in which I had sailed in the windy Chicago-Mackinac Race of 1970. Bill and I refurbished her and then raced together in the Southern Circuit. It was fun for me. We'd fly to the SORC in his private jet. He has three degrees from MIT, and we had interesting conversations about business.

That SORC wasn't very successful for us. We broke a centerboard in the Gulf Stream in the St. Pete-Lauderdale Race, and we hit the bottom with the rudder in a canal heading out to the start of the Miami-Nassau Race. We sailed the race with half a rudder. Nevertheless, Bill seemed to enjoy it. In fact, it seemed to whet his appetite for more. He later blamed me for getting him into sailing, where he spent all this money on the boats and two America's Cups. He defended the Cup in 1992.

One commission I didn't get was Koch's maxi that would be called *Matador²*. Maxis were the largest yachts that would then race under the IOR. Koch set up a design contest, which included nearly every major designer. My design—one of 20, I understand—ended up being 90 feet long, which was 10 feet longer than the next largest design, and weighed all of 160,000 pounds, which was twice as heavy as the typical IOR maxi. Then, he built 22-foot scale models of all of them and

Palawan VII under construction at the Little Harbor yard in Taiwan
1991

Little Harbor Custom Yachts

In the late 1970s Ted started building his designs in Taiwan, under the name Little Harbor Custom Yachts. At first he had them built by existing yards, including Lien Hwa and Alexander Marine. Later, Ted formed his own company in Taiwan, Little Harbor Marine Enterprises, managed by Bruce Livingston Jr.

Shown here in chronological order is the complete line of Little Harbor sailboats built under the Little Harbor Custom Yachts name.

Little Harbor 38
1980

Little Harbor 75
1980

Little Harbor 62
1980

Little Harbor 50
1982

Little Harbor 44
1983

Little Harbor 46
1985

Little Harbor 53/54
1984

Little Harbor 42
1986

Little Harbor 63
1987

Little Harbor 58/60
1989

Little Harbor 75 *Palawan*
1991

Little Harbor 52
1991

Little Harbor 68/70
1993

Ted Hood 51
1995

Little Harbor 75 *Palawan VII*
1991

tested them at the David Taylor Tank in Annapolis. My design, I heard, tested the best in the tank. At some point, he rigged the models, ballasted them, and raced them together in a fleet race at Osterville on Cape Cod, where he lives. It must have been some sight. He never built my design, however, believing it was too extreme and would kill the Maxi Class. Instead, he built the 80-foot *Matador*[2] to the design of Bill Cook, Buddy Duncan, Penn Edmonds, and Dr. Jerome Milgram. The boat was so successful it killed the Maxi Class.

Palawan VII was the only really big one-off custom yacht we built in Taiwan. This 75-footer was designed for Thomas J. Watson Jr., CEO of IBM. I had, over the years, built sails for him. When it came to yacht design, however, he was a long-time customer of Sparkman & Stephens. He gave S&S, another designer, and us the specs for what he wanted, and he chose our design. This boat was for his wife, Olive. He'd fly his own helicopter up to Portsmouth, Rhode Island, where we relocated in 1986, and land right here on the property, next to the high-tension wires. Often Olive would accompany him. She was a very strong woman. Tom would've had trouble without her. She set him straight when he needed it. Watson was also a stunt pilot in fixed-wing aircraft.

Watson was a most experienced yachtsman. With earlier *Palawans*, he made a circumnavigation of Newfoundland in 1971 and cruised to Greenland in 1974, reaching 77° 38' north, a record at the time. He sailed from Helsinki, rounded Cape Horn, reached Antarctica, and finally returned to the Chilean archipelago. He sailed from Newfoundland to Churchill on Hudson Bay, and, in his mid-sixties, single-handed *Palawan* from Bermuda to Antigua and back. In 1986, he received the prestigious Blue Water Medal, presented by the Cruising Club of America.

Our *Palawan* was a heavy boat—as is my way—with shallow draft and two centerboards. The forward one was used when sailing upwind. The aft one was a trimming board, to help steering when sailing in rough conditions off the wind. He called me once and complained that the boat didn't steer that well off the wind in rough going. I said, "Did you try the aft centerboard?" No, he hadn't—I think he had forgotten it was there. He tried it, and later he said that the boat steered fine with the aft centerboard down.

She had a big variable-pitch propeller on the centerline that did its work in an aperture cut in the rudder.

Of special interest to Tom Watson was the motion of this boat in a seaway. As I explained to him in a letter, "We feel that our design's good beam, shallow draft, heavy construction and a large amount of lead ballast centered near the center of gyration [will] tend to slow the motion of the boat.

The CCA stability study came to the conclusion that the light displacement, light-weight hull with a heavy keel extended deep down and light mast and rig add a great more tendency to capsize in rough conditions than our type of design. The reason being that the quick motion of the lighter boat would react much quicker to a wave flipping it over before the next wave passed by, whereas the wave would pass by the heavier, shallower slow motion boat. . . . We all know how bad a sailboat is without a mast. This is basically the same theory that makes the boat much more comfortable in a seaway."

Paul Wolter, his captain, built a mockup of the boat, as he did for *American Promise*, on the third floor of our building in Rhode Island, which was then empty. It showed the whole cockpit layout, the pilothouse, where the windows would be, the nav. station, the main saloon, and the aft stateroom.

After Tom Watson died, a German bought her and sailed around the world, and then Joe Hoopes bought the boat. On her, he won his class by four hours in the 2002 Newport-Bermuda Race. He started the race with the bimini top up, a first, I'm sure.

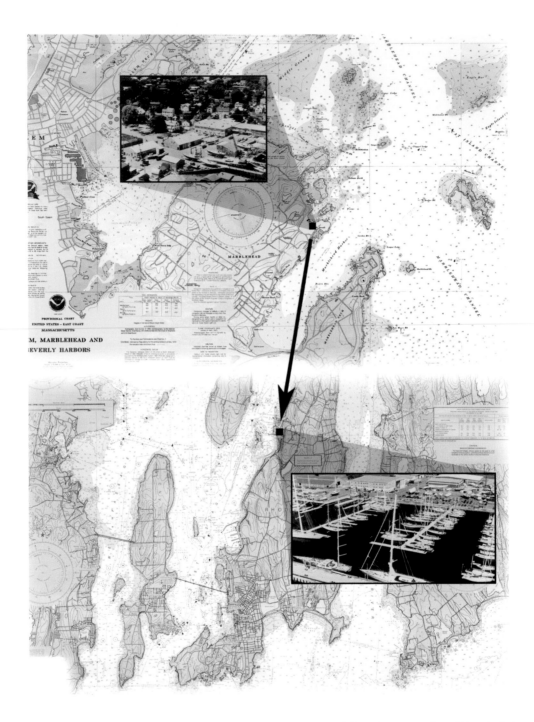

After many years in Marblehead, Ted, his business, and family moved to Rhode Island
1986

Goodbye Marblehead

Perhaps, the greatest single individual in building Marblehead's reputation as the "Yachting Capital of America," Ted Hood continues to be recognized in yachting circles around the world . . . . In 1965 he announced plans to develop Riverhead Beach into a world-class marina at no charge to the town. His plan met with vociferous contention and opposition and ultimately went down in humiliating defeat at Town Meeting. Afterward, Marblehead's favorite son sold all of his boat-related businesses in Marblehead and transferred his base of operations to [Portsmouth,] Rhode Island, where his plans were welcomed, and his companies have continued to grow in scope and importance in the world of yachting. Marblehead's industry suffered serious stagnation and, perhaps, ultimately the town's resistance to Ted's plans reduced the once world famous racing center to a field of moorings for seasonal enjoyment of day sailing and buoy racing.

– Marblehead Magazine

In 1954 I purchased the Little Harbor property in Marblehead, which primarily consisted of the foundation of the Burgess-Curtis aircraft factory. The factory, which manufactured seaplanes during World War I, burned to the ground on the night of the "False Armistice," November 7, 1918. The timing of that fire likely accounted for idle but persistent speculation in Marblehead about the real cause of the fire.[1] That, however, happened long before my time.

When I bought the yard, primarily to house my sailmaking business, there was little or no zoning in Marblehead. I could have constructed a skyscraper on the property if I had wished to do so.

Times change, however. More and more houses were built around the Little Harbor property, and residents began complaining about the noise, dust, the comings and goings, and

---

[1] The real armistice that ended World War I occurred four days later, the 11th day of the 11th month, 1918.

Little Harbor Boat Yard, Marblehead
1950s

the goings-on. After 30 years in Marblehead, we could grow no more. For me, standing pat holds little interest; never has.

I had long dreamed of building a really good boatyard, a place to build, service, moor, store, and work on yachts. I had seen my fair share of yards that weren't run very well. Often, I would go out on new yachts, sometimes with Rod Stephens, Olin's brother and a principal in the yacht-design firm of Sparkman & Stephens. A no-nonsense guy, Rod would be at the boatyard to check his firm's latest yacht; I would be there to check our sails.

We'd arrive promptly at the appointed time and often find that the boat was not ready. Someone was varnishing or doing something else to the boat. Rod would have planned on a six-hour inspection, six hours would come and go waiting for the boat, and he'd take off for his next appointment. He'd charge for his time, too. I couldn't quite charge for standing still, but I wanted to. From such experiences, which were far more common than you might think, I concluded that there were many ways to improve the organization and the level of service in the typical boatyard. How I detest such inefficiencies. I was eager to run a yard the right way.

However, Little Harbor wasn't a good place for a sizable boatyard or marina. It didn't have deep water; you had to come in or leave at high tide.

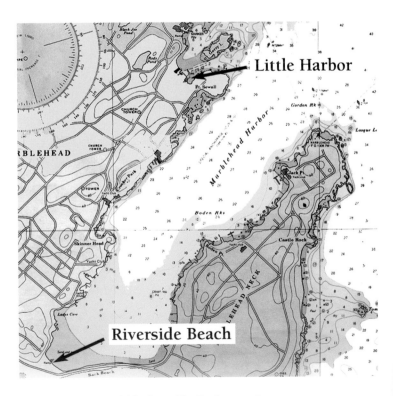

Marblehead Harbor, Ted's home for many years
1943-1985

View of Marblehead Harbor, looking south, showing Ted's Little Harbor operations (see arrow)
1970s

In the 1970s I made plans to build a marina down by the cemetery on the west shore of Marblehead. I also considered Riverhead Beach at the south end of the harbor along the causeway to the Neck, unused town land at the upper end of Salem Harbor, Derby Wharf in Salem, and the old Coast Guard station in Salem, but the towns weren't interested. So I began to think about expanding elsewhere.

I did not wish to leave this area, where several generations of Hoods had lived and worked, but I thought I could develop a second base of operation closer to my primary markets: Rhode Island, Connecticut, and New York. This would be a satellite facility where I would build, service, moor, and store boats. I also hoped to have office space for other marine-related businesses and stores selling nautical gear and equipment. A one-stop "marine-mart" is how I envisioned it.

Prime property for such development was a piece of the sprawling Quonset Point-Davisville property in North Kingstown, Rhode Island. It had once been a naval air station and home of the Seabees. As I was considering this, another piece of property in Melville, a section of Portsmouth, Rhode Island, on the other side of Narragansett Bay from Quonset,

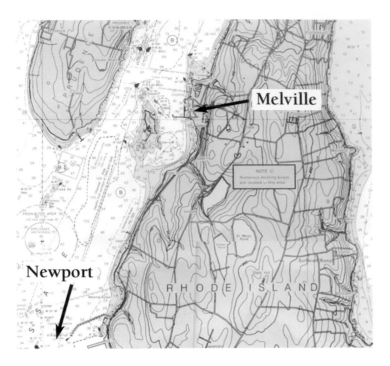

Ted's new home, the Melville area of Portsmouth
1985

came up for development. This was part of the Newport/Melville Naval Complex. It was about six miles north of Newport, home of the America's Cup from 1930 to 1983. Like its better-known neighbor Newport, Portsmouth also featured great sailing waters, although few people knew about Portsmouth's charms in this regard at the time.

Melville was acquired by the U.S. Navy in 1902 and became one of the Navy's largest coaling stations. Later, it was the U.S. Navy Center for PT Boat Training. Among its graduates was Lieutenant John F. Kennedy of PT-109 fame—later the 35th president of the United States. The site was also used during World War II for manufacturing harbor-defense nets and for storing fuel for the Atlantic Fleet. The Melville property had been declared surplus by the Navy after the fleet departed in 1973. The price was set at $1.3 million for a 100-year lease. Town and state officials would select the most congenial bid for the property.

I had a potential partner from Massachusetts, who was interested in joining me. He saw this as an investment opportunity, however, and had no desire to be an active participant. Then it occurred to me that my proposal might have a better chance of success if I had a local partner who was well connected and well respected. That led me to Everett Pearson, whom I had come to know over the years through sailing and yacht design, and by making sails for his boats.

Everett Pearson and his cousin Clint Pearson started building boats in Rhode Island in 1957, using the new fiberglass material rather than the traditional wood. This was seven years after I started making sails in Marblehead out of cotton, then nylon, orlon, and in 1952 Dacron or polyester, a new material for that application. New materials have a way of upsetting the existing order.[2]

A family friend showed the Pearsons an article in *Popular Mechanics* about fiberglass boatbuilding. The Pearsons first built eight-foot runabouts out of "glass-reinforced plastic" (grp), as fiberglass was then known. Soon came an order for a 28-foot fiberglass sailboat, designed by Carl Alberg. It seemed like a good boat to build and to display at the 1959 New York Boat Show. Before completing the boat, however, the cousins ran out of money and had to borrow the remaining few dollars from a family friend, who ran a funeral parlor.

At the New York Boat Show they took orders for 18 of these sailboats, which came to be called the Triton. The price was under $10,000. In time more than 700 Tritons would be built. Overbuilt might be a better word, as no one knew the tolerances of fiberglass in those early days. Many Tritons are still sailing.

If the public was impressed by fiberglass—in particular its ease of care when compared to wood—L. Francis Herreshoff,

---

2 Much of the information on the Pearson cousins comes from an article in the Brown University alumni magazine, entitled "Movers, shakers, builders: Alumni in the Rhode Island boatbuilding tradition."

The Melville Naval Refueling Base, Portsmouth
1985

The Ted Hood Marine Complex
1997

the famous Marblehead yacht designer and youngest son of the legendary designer and boatbuilder Nathanael Herreshoff, wasn't. The influential L. Francis, who lived and worked in Castle Brattahlid at Crocker Park in Marblehead, termed the new fiberglass material "unlovely" or, more descriptively, "frozen snot." It's funny how the latter line stuck, long after the aesthetics of fiberglass boatbuilding ceased to be an issue.

The Pearsons began building fiberglass Tritons in Bristol, Rhode Island. In time, they sold the company to Grumman, which moved production to Portsmouth, Rhode Island. Clint started Bristol Sailboats in 1966. I designed at least six production models for Bristol, of which more than 1,000 copies were produced. Everett stayed on working for Grumman.

After leaving Grumman, Everett built a 58-foot sailboat for Neil Tillotson, a boat-loving businessman. This began a relationship that led to the formation of Tillotson-Pearson in Warren, Rhode Island.

Tillotson was an interesting man. Everett and I would have meetings with him when he was in his mid-80s, and he'd be telling us what we were going to be doing 20 years later. I was in my early 60s, as was Everett, but I'm sure he thought of us as "boys." Tillotson sold a building and property he owned on the waterfront in Boston with the provision that he be allowed to stay there until he died. No one thought he was going to live until he was 102; he only recently passed away. The rest of the Boston waterfront had been redeveloped in grand fashion except this one pier with a falling-down building on it—Tillotson's office.

Pearson—later Tillotson-Pearson and now TPI—manufactured fiberglass yachts for such well-known companies as J-Boats, including the precedent-setting J/24. At one point, they were producing six J/24s a day. They also built the Etchells and yachts for Freedom, Alden, Rampage, Jeanneau, and Sundeer.

Tillotson-Pearson lasted until 1993, when Tillotson, in his 90s, sold out to John Walton, a son of Sam Walton, the founder of Wal-Mart. John Walton and a brother were manufacturing folding trimarans. Despite being worth, presumably, billions—or perhaps because they're worth billions—the sons of John Walton treated the boating business as a business, not a hobby. I can respect that. With Walton in the picture, the company became TPI Inc., with Everett Pearson as president.

But back to the Hood-Everett Pearson proposal for the Portsmouth property. Thirty proposals were submitted; one of them, as I recall it, was a place to unload coal. Town officials picked our plan to start a service yard and to take care of boats. In addition to the cost of the property, we had to promise to spend $7 million within seven years and have 200 people on the payroll. As it turned out, I invested $6.5 million, and Everett put in about $500,000. We each agreed to pay 50 percent of the taxes and any expenses.

Hood Enterprises, Inc., and TPI formed a partnership called Melville Marine Industries (MMI). That partnership bought the property, then the principals split the property with long-term subleases—some land going to me, some to Everett, and some staying with MMI. The land I got I developed into the new boatyard and eventually a boatbuilding facility. The land Everett got already had a building on it, and TPI put Alden Yachts production there (TPI owned Alden Yachts).

Thus began my life as a commuter between Marblehead and Portsmouth. That's not a daunting trip in terms of miles, but getting around or through Boston—take your pick—could make it difficult. I couldn't come down to Rhode Island every day. While the sail loft had been sold to Jack Setton, I was still running a business in Marblehead with about 35 employees. I commuted back and forth on many days.

The most prominent building we inherited was an old boiler factory, built by the Navy, as well as three or four other units of varying worth and decay. I had to pay $65,000 to tear down the boiler factory, and the guy who did the work lost money. The structure was riddled with galvanized reinforcing rods, and the poor man was hammering away for two months. The Navy had built it to last.

I was the general contractor. As an assistant, I hired a young man named Rick Hall, who wanted to learn the construction business, and we subcontracted much of the work. Prices were good back then. We hired a foundation guy, a cement-floor guy, and then a steelworker to come in and erect the buildings. There were challenges, however, because there were so many easements, according to the Navy. There were electrical easements, sewer easements, water easements, and more. You couldn't put things where you wanted to, you had to fit them between easements.

I think we ended up doing it for 60 percent of the lowest bid. Looking back on it, we might not have succeeded if I had to pay 100 cents on the dollar.

The first thing we did was to build a three-story building for offices and shops, overlooking the waterfront. I had them put in an elevator, too, for my old age.

As the first building was going up, we built a retaining wall at the water's edge to our own design. All the outside designers with whom I consulted had expensive ways of doing the retaining wall, but I got approval to do it my way. There was a rough beach, which I had to dredge. Then I went to the low-water mark and put in a five-foot-high L-shaped foundation. We poured it at low tide with all sorts of reinforcing rods sticking out of the top. A foundation wall was poured above it, tied to the reinforcing rods and extending well above the high-water mark. The base of the L faced the land. We backfilled this area with earth and large stones, but not before we further buttressed the seawall with tie-rods anchored to the land. Eighteen years later, it's still standing, as good as new.

Next, we built a 100-slip marina. My dream was to build a

MARBLEHEAD REPORTER

Vol. 21, No. 44   3 sections, 128 Pages   Thursday, August 14, 1986   A publication of North Shore Weeklies, Inc.   35¢

Hood prepares to shove off

Town loses another chunk of harborfront tradition

By KENNY WOOTON

The end of this month will mark the end of an era in Marblehead's centuries-old association with the sea.

In a few weeks, Ted Hood will begin moving his company — Hood Enterprises — to new quarters in Rhode Island. He'll take with him, not only one of the town's largest industries, but a decades-long tradition which has done much to make Marblehead a world-class name in yachting.

Hood said he has grown weary of the town's resistance to his plans for expanding and improving his Little Harbor facility. He says that resistance has made it impossible for him to run a viable operation.

"I've done all I can," he said in an interview recently. "I don't like to be leaving, but I really don't have much choice, other than to retire."

For three decades, Hood and his companies have been a major force in the yachting industry the world over. Operating under the umbrella of Hood Enterprises, Hood Sailmakers, Marblehead Manufacturing, Little Harbor Yacht Sales, Little Harbor Custom Yachts, Hood Yacht Systems and the Little Harbor Design have made a significant contribution to Marblehead's reputation as "The Yachting Capital of America."

Hood no longer owns Hood Sailmakers or Marblehead Manufacturing, but the rest of his companies generate between $15 and $20 million in annual sales and employ about 100 people.

According to Hood, the boatyard operation will begin moving at the end of this month. Ted Moore and Alan Chew, who purchased the property from Hood last year, have said they plan to operate a boatyard of some scale on the site for an inde-

finite period. They have already begun construction on three house lots in the corner of the property farthest away from the water.

Also leaving with the boatyard will be Little Harbor Custom Yachts — the division of the company that fits-out and finishes Hood's Taiwan-built Little Harbor line of luxury yachts.

The Little Harbor Design Group — the company's yacht design division — will go next, Hood said, "in a couple of months."

Hood Yacht Systems, which manufactures spars and rigging, is located in the same building as Hood Sailmakers on Lime Street and will be the last to go, probably in six months, said Hood.

He said in addition to the staff of the design office, as many as six yard workers and about half the 30-person Yacht Systems staff would be moving to Rhode Island with him. Little Harbor Yacht Sales — Hood's used boat brokerage — may go, but Hood is not sure if or when.

Hood said he doesn't want to leave Marblehead. He pointed out that 11 generations of his family have lived within 10 miles of the town.

"It takes a lot to move after all that," he said.

The beginnings

Hood's business relationship with the town began back in 1950 when Hood and his father — operating as Freddie Hood Sailmakers — moved into the Maddie's Sail Loft Building

on State Street and started making sails for the family's International One Design racer and for others in the class.

Two years later, the Hoods purchased four looms from the old Pequot Mills in Salem and began manufacturing their own cloth — then a unique approach to the business.

When the Hoods began making sails, synthetic fabrics such as Orlon and Nylon had begun to replace cotton as the preferred material for sailmaking. But the advent of Dacron in the early '50s revolutionized the industry, and Hood and his father pioneered its use.

Overwhelmed with business and in need of room to expand, the Hoods purchased Little Harbor Boatyard, then just over an acre along the water, next to the Richard Price Boatyard and in front of Goodwin's house-moving company. The site already had a marine railway and the Hoods built a 100-by-43-foot building to house the cloth-making operation and sail loft.

The company experienced tremendous growth between 1954 and 1960. More looms were added, and the original sail loft building was extended out to the seawall at Little Harbor. Hood's brother moved his molded foam company onto the site as well.

At one point, Hood wanted to move the whole sail and cloth-making operation to land he owned on Lime Street but decided against moving the sail loft there when the town took part of the land by eminent domain to build Powderhouse Court.

The company took another giant step in 1957 and 1958. Hood served on the crew and made all the sails for America's Cup defender Vim. Although Columbia ended up beating Vim out for the honor of defend-

Continued on Page 22

Hood shoves off at month's end

Continued from Page 1

ing the Cup, she used some of Vim's sails, establishing the company as a winner in the eyes of the sailing community.

Ted Hood dominated America's Cup competition for almost two decades, designing defenders Nefertiti and Independence, skippering Courageous to a successful defense in 1974 and placing sails on defenders through 1977.

Little Harbor Yacht design got its start in 1959 when Hood designed his first offshore racer. Hood Yacht Systems started with the same project when Hood designed and built the spars for the boat.

Expanding abroad

The company experienced worldwide expansion during the 1960s. Affiliated sail lofts were opened in Australia, England, Japan, France, Sweden, Germany and South America, in addition to sites all over North America. It also bought up the Price boatyard and the Goodwin property, increasing the Little Harbor yard to over 3½ acres.

Cloth for most of the lofts was supplied by a Hood-owned mill in southern Ireland and by Marblehead Manufacturing (the outgrowth of Hood's local cloth-weaving operation).

In 1970, Hood sold part of the business — the sailmaking operation, the yacht systems division and

Marblehead Manufacturing — to the CML Group, who planned to include it as part of a leisure-oriented enterprise. Hood kept the design office, the boatyard and the real estate on Lime Street.

But five years later he bought it back. "I was happy to buy it back, and they were happy to sell," said Hood.

Changes begin

Four years ago, Frenchman Jack Setton came into Little Harbor for a spars and rigging for his new boat and expressed an interest in investing in some marine-related businesses. Hood said he wasn't considering selling any of his operation at the time, but when a Setton employee called back several weeks later inquiring about a possible purchase of part of the sailmaking business, Hood thought it over and changed his mind.

He sold Setton 60 percent of Hood Sailmakers. Hood kept 30 percent and New Zealander Chris Bouzaid, a sailmaker who had been with him for a number of years, maintained a 10-percent interest.

Setton moved the sailmaking operation to its present location on Lime Street in 1983, bought out Bouzaid in 1984 and closed down Marblehead Manufacturing's Lime Street and New Bedford mills. Six months ago, Hood bought back the yacht systems operation and sold

his remaining interest in Hood Sailmakers to Setton.

Hood told the Reporter last October shortly after he sold the boatyard that resistance from voters and town officials to his ideas for expansion and improvements had made it impossible to make the boatyard a viable operation.

"To keep it viable," he said, "you would need deep water, a breakwater, a dock, a bigger travel-lift (and) bigger buildings." He added, "Even if I were willing to spend the money, I probably couldn't get the permits."

He said this week that without the improvements he couldn't lure the bigger boats. And without the bigger boats, he couldn't keep the yard profitable.

"I'm 59," he said. "I could probably retire. I've been frustrated with this place. I've always wanted to run a really top-notch place, but I haven't been able to do it here for a lot of different reasons.

"I should have stopped 15 years ago and moved someplace else," Hood said as the era closed.

He bought the property in Rhode Island four years ago and plans to eventually develop it into an 80-acre marine industrial park. The site is on Narragansett Bay about six miles north of Newport. It has about a mile of waterfront. Hood has devoted about 10 acres to his boatyard operation.

Marblehead's reaction to Ted's move
1985

huge 1,500-slip marina, to the south, but that dream would have to wait.

Already I was thinking about moving lock, stock, and barrel to Portsmouth. For sailing, the winds there are better than at Marblehead. More important, there was room to grow. We couldn't expand anymore in Marblehead; we were just crowded out. I wasn't ready to retire; I'm still not. My children, all of whom worked or had worked in the business to varying degrees, came to support me in this relocation. Talk about winds of change. I was then 60 years old and had lived on the North Shore my entire life, as had several generations of Hoods before me.

But once the first three-story building was up, I severed my ties to Marblehead. Sue and I found a condominium in Portsmouth. Later we completely rebuilt a house facing the Sakonnet River on the eastern edge of Aquidneck Island. The new yard was on the western edge, facing Narragansett Bay. I would watch the sun rise at home over the Sakonnet River, and often I would see it set at the boatyard on Narragansett Bay. Life was busy and good, and I was building something truly substantial. It was a wonderful time.

By this point, I had found a local developer to buy the Little Harbor property in Marblehead. He divided it into lots and built houses, mostly. The sail-loft building is still standing—it's all offices now—and a small boatyard remains. I took all that money from the sale of the Marblehead property and invested it in Portsmouth.

Other buildings followed in Portsmouth: a 120-by-200-foot storage shed, directly behind the office building; a high-tech paint shop, where boats up to 150 feet can be accommodated, and sanding is separated from a climate- and dust-controlled paint facility; a storage shed; and another building of 60,000 square feet with offices and shops. Today, it houses North Sails, US Sailing, Cay Electronics, S&S Fabrics, Newport R&D, and other marine firms, including my current business, Portsmouth Marine.

We had seven years to spend $7 million and employ 200 people in Portsmouth. Within five years we had met those goals. Besides building boats, Everett Pearson was also building windmill blades for power generation. He had plans to build them here, along with the Waltons' trimarans. He ended up reclaiming one of the Navy buildings for Alden to the north of the first office building. A second new building for Alden followed. Everett eventually sold out to the Waltons. In 2003, I bought the Walton brothers 50 percent interest in MMI, the partnership between Hood Enterprises and TPI that owned the remaining undeveloped land.

Left on the property when I moved in were a tired freighter and a 320-foot LST (Landing Ship Tank) at the end of the dock. This gave me an idea. A large ship, I reasoned, would help to protect the marina from waves from the southwest. But I was not going to use that tired freighter or LST. I

The Little Harbor Yard in Taiwan
1990

went to Norfolk, Virginia, to look into buying a mothballed Navy ship. You could get them for practically nothing, as long as you promised not to put them into competition with regular shipping. I looked at a 450-foot LST, used to carry troops and supplies. The entire inside could accommodate tanks, and it had a great ventilation system. I thought this could be a great breakwater, as well as a workshop. You could store 30 50-foot boats in there. However, people said I was nuts to buy something like that—how often I have heard that in my life. I should have bought it and shooed the old freighter and the smaller LST away.

I got to know the man who owned the freighter and LST. He had plans to have the LST towed to Haiti and Guyana. For the trip to Haiti, the 320-foot LST was loaded with cars, televisions, and furniture collected from Haitians living in the Rhode Island-Massachusetts area to deliver to their relatives back home. The LST was very late in its departure. The local Haitians were getting upset about the failure to depart and were expressing their anger in my boatyard. I couldn't blame them, but it was scary.

Eventually, the LST left Rhode Island. In Haiti, it attracted a lot of attention. At some point a man was killed when a crane fell on top of him. Others rushed over. This precipitated a near riot. The owner had to call the police and eventually the U.S. Army to protect him and his cargo. Then he went on to Guyana, where he had to hire an armed guard. He asked the guard what he would do if the cargo was threatened or the ship boarded. "Shoot 'em!" the guard said. "Not on my boat!" he replied.

In Guyana, he picked up greenheart pilings for me to build the 1,500-slip marina. That's a lot of pilings. Eleven years later, they're still waiting on the dock here for the new marina. After the LST returned to my yard in Rhode Island, it and the freighter were only to be here for two months, but the owner abandoned them. The freighter sank, and both of the ships eventually had to be chopped up and trucked away by a salvage company.

Since 1979, we had been building about 12 boats a year in Taiwan. Then things started slowing down in this regard, until we were only doing six boats a year. Around 1992 I said to Bruce Livingston, my manager there, that we needed to lay people off, but he pointed out that Taiwanese law required huge severance payments. Thus, we were losing money every day we were operating there.

At some point, we ran into people from American Marine, builders of the Grand Banks yachts in Singapore, and they were facing the same problems: slowing demand and a large workforce. We decided to try to work together. They came to our yard, we went to theirs, and we started building our Little Harbor yachts at their facility. So we shut down our Taiwanese yard and ended up paying all the severance pay anyways.

American Marine estimated they could do the job in 10

percent more hours than it took us in our very efficient yard in Taiwan. So we sent American Marine the tooling for the Little Harbor 42, 46, 52, 54, 60, and 70. They built Dodge Morgan's second boat, the Little Harbor 52 *Wings of Time*, and four others, including a 60- and a 54-footer.

As it turned out, they needed twice as many hours. After five boats, it was apparent this wasn't going to work. But now we had a problem in that we had sold boats at American Marine's prices, and American Marine had quit. At first we considered shipping the tooling to New Zealand, but we could not come to agreement with the yard there.

At that point we had a Little Harbor 60 that was partially built in Singapore and a Little Harbor 70 that was not started. We shipped back the unfinished 60 and the tooling for the 70. We finished the 60 and built the 70 in Portsmouth at a big loss, since they had been priced to build in Singapore.

These boats were built by our boatbuilding operation in Portsmouth, Ted Hood Yacht Builders—the crew that had built the Black Watch powerboats, and were now building our Little Harbor powerboats (see chapter 13). They were great boatbuilders, mostly Portuguese, and were quite efficient. But the labor cost per hour was almost three times the cost in Singapore, and these were very labor-intensive boats to build.

Bruce Livingston, the American who had been running our yard in Taiwan and was later our representative in Singapore at American Marine, came here to Portsmouth to run boatbuilding. Livingston departed after a year because his Taiwanese wife didn't enjoy the culture. American Marine knew him and hired him back to run their new factory in Malaysia. Ted Grant, the longtime production manager at Ted Hood Boatbuilders, took over from Bruce and did a great job.

The losses from closing Taiwan in 1993, followed by the losses in moving back to the U.S. in 1995, put us into a huge cash crunch that started in the fall of 1995 and didn't end until the spring of 1997, when we were helped out with a loan from one of our customers. With that loan we were able to pay off our bank debt and have a bit extra. Plus, in 1997 we started to make good money again, which carried through until we sold the business in March 1999. The years 1998 and 1999 were the most profitable ever, with my son Rick as president. He had assumed that title in 1991.

A number of companies accompanied me from Marblehead, or would be formed in Portsmouth in due time. Ted Hood Design Group designed sail- and powerboats up to 150 feet for Little Harbor Custom Yachts and other leading boat manufacturers worldwide. Little Harbor Custom Yachts, marketed and built custom sail and power yachts. Ted Hood Yacht Builders built semi-production and custom one-off yachts in both power and sail from 26 feet through 85 feet. This came to include Black Watch Sportfishing boats and our Whisperjet line of water-jet-powered yachts. Little Harbor

Little Harbors under construction in Portsmouth
1997

The Ted Hood 51 was the last of the sailboats built by Little Harbor
1995

Marine would become New England's largest and best-
equipped marine-service yard. In its 10 acres would be 65
well-protected, fully equipped deepwater slips; two acres of
fire-protected (sprinklers) indoor and insulated storage; large
workshops; five acres of outdoor storage; 35-, 40- and 160-
ton Travelifts; and a highly skilled labor force of carpenters,
riggers, machinists, mechanics, electricians, fiberglass special-
ists, and painters. Little Harbor Yacht Sales was an on-site
yacht-brokerage service for high-end previously owned sail-
and powerboats. Hood Yacht Systems, which we had bought
back from Hood Sails (Jack Setton) in 1986, sold the Stoway
Mast, Gemini and SeaFurl systems, etc. My oldest son, Rick,
was running that division in 1987, the year we moved it from
Marblehead to Portsmouth, until he became president of
Hood Enterprises. We sold Hood Yacht Systems in 1992 to
Pompanette, Inc.

I had realized my dream of building a one-stop "marine-
mart." However, 12 years after this facility was established in
Portsmouth, the name on the door read "Hinckley," rather
than "Hood." One of our strongest competitors, Hinckley
Yachts of Southwest Harbor, Maine, made an offer to purchase our company. We discussed the idea of selling the company at a family meeting at my home in Portsmouth. I was
then 72 years old and had, in truth, risked everything in the
move from Marblehead to Portsmouth in 1986. No one in the
family had a strong desire to continue running the operation.

After a couple of lucrative years, we thought the business was at its peak. We all remembered the cash-crunch years of the recent past and did not want to live through that again—so we accepted Hinckley's offer in 1999.

Selling the company might have been a good business decision, but it was probably a bad move for me, personally. I'm still bursting with ideas, and it is much harder now to develop them, working mostly alone without an organization behind me.

I'm on to the next thing. Our MMI, which was not sold to Hinckley, owns about 44 acres to the south of the Hinckley yard, on Weaver's Cove in Portsmouth. This includes one mile of ocean frontage on Narragansett Bay. Here I have plans to build a 1,495-slip marina—I already have the pilings!—as well as 100 to 175 units of luxury housing, an inn/yacht club with a restaurant and function facilities, a commercial-support area for marine-related businesses, and an area for seasonal shows, auctions, and open-air events.

Standing pat holds little interest…

The purchase of Black Watch marked the beginning of Ted's powerboat business
1987

Chapter 13

Powerboats

"I should admit that I have an affinity for Little Harbor yachts. As a former commercial fisher-man—weary veteran of dozens of crab and halibut seasons in the North Pacific—I recognize in their classic Downeast lines echoes of a lobsterboat's ready attitude and able spirit. Combine that with speed, agility and expertly wrought details, and you've got the embodi-ment of a 'retired' fisherman's fantasy: A purposeful craft whose business is pure pleasure."

— Tim Clark, Power & Motoryacht

The custom- and semi-custom sailboat businesses were peaking by the mid 1980s. By the early 1990s, Hinckley, which had started in 1928 building powerboats, was once again building more of them than the sailboats that made it famous, as was Alden, my neighbor in Portsmouth. My Little Harbor line of sailboats wasn't immune either.

For me, the boating business has been a series of small companies with similar interests. The danger, of course, is that a sneeze in one division often means a bad cold some-where else. We felt the chill not only on the boatbuilding front, but also at Hood Yacht Systems, where we had been able to count on selling 50 of our not-inexpensive Stoway masts each year.

I'm a builder, as I've said. It makes little difference to me if I'm building houses, sailboats, or powerboats, as long as I'm building something. They're all of interest to me. Plus, I have no prejudice against powerboats. Sailboat and powerboat design, you shall see, converged in the 1950s. I saw it was time for me to head in a different direction–powerboats.

Inspiration came from other boatbuilders, to be sure, as well as from my wife, Sue. Around this time, Sue wanted a small powerboat to explore the Sakonnet River, which our house overlooks. That led me to Black Watch, across the bridge in Bristol, Rhode Island, which was selling a Ray Hunt deep-vee design. This shape, 46 years old as I write this, is still the gold standard for planing powerboats running in rough water. As mentioned in an earlier chapter, not only did I buy the boat, I bought the company. It only cost me about $350,000 to purchase the name, tooling, and designs of the struggling powerboat company.

Readers will recall my early association with C. Raymond Hunt, champion sailor and designer of the International 110, 210, Concordia Yawl, and the ubiquitous tri-hulled Boston Whaler—specifically, the 13 and 16 which put that company on the map.

Hunt was an interesting guy, if different. In Marblehead, he cast a long shadow. He was hard to pigeonhole and always experimenting in new directions, like with the 110- and 210- Class sailboats, which were designed to be built using the new marine-quality plywood. Hunt was unschooled in yacht design, but he was a gifted sailor. In some ways I've followed in his independent footsteps; in other ways I've steered far away from the path he took.

In 1949, Hunt designed *Sea Blitz*, a 42-foot powerboat built by Quincy Adams Yacht Yard for my friend Bradley Noyes. Powered by a 1,500-horsepower Packard engine taken from a PT boat, she could attain speeds of 60 knots and cruise at 40. At such speeds, you had to bend your knees to absorb the shock when the boat hit a wave. *Sea Blitz* was interesting to me as a most creative solution to the problem of speed at sea.

Brad, Ned Stephenson, Nick Winslow, and I took *Sea Blitz* from Marblehead to New London, Connecticut, for the Harvard-Yale crew race, officially called "the Harvard-Yale Regatta." We were speeding into the Thames River, which did not please the Coast Guard. When a Coast Guard patrol boat gave chase, Ned, Nick, and I, who were fresh out of the Navy, changed into our old Navy uniforms—Brad was wearing a gray-flannel suit with a neck tie, and we stood at attention at the rail. The Coast Guard didn't know what to make of us. After looking us over they dismissed us with a friendly wave. It was fun, and the spectators seemed to enjoy the boat. It was something new and distinctive.

Sea Blitz was a transitional design between the "Huntform" and the deep-vee. Before Hunt had his say, powerboats tended to have sharp bows and flat bottoms. That was a good, easy-planing shape in flat water, but it pounded in rough water and was hard to steer downwind, where it was subject to broaching.

The so-called Huntform was more bell-shaped than veed. Think of an upside-down bell. Hunt employed it on a power-boat he designed for himself to fish for lobsters during World War II. The Huntform could go farther offshore and run faster than conventional lobsterboats.

A 20-foot model of the Huntform was tested by the Navy's Bureau of Ships, at the request of Charles Francis Adams, the former secretary of the Navy (1929 to 1933). The

Ted, Brad Noyes, and Ray Hunt in Bermuda
1950

model reached speeds of a destroyer, but since it was beamier and featured a bottom with a chine, it was more stable. If impressed, the Navy never built it because, as I understand it, they feared a loss of time to change production techniques to accommodate the chine. That was said to be a disappointment for the designer, who invested personal money, of which there was never an abundance, in the project.

Perhaps because he was a sailboat designer with no pre-conceptions of powerboat form, Hunt was a revolutionary who changed planing-powerboat design forever by introducing a deep-vee underbody, reminiscent of a displacement sailboat. This is where sailboat and powerboat design converged.

The deep-vee shape proved very effective in rough seas. The archetypal Hunt deep-vee ended up showing 24 degrees of deadrise, or vee, which was carried all the way aft. By way of comparison, the deadrise on the Noyes *Sea Blitz* was about 14 degrees.

While a deep-vee runs well in waves, the tradeoff is that it requires more power for the boat to get up on a plane. To help solve this problem, Hunt used "lift strakes" to help facilitate early planing. Lifting strakes, too, became a standard feature of planing powerboat design.

Before the 1958 America's Cup competition, my fellow crew-member on *Vim*, "Spinnaker Dick" Bertram, had been looking for a powerboat to take guests out to watch the racing. I had one I was interested in selling. The governor of New Hampshire had a 42-foot lapstrake-plywood Chris-Craft with twin engines. It had run into some rocks and sunk. I bought it cheap from the insurance company and fixed it up–this was practically a family tradition. Bertram bought it from me and called it *Moppie*, which was the nickname of his wife, Pauline.

The Chris-Craft proved sufficient until a Hunt-designed deep-vee prototype made a grand entrance during the 1958 America's Cup trials. So impressed was Bertram that he ordered a similar powerboat from Hunt the next day. This 31-footer became another *Moppie*, and this *Moppie* became the basis of Bertram Yachts.

In those days, sailboat designers like Hunt drew powerboats; sailors like Dick Bertram started very successful powerboat companies. No one thought it odd.

The proof of the high-deadrise deep-vee concept came in the Miami-Nassau powerboat race of 1960, which started in nasty weather. *Moppie* won this 160-mile race in record time, while one-third of the fleet never finished. Another Hunt-designed deep-vee hull, a 24-footer skippered by Jim Wynne, finished second.

Hunt enjoyed taking potential customers for rides on his deep-vee powerboats. When running downwind in heavy seas, the orientation where a powerboat is most likely to broach, he would pretend his shoelaces needed retying and would bend down, leaving the helm to fend for itself. It used to scare his

Sea Blitz
1949

Ray Hunt's deep-vee _Hunter_—note the lift strakes on the hull
1957

clients inordinately, but he could offer no better proof of the safety of the deep-vee hull.

This was about all the marketing and promotion Hunt, a most private man, could stand. I, on the other hand, saw marketing, promotion, and advertising as an "evil," perhaps, but a very necessary one for survival in this business. And if this stuff didn't come naturally to me—and it didn't—I certainly surrounded myself with people for whom it did, like Dick Carter.

The deep-vee concept was much copied and, indeed, still is. Hunt tried to patent the deep-vee hull. It was not to be, however. In 1958, _Skipper_ magazine columnist V. B. Crockett visited Hunt in his office in Padanaram and idly inquired what was new. Hunt made the mistake of telling him. Crockett's column on the deep-vee concept appeared in the July 1958 issue of the magazine. Hunt didn't know it, but the patent clock started ticking at that point.

More than a year later, Hunt applied for a patent, which he received, and busied himself suing infringers with some success. The article, however, invalidated the patent, as the rules specified applications for patents must be made within a year of the invention being used or written about.

I've had a number of patents in this business—the cross-cut-spinnaker, double-swivels on headsail-furling devices, and the Stoway mast—but the Hunt experience is one reason why I've never invested too much energy in defending them. The market is too small and litigation too expensive to make it worthwhile. Honorable companies respected patents and made payments. As for the rest, best forgotten. As mentioned earlier, Harken paid royalties for years on our double-swivel patent for headsail roller-reefing systems. Olaf and Peter Harken are good guys.

So, in 1987 I found myself in the powerboat business, selling Black Watch powerboats with a Hunt deep-vee hull designed by C. Raymond Hunt Associates in Boston. I felt on solid ground, if that's the proper word for it. The boats seemed true to my roots. Obviously, you wouldn't go to Hood or Little Harbor for the latest in Italianate styling. They were beautiful boats, I like to think, but their beauty was more than skin deep. As Louisa Rudeen wrote about our powerboats in _Motorboating & Sailing_, "It's no small feat to be classic and cutting-edge at the same time." That's the note we tried to hit.

Black Watch had a nice 30-footer. We started building it in Portsmouth. Marketing and promotion were important, particularly in those early days. Like the other sailboat manufacturers who started building powerboats, we had credibility issues. Unlike the 1950s, when Ray Hunt designed the best powerboats or Dick Bertram started Bertram yachts, now there is an "east is east and west is west" prejudice in this business when it comes to powerboats and sailboats.

Next, we developed a 26-footer. That was a remarkably seaworthy boat for its size. We sold dozens of them, both with outboard motors and with inboard engines. With twin

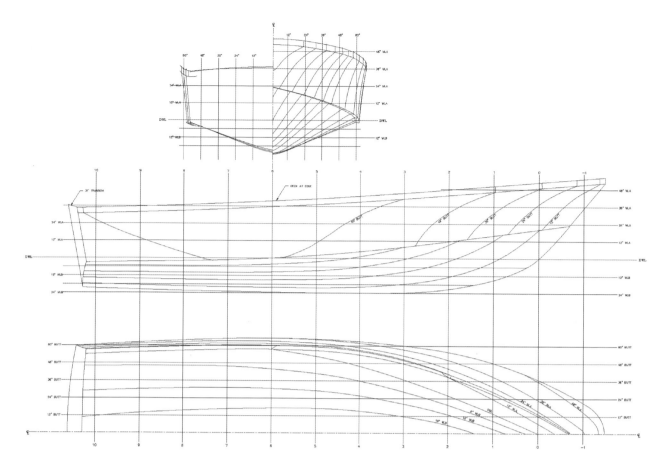

The Black Watch 30, a typical Ray Hunt deep-vee hull
1987

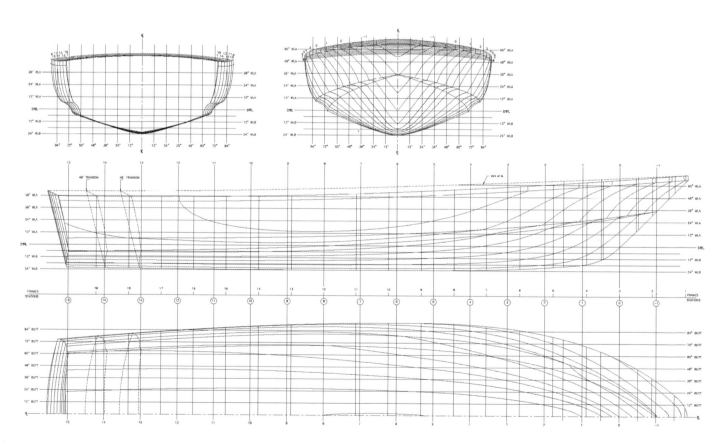

The Little Harbor 52 Whisperjet hull design
1997

150s, the 26 could do 60 knots, although I certainly wouldn't recommend that, as it seemed dangerous. I took one to Block Island for Race Week. I used it as a "mother ship"–a small mother ship. It had two good bunks and was very comfortable. I sold one to my friend Brad Noyes; he'd cruise on it for weeks at a time with his wife.

In time we produced eight versions in the Black Watch line, either in sportsfisherman or flybridge configurations, in sizes of 26, 30, 33, 36, and 40 feet. We did it by stretching the mold. We took the 30-foot mold and stretched it to a 33 and a 36, and, eventually, to a 40.

It isn't that difficult to make one mold longer. We had a transom for a 30-footer, another for the 36-footer, and so on, that would be dropped into place. The trick was in making the one mold proportionally wider for the larger hulls. To do this, we added two-tapered molds to the bottom of the structure where it was split to pull the boat apart. The pieces had flanges that were bolted together. Being knife-shaped with the point facing forward, they added nothing at the bow, maybe 3 inches amidships, and up to 18 inches of beam aft if we were building a 40-footer. I don't know of anyone else who did it that way. Using one expensive mold to build five different hulls was a Yankee-type approach to boatbuilding.

To build a light and strong hull for our Black Watch line, we used core construction–the boatbuilding version of the I-beam–two layers of fiberglass separated by a light core material, like Balsa, Airex foam, or a honeycomb. Like the I-beam, it is very strong for its weight.

We had built the first-ever Airex-cored fiberglass sailboat in the early 1960s. Frans Maas, in Holland, who was building our boats in steel then, said, "You know that North Sea Patrol boats are being built out of this material?" I said, "If it's good enough for them, it should be good enough for us." So we built a 36-footer for an owner. That boat is still sailing in Nova Scotia.

In the Black Watch 40, the biggest boat in that line, we used knitted bidirectional E-glass, Airex, and baltek coring, and Kevlar, the material used in tires and bulletproof vests. Production-built boat hulls are built inside a female mold. Our first layer was bidirectional knitted E-glass. Knitted is better than woven, since there is no crimp. (Crimp is akin to that type of telephone cord that grows longer when you pull on it, which is not good for sails or for hulls.) Then we'd take the foam and give it a light layer of resin. Next, a thin layer of putty was added to the hull, and the core was attached. These pieces of foam were vacuum-bagged, which held the foam to the inside of the hull until the material cured. The final layer was Kevlar, which is good under tension but not compression. That's why it was the inside layer. The E-glass is better under compression. Imagine running your boat into a piling. The knitted E-glass on the outside resists the compression; the Kevlar takes the tension on the inside to resist the bulging.

Little Harbor 40 Whisperjet, sportsfisherman version
1997

1987 – 1999
The Power Yachts

By the late 1980s the sailboat business had quieted considerably. Other builders, such as Hinckley, had shifted from sail to power. Ted moved into the powerboat arena as well, first with his purchase of Black Watch in 1987, and then with the expansion of his Little Harbor line into power, culminating in the Whisperjet line of water-jet-driven power yachts.

Black Watch 26
1988

Black Watch 40
1989

Black Watch 30
1987

Little Harbor 34 Whisperjet
1996

Little Harbor 38 Whisperjet
1996

Little Harbor 40 Whisperjet
1997

Little Harbor 44 Whisperjet
1997

Little Harbor 52 Whisperjet
1998

Little Harbor 55 Whisperjet
1998

**Patrol boat for the Taiwanese Coast Guard,
underway (top) and undergoing rollover test**
1992

Black Watches were nice boats: well-made, well-designed, pretty, and practical. We worked hard on such amenities as fit, finish, and sound-deadening. You shouldn't have to shout above the engines. The boats were full of thoughtful touches, gleaned from a lifetime at sea and listening to others. For example, our Black Watch 40 sportsfisherman had an airy fish tower, with easy access and a clear 360-degree view. To navigate a low bridge, however, it was designed to fold down. The Bimini top would swing forward while the outriggers dropped aft horizontally. The walkarounds on these yachts were kept wide, for reasons of safety, and the rails were high and secure. We worked hard to find the best nonskid surfaces.

However, we didn't make any money from Black Watch. The guy I had running it gave everyone a discount with the idea of promoting the line. "Gave away the farm," you might say. And I did.

The sportsfishing market fell hard in the late 1980s. What's a builder to do? For me it meant building something different. I was already doing that. Contacts I had made in Taiwan led to a contract with the government there to construct eight 40-foot "Interdictor" patrol boats. We built them in Rhode Island, not in Taiwan. They had to be extremely fast, but also extremely safe.

Safety first: In this case, that meant they had to be self-righting in the event of capsize. We accomplished this through a trunk cabin that was higher than it might ordinarily be. This was to raise the center of buoyancy, ensuring the boats would be self-righting in the event of capsize. Then, the engines had to start after rolling over. To accomplish this, we added a position-sensitive mercury solenoid to shut off the engine in a rollover.

We specified Arneson surface-drives for the patrol boats. In this application, only a skeg and the bottom of the propeller, which does the work, are in the water. The top half of the prop is out of the water, increasing prop efficiency 15 to 20 percent when compared to a conventional submerged propeller. The result is much better fuel economy, better acceleration, and higher top-end speed.

The shaft can be adjusted vertically to trim the hull to the load and to the seas. It also can reduce draft for shallow running. For steering, the entire drive moves horizontally. This is a better system of steering than having to bounce the flow off a rudder in the conventional manner. Also with the Arneson drive, the propeller is farther aft, which increases leverage, further abetting steering.

Also during this time, we won two contracts to build boats for the U.S. Navy. One contract was to build "whaleboats" (launches). The other was for 60-foot target drones–remote-controlled boats that would pull a target used for gunnery target practice. The commercial and military work we took on at that time helped greatly in keeping us alive until we were able to recover in the pleasure-boat business.

The Arneson drive used on the Taiwan patrol boats was very interesting to me and led directly to our building power-boats with jet drives that were shaftless and rudderless. I had long wanted to do that, but, again, people told me I was nuts. Then Hinckley, a good competitor of ours at the time, and a company with strong roots in sailing that was beginning to take an interest in powerboats, did it with their "Picnic Boat."[1] I called our offerings "Whisperjets," and they proved quite popular. Jet propulsion was in use at the time on mega-yachts but not, generally, on powerboats in smaller sizes.

Jets have few moving parts. They are safer, as they eliminate the need for spinning propellers beneath the hull. Without propellers, they are unaffected by running over lobster pot buoys, anchor lines, and other such hazards. Steering is accomplished by aiming the nozzle, which allows for very shallow running, even at cruising speed, making gunk holing such an appropriate activity. For example, our Little Harbor Whisperjet 55 drew a thin two feet, 6 inches; our 38, one foot, 10 inches. Both could operate at cruising speed in very shallow water.

It is more expensive than propeller power, but jet power offers superior maneuverability, making it relatively easy work to slip-slide into a tight berth. Jet power also offers less noise. It was no accident that we called our jet boats "Whisperjets," even trademarking the name. Jet power is also more efficient in some ways, not the least of reasons being the clean running surface below the water.

There were problems to solve, however, before offering them to the public. Foremost was the type of jet. The first jet boat we built was a 26, with a single jet. We went to the jet-engine people and asked what they would recommend we put in. They suggested a Kodiak, which is sort of a copy of a Hamilton. "Just as good," we were told. But we couldn't get the performance we desired, so we had to start over.

Then we tried a jet from North American Marine Jet, developed, I believe, by Jacuzzi. The Navy went to them for jet engines for boats used in Vietnam. That didn't work well for us, either. Finally, we ended up using a Hamilton; it wasn't because they were any better, but we used a larger size than was recommended by the manufacturer. Because bigger jets cost more, everyone was going to smaller ones. It was better, we learned, to have oversized jets. To learn that important lesson cost me $500,000 over two years.

The typical configuration ended up with twin diesels that turn drive shafts powering the water jets. The drive shafts do not spin in neutral. Once in gear, water is sucked into the jets

60-foot U.S. Navy target drones
1993

[1] Actually, Hinckley began building wooden workboats in Maine in 1928 for the fishing industry. For World War II, it built more than 500 picket boats, towboats, and yawls for U.S. forces. In the 1950s, Hinckley started building wooden sailboats and then, in the mid-1950s, fiberglass sailboats. In 1960, Hinckley launched its first Bermuda 40 yacht, which proved extremely popular and enduring. In 1994, Hinckley came "full circle" by introducing its Picnic Boat with a water-jet propulsion system. I sold my companies to Hinckley in 1999.

Little Harbor 38-foot Whisperjet
1996

from intake grids on the bottom. Multi-vaned impellers, which work on the same principle as the fan in a jet engine, compress the water and force it from the nozzle at high speed to drive the boat. Steering is accomplished by turning the jet nozzles with a steering wheel. For reverse, baffles called "buckets" drop a little or a lot to redirect the thrust forward, and the boat goes backwards.

And do they ever work as brakes. Our Whisperjets could stop faster than a car by simply dropping the buckets. Like Ray Hunt before me, who would idly demonstrate the surprising ability of his boats, I enjoyed showing potential customers how our Whisperjets could stop on a dime—but not before I warned them with a "Hold on!" You have to be careful when you do that.

Similarly, I would direct customers to aim for a lobster pot buoy. Reluctantly they would, as it is not natural to steer for an obstruction. The buoy would pop out on the other side, obviously not wrapped around the prop, rudder, or shaft because there weren't any. The buoy was undamaged.

Robert C. Wright, the president of NBC, was interested in buying one of our Whisperjets. He had an outboard that he used in the shallow waters of Nantucket Sound, and he kept running aground. When testing our Whisperjet, he was running through a very shallow area and sucked up a big piece of kelp. All of a sudden the boat slowed to half speed. Fortunately, you could back-flush it, and off we went. And fortunately he bought the boat, a 38-foot Whisperjet, so he could get to his shallow-water dock.

Side-slipping into a dock is accomplished by putting one of the buckets in reverse. Then you balance the other one with a gradual forward adjustment. With occasional help from the steering wheel, the boat slips sideways neatly into a space. Later on we incorporated the "JetStick"—developed by Hinckley—a joystick that operates the buckets, steering, and bow-thruster, which made this maneuvering even easier.

If that sounds difficult, it wasn't; only different. Unlimited training came with the purchase of these boats. It was actually harder for an experienced person to learn than for an inexperienced one.

Our Whisperjets featured a novel dual-chine configuration. They were narrower underwater, to reduce drag. This means that less power was required to maintain planing speeds, resulting in greater fuel economy—around 5 percent better. Then there was an extension just above the waterline, allowing the more generous accommodations of a beamier vessel and providing stability during turns.

The chines were further shaped to reduce the annoying noise of waves slapping against the hull. Aboard our prototype boat at anchor in Nantucket Harbor, I heard this all-too-common and unpleasant slap, slap, slap of the water against the hull. I got into my bathing suit to investigate. Where the water hit the chine, just above the waterline and where the

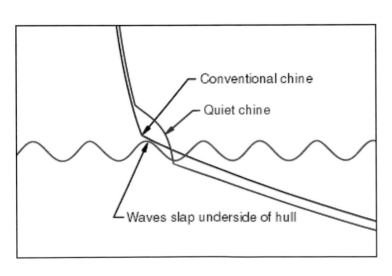

"Quiet Chine" design
1996

lifting strakes are, it was making this awful noise. So I changed that area, angling it to about 30 degrees, which eliminated the slapping. We termed the new design "Quiet Chines."

But the sections were not shaped to reduce bearing surface, and the shape helped in a fast, sharp turn. The chine design made it feel like the boat was running "on a rail."

In powerboats, noise and vibration are the enemies. The jet-propulsion system keeps noise and engine vibration well aft, providing a relatively quiet and comfortable ride above and below deck. Noise and vibration were further reduced by a buffer material made of rubber, mounted on all hard surfaces. This includes the engines as well as the fuel filters and pumps. Typically, we added Nidacore sound-proofing to the sole above the engine room to lessen noise further.

We worked hard on engine and water-jet access. A hydraulic system would open the engine compartment fully at the touch of a button. The jet drives were similarly accessible through a large hatch aft.

Like the Black Watch, the boats were made of high-tech materials. We utilized, for example, non-woven glass laid in a vinylester resin. For core materials, we employed Corecell A550 cores for the hull and the deck. The structure, complete with a laminate of Kevlar, was vacuum-bagged. The hull was further reinforced with composite stringers and fiberglass-laminated marine plywood bulkheads.

We sold about 50 Whisperjets in these lengths: 30, 33, 36, 38, 40, 42, 46, 52, and 55, all of which we built in Portsmouth. Then we made a new mold for a 44, which we built in Taiwan. It was a million-dollar yacht. We built about 10 of them there and made a tidy profit of about $300,000 each, and still provided good value to our customers.

So things had changed. In 1959, I had designed and built my first *Robin*, a sailboat. By 1999, we were building nothing but powerboats.

Ted Hood
2003

Epilogue

Through Hand And Eye

I am very fortunate to have been able to do work that I love and be financially successful at it. Each venture I undertook I pursued primarily because it interested me, not because I thought I would make money doing it. In fact, many times I have done things that appeared risky–and "crazy" to some–and yet somehow I have made it this far. Some paths were more successful than others–in fact some were failures. But I did not dwell on failures–I just moved on to the next thing that grabbed my interest.

As I write this I am 78 years old and still "crazy" I guess. We sold our business six years ago, but I realized that for me that was a mistake. I like to build things. It's not good enough for me to just have ideas and not see them built. My eyes see these ideas, but my hands crave to build them.

To build things I needed an organization, and so I created my current company, Portsmouth Marine, to help me build my ideas.

In the last four years I have been studying displacement catamaran hulls. The shape has become popular for big ferry boats and even for Navy vessels. I believe it has a future in yachts. Advantages are speed, economy, and load-carrying ability of displacement types. With a displacement hull, rather than the more common planing hull, you get a lot of room inside. However, since all the accommodations are above the waterline, the waterline remains very narrow, contributing to fuel economy. But six inches above the waterline, the beam widens quickly, which allows abundant accommodations. So a displacement catamaran hull offers the best of both worlds.

My first catamaran design, a 52 footer, I had built in Poland in 2003. Then I moved to a yard in Turkey and catamaran number two, a revision of the first design, was launched this summer.

I am also working on a new type of sailing yacht that will be very fast under sail and power. Many people, like me, would like to keep sailing later in life, but want to be able to get out of the elements and keep to a schedule, even if there is no wind, or too much wind. A well-designed motorsailer is

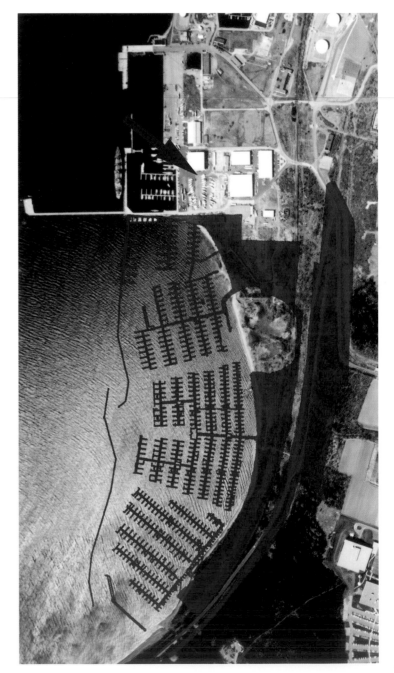

188

really the answer, but there are none that satisfy the need to both sail well and power well. I have designed such a boat in 48- and 55-foot versions, and I think people are going to appreciate the no-compromise benefit. Either way, I will know soon because I am currently building the first 55-footer in Istanbul and will be performing sea trials in March 2006. It is amazing how much design time I have in this boat! The more the better!

After I get the 49- and 55-foot fast motorsailers going, I am hoping to find a client interested in my long-range expedition trawler yacht. I see an opportunity for a good offshore yacht—with fuel economy at 9- to 10-knot speed—that makes sense for the cruising couple, with or without a crew. I have plans for 61- and 71-foot versions that feature a unique no-up-and-down layout. Some of the most popular designs today have 20 steps on the main level—mine has one! You will also be able to walk with full headroom from the engines to the bow thruster. This is something new in the 61-foot range. A very exciting new development in the marine business is diesel-electric propulsion which I am working on incorporating in all of these new designs.

We also distribute the fine Selene Trawler line on the east coast. I have been involved with Selene for the past six years, and know the builder from my days in Taiwan. I have enjoyed contributing ideas to the design of their yachts.

Finally, our MMI owns about 44 acres to the south of the Hinckley yard, on Weaver's Cove in Portsmouth. This includes one mile of ocean frontage on Narragansett Bay. Here I have plans to build a 1,495-slip marina, as well as 100 to 175 units of luxury housing, an inn/yacht club with a restaurant and function facilities, a commercial-support area for marine-related businesses, and an area for seasonal show and auctions for open-air events. I am working with a developer to get that project built—which is a multi-million dollar project and well beyond my means.

I guess retirement will have to wait a little longer to claim me. In fact, it will never claim me. I have to keep designing—and building.

Shown at left are some of the many projects that Ted is working on today, including (clockwise from upper left):

52-foot power catamaran, 55-foot fast-power-fast-sail motorsailer, MMI marina development (in blue —the red arrow shows the location of Little Harbor, now Hinckley), 61-foot power expedition yacht, and 55-foot sail expedition yacht.

Selected Bibliography

Books

Bertrand, John, and Patrick Smith. *Born to Win: A Lifelong Struggle to Capture the America's Cup*. New York: Hearst Marine Books, 1985.

Conner, Dennis, and Michael Levitt. *The America's Cup*. New York: St. Martin's Press, 1998.

Conner, Dennis, and John Rousmaniere. *No Excuse to Lose*. New York: W. W. Norton, 1978.

Jones, Theodore A. *Challenge '77: Newport and the America's Cup*. New York: W. W. Norton, 1978.

——. *Racing for the America's Cup, 1974*. New York: Quadrangle, 1975.

Lawson, Thomas W., and Winfield M. Thompson. *The Lawson History of the America's Cup, a Record of Fifty Years*. 1902; reprint, Dobbs Ferry: Sheridan House, 1986.

Marchaj, C. A. *Aero-Hydrodynamics of Sailing*. New York: Dodd, Mead, 1980.

McNamara, John J. "Don," Jr. *White Sails, Black Clouds*. Boston: Burdette, 1967.

Mitchell, Carleton. *The Summer of the Twelves*. New York: Charles Scribner's Sons, 1959.

Morgan, Dodge. *The Voyage of American Promise*. Boston: Houghton Mifflin, 1990.

Parkinson, John, Jr. *The History of the New York Yacht Club*. 2 vols. New York: New York Yacht Club, 1975.

Somer, Jack A. *Ticonderoga*. Mystic: Mystic Seaport, 1997.

Vaughan, Roger. *Ted Turner: The Man Behind the Mouth*. New York: W. W. Norton, 1978.

——. *The Grand Gesture*. New York: Sports Illustrated Books, 1975.

Watson, Thomas J., Jr. *Pacific Passage*. Mystic: Mystic Seaport, 1993.

Whall, Hugh. *The Southern Cross, Australia's 1974 Challenge for America's Cup*. Annapolis: Admiralty Publishing House, 1974.

Whidden, Tom, and Michael Levitt. *The Art and Science of Sails*. New York: St. Martin's Press, 1990.

Magazines/Newspapers

America's Cup Issue. *Yachting*, September 1958.

"America's Cup Races-Biggest Show on the Seas." *Life*, September 29, 1958.

Angrist, Stanley W. "It's all in the Earn-out (CML Group Company profile)." *Forbes*, April 25, 1988.

Bailey, Anthony. "Sailmaker." *New Yorker*, August 26, 1967.

Burill, B. D. "Ted Hood Sailmaker to the Twelves." *Yachting*, September 1970.

Cady, Steve. "Controversial Cup Challenge." *New York Times*, August 29, 1974.

Clark, Tim. "Retro Rocket." *Power & Motoryacht*, January 2001.

Edey, Maitland A. "Article of the Week: Sea Dog Eat Sea Dog for the America's Cup." *Life*, July 13, 1962.

——. "Inches, Ounces, Seconds." *Life*, August 25, 1958.

Gemert, Lee Van. "Write-up." *Boating New Zealand*, February 2000.

Gribbins, Joseph. "Ray Hunt - New England Archimedes." *Nautical Quarterly*, Spring 1984.

"Hood Wins Mallory Series." *Yachting*, August 1956.

Klein, Larry. "A New Boat and the Man Who Is Her Designer and Sailmaker-and Skipper." *Newsweek*, August 6, 1962.

Levitt, Michael. "Another Chance." *Nautical Quarterly*, Summer 1987.

——. "Ted Hood Doesn't Live Here Anymore." *Nautical Quarterly*, Autumn 1987.

Lund, Mort. "Men Behind the X Factor." *Sports Illustrated*, July 14, 1958.

"Marblehead Marvel." *Time*, August 17, 1959.

McAllister, Jim. "Beans, Planes and Automobiles Were all Made Here Once." *Salem News*, January 12, 2005.

Mitchell, Carleton. "America's Cup: The Defenders." *Sports Illustrated*, May 12, 1958.

——. "The Twelves Shake Down." *Sports Illustrated*, July 28, 1958.

Morris, Everett B. "Just Weren't Good Enough-*Nefertiti*'s Skipper." *New York Herald Tribune*, August 27, 1962.

Mosbacher, Emil "Bus." "Mosbacher on Crews, Sails, Pressures. . . ." *Nautical Quarterly*, October 1977.

Newsweek, July 7, 1958.

Newsweek, July 28, 1958.

Philips, Dave. "Meet the Skippers." *Providence Journal*, September 8, 1974.

——. "Yachting's Affection Goes to Gallant old *Intrepid*." *Providence Journal*, September 3, 1974.

Rudeen, Louisa. "Jet Classic." *Motorboating & Sailing*, August 1997.

Silk, George. "Color Spectacle-Cutting the Waves for a Classic Cup." *Life*, August 24, 1962.

Smith, Red. "The High Moral Plane of Yachting." *New York Times*, September 4, 1974.

——. "Victory at Sea (At Any Price)." *New York Times*, September 1, 1974.

Swift, E. M. "Dodge Morgan." *Sports Illustrated*, April 21, 1986.

Wallace, William N. "Aussie Spies Steal Aboard *Courageous*." *New York Times*, September 5, 1974.

——. "Hood Replaces Bavier as *Courageous*' Skipper." *New York Times*, September 1, 1974.

"*Weatherly* in Four?" *Newsweek*, September 17, 1962.

Whittier, Anthony. "*Niña* - A Great Reckoning in a Little Room." *Nautical Quarterly*, Winter 1980.

Wooten, Kenny. "Adventure Capitalist." *Yachting*, 1995.

Websites

The Hinckley Company
        http://www.hinckleyyachts.com/.

"The Legacy of John G. Alden" http://www.aldenboats.com/history/ourhistory.html.

"Movers, Shakers, Builders: Alumni in the Rhode Island Boatbuilding tradition" (article on Everett and Clint Pearson from *Brown Alumni Magazine*) http://www.brown.edu/Administration/Brown_Alumni_Magazine/95/5-95/goetzide.html

"People, Places & Things," *Marblehead Magazine*
        http://www.legendinc.com/Pages/MarbleheadNet/MM/PeoplePlacesThings/TedHood.html

Illustration Credits

Legend:
THF: Ted Hood Family Collection, unidentified
    photographers
THB: Ted Hood Business Collection (brochures, business
    files, product photos), unidentified photographers

Page 10, Michael Levitt photo
Page 14, THF
Page 16, THF
Page 17, all, THF
Page 18, THF
Page 19, Willard B. Jackson photo, Peabody Essex Museum
Page 20, all, THF
Page 21, upper left, THF
Page 21, lower right, THB
Page 22, © Mystic Seaport, Rosenfeld Collection,
    1984.187.87663F
Page 23, all, THF
Page 24, THF
Page 25, all, THF
Page 26, THF
Page 27, Ronald E. Stroud photo
Page 28, all, THF
Page 30, THB
Page 32, THB
Page 33, lower left, Colin Ryrie photo
Page 33, upper right, Ted Jones photo
Page 34, © Mystic Seaport, Rosenfeld Collection,
    1984.187.160110F
Page 35, THB
Page 36, THB
Page 37, THB
Page 38, THB
Page 39, all, THB
Page 40, upper left, David Rosenfeld photo
Page 40, lower left (both), THB
Page 41, George M. Loring photo
Page 42, Bahamas News Service photo, Mystic Seaport,
    1996.31.6945
Page 44, © Mystic Seaport, Rosenfeld Collection,
    1984.187.17332
Page 45, THB
Page 46, all, THB
Page 48, © Mystic Seaport, Rosenfeld Collection,
    1984.187.151576a
Page 50, all, THF
Page 51, © Mystic Seaport, Rosenfeld Collection,
    1984.187.151594F
Page 52, upper left, Bermuda News Bureau
    photo by Perinchief

Page 52, lower left, THF
Page 53, THF
Page 54, © Mystic Seaport, Rosenfeld Collection,
    1984.187.160303F
Page 55, Carleton Mitchell Collection, Mystic Seaport,
    1996.31.5266.36
Page 57, © Mystic Seaport, Rosenfeld Collection,
    1984.187.159364F
Page 58, top, © Mystic Seaport, Rosenfeld Collection,
    1984.187.161320F
Page 58, lower left, THF
Page 59, upper right, THF
Page 59, bottom, © Mystic Seaport, Rosenfeld Collection,
    1984.187.161250F
Page 61, © Mystic Seaport, Rosenfeld Collection,
    1984.187.161178F
Page 62, © Mystic Seaport, Rosenfeld Collection,
    1984.187.161306F
Page 64, © Mystic Seaport, Rosenfeld Collection,
    1984.187.163836F
Page 66, top, THF
Page 66, lower right, © Mystic Seaport, Rosenfeld Collection
    1984.187.156267F
Page 67, Lenscraft Photos, Inc., Boston, MA
Page 68, © Mystic Seaport. Rosenfeld Collection,
    1984.187.159853F
Page 69, THB
Page 70, THF
Page 71, THF
Page 72, THF
Page 73, THF
Page 75, Howay Caufman photo, *Sports Illustrated*
Page 76, THB
Page 77, all, THB
Page 78, Norman Fortier Collection, New Bedford Whaling
    Museum
Page 80, THF
Page 82, upper left, © Mystic Seaport, Rosenfeld Collection,
    1984.187.172847F
Page 82, lower right, © Mystic Seaport, Rosenfeld Collection,
    1984.187.171818f29
Page 83, upper left, © Mystic Seaport, Rosenfeld Collection,
    1984.187.171819f33
Page 83, upper right, © Mystic Seaport, Rosenfeld Collection,
    1984.187.171821f24
Page 83, bottom, © Mystic Seaport, Rosenfeld Collection,
    1984.187.171818f11
Page 84, THF
Page 85, THF
Page 86, THF
Page 87, © Mystic Seaport, Rosenfeld Collection,
    1984.187.172689F

Page 88, THF

Page 89, upper left, THF

Page 89, lower right, THF

Page 90, © Mystic Seaport, Rosenfeld Collection,
    1984.187.172694F

Page 91, John Osgood photo

Page 92, THF

Page 93, John Osgood photo

Page 94, © Mystic Seaport, Rosenfeld Collection,
    1984.187.173296f21

Page 95, © Mystic Seaport, Rosenfeld Collection,
    1984.187.176808f22

Page 96, Onne van der Wal photo, www.vanderwal.com

Page 98, upper left, © Mystic Seaport, Rosenfeld Collection,
    1984.187.173914F

Page 98, lower left, THF

Page 99, © Mystic Seaport, Rosenfeld Collection,
    1984.187.184188F

Page 100, upper left, © Mystic Seaport, Rosenfeld Collection,
    1984.187.163836F

Page 100, upper right, THF

Page 100, bottom left, THF

Page 100, bottom center, Norman Fortier Collection, New
    Bedford Whaling Museum

Page 100, bottom right, Howay Caufman photo,
    Sports Illustrated

Page 101, top left, Pierre Fouquin photo

Page 101, top center, THF

Page 101, top right, THF

Page 101, middle left, THF

Page 101, middle center, THF

Page 101, middle right, Edwin Hills photo

Page 101, bottom left, THB

Page 101, bottom right, THB

Page 102, THB

Page 103, THB, based on illustration in C. A. Marchaj's
    Aero-Hydrodynamics of Sailing

Page 104, Gloria McDougal photo

Page 106, © Mystic Seaport, Rosenfeld Collection,
    BOX.1984.187.10.13.16

Page 108, © Mystic Seaport, Rosenfeld Collection,
    1984.187.191282f26

Page 109, © Mystic Seaport, Rosenfeld Collection,
    1984.187.187634f8

Page 110, upper left, © Mystic Seaport, Rosenfeld Collection,
    BOX.1984.187.99.9.13

Page 110, bottom, © Mystic Seaport, Rosenfeld Collection,
    1984.187.190975f17

Page 111, © Mystic Seaport, Rosenfeld Collection
    1984.187.191133f17

Page 112, top, © Mystic Seaport, Rosenfeld Collection,
    BOX.1984.187.100.12.8

Page 112, lower right, © Mystic Seaport, Rosenfeld
    Collection, BOX1984.187.99.10.8

Page 114, © Mystic Seaport, Rosenfeld Collection,
    1984.187.191198f20

Page 115, © Mystic Seaport, Rosenfeld Collection,
    1984.187.191094f10A

Page 117, © Mystic Seaport, Rosenfeld Collection,
    1984.187.190989

Page 118, © Mystic Seaport, Rosenfeld Collection,
    1984.187.191163f5

Page 120, THF

Page 122, top, © Mystic Seaport, Rosenfeld Collection,
    1984.187.191288f25a

Page 122, lower right, © Mystic Seaport, Rosenfeld
    Collection, 1984.187.192021f10

Page 123, upper left, © Mystic Seaport, Rosenfeld Collection,
    BOX.1984.187.99.23.3

Page 123, bottom, © Mystic Seaport, Rosenfeld Collection,
    1984.187.191307f27a

Page 125, © Mystic Seaport, Rosenfeld Collection,
    1984.187.192060f26a

Page 126, THF

Page 128, George M. Loring photo

Page 130, THB

Page 131, all, THB

Page 132, upper left, THB

Page 132, lower left, courtesy of Ed Botterell

Page 133, all, Richard Hood

Page 134, THB

Page 135, THB

Page 136, courtesy of Chris Bouzaid

Page 138, THF

Page 140, all, THF

Page 141, THF

Page 142, THF

Page 143, THF

Page 144, all, THF

Page 145, Tom Leutwiler Collection, Mystic Seaport

Page 146, THF

Page 147, © Mystic Seaport, Rosenfeld Collection,
    1984.187.191983f13a

Page 148, THF

Page 150, THB

Page 152, THB

Page 153, all, THB

Page 154, all, THB

Page 155, THB

Page 156, upper left, THB

Page 156, upper center, THB

Page 156, upper right, THB

Page 156, lower left, Chris Cunningham photo

Page 156, lower right, THB

Page 157, upper left, THB

Page 157, upper center left, THB

Page 157, upper center right, THB

Page 157, upper right, THB

Page 157, middle left, Onne van der Wal photo,
        www.vanderwal.com

Page 157, middle right, © John Corbett,
        www.corbettphotography.net

Page 157, lower left, THB

Page 157, lower right, THB

Page 158, Onne van der Wal photo, www.vanderwal.com

Page 160, Richard Hood

Page 162, top, THB

Page 162, lower right, Richard Hood

Page 163, THB

Page 164, Richard Hood

Page 165, all, THB

Page 167, *Marblehead Reporter*

Page 168, all, THB

Page 169, Allison Langley photo

Page 170, Onne van der Wal photo, www.vanderwal.com

Page 172, THB

Page 174, THF

Page 175, all, courtesy of Bradley Noyes

Page 176, © Mystic Seaport, Rosenfeld Collection,
        1984.187.156481F

Page 177, all, THB

Page 179, THB

Page 180, all, THB

Page 181, all, THB

Page 182, all, THB

Page 183, all, THB

Page 184, upper left, THB

Page 184, lower left, Richard Hood

Page 186, Onne van der Wal photo, www.vanderwal.com

Page 188, all, THB

Index